CORIOLANUS

The RSC Shakespeare

Edited by Jonathan Bate and Eric Rasmussen

Chief Associate Editors: Jan Sewell and Will Sharpe

Associate Editors: Trey Jansen, Eleanor Lowe, Lucy Munro,
Dee Anna Phares, Héloïse Sénéchal

Coriolanus

Textual editing: Eleanor Lowe and Eric Rasmussen

Introduction and Shakespeare's Career in the Theater: Jonathan Bate

Commentary: Eleanor Lowe and Héloïse Sénéchal

Scene-by-Scene Analysis: Esme Miskimmin

In Performance: Jan Sewell (RSC stagings) and Peter Kirwan (overview)

The Director's Cut (interviews by Jonathan Bate and Kevin Wright):
Gregory Doran and David Farr

The RSC Shakespeare

William Shakespeare

CORIOLANUS

Edited by Jonathan Bate and Eric Rasmussen

Introduction by Jonathan Bate

The Modern Library
New York

2011 Modern Library Paperback Edition

Copyright © 2007, 2011 by The Royal Shakespeare Company

Published in the United States by Modern Library, an imprint of
The Random House Publishing Group, a division of
Random House, Inc., New York.

MODERN LIBRARY and the TORCHBEARER Design are registered trademarks
of Random House, Inc.

"Royal Shakespeare Company," "RSC," and the RSC logo are trademarks
or registered trademarks of The Royal Shakespeare Company.

The version of *Coriolanus* and the corresponding footnotes
that appear in this volume were originally published in *William Shakespeare:
Complete Works*, edited by Jonathan Bate and Eric Rasmussen, published
in 2007 by Modern Library, an imprint of The Random House
Publishing Group, a division of Random House, Inc.

ISBN 978-0-8129-6934-4
eBook ISBN 978-1-5883-6881-2

Printed in the United States of America

www.modernlibrary.com

2 4 6 8 9 7 5 3 1

1099

CONTENTS

INTRODUCTION

THE LANGUAGE OF POETRY AND THE LANGUAGE OF POWER

The nineteenth-century critic William Hazlitt said that anyone who was familiar with *Coriolanus* could save themselves the trouble of reading Edmund Burke's attack on the French Revolution and Tom Paine's defense of it, because Shakespeare gives you both sides of the question. The play anatomizes the strengths and the weaknesses of both absolutism and republicanism, interrogates both the principle of aristocracy and that of democracy. The plebeians and their elected representatives, the tribunes, have arguments as good as those of the patricians who, at the beginning of the play, have been hoarding grain for no good reason.

But ultimately, Hazlitt contended, Shakespeare had a leaning toward the side of arbitrary power, that of Coriolanus himself. Perhaps in contempt of his own lowly origins, or out of politic fear of the consequences of "confusion" in the state, Shakespeare gives charisma to aristocratic swagger. Stage directions such as *"Citizens slink away"* and *"Enter a rabble of plebeians"* suggest where authorial sympathies do not lie. "The language of poetry," Hazlitt said, "naturally falls in with the language of power." All the memorable poetry belongs to Coriolanus, none to the tribunes. Whatever the force of the arguments on either side, the audience is swept away by the energy of the play's warrior hero. In particular, there is something irresistible about his solitary intensity. "*Alone* I did it," he vaunts, remembering the deed that gave him his name: the conquest of Corioles, achieved when the plebeian soldiers ran away and the gates of the enemy city clanged shut behind him. In its way, his arrogance is as magnificent as his courage. Accused of being an enemy to the people, he is banished from the city for which he has been prepared to lay down his life on the battlefield. His reply turns the sentence on its head:

> You common cry of curs, whose breath I hate
> As reek o'th'rotten fens: whose loves I prize
> As the dead carcasses of unburied men
> That do corrupt my air: I banish you,
> And here remain with your uncertainty.

The brilliance of the writing is in the detail: not only the glorious turn in the verb from passive "banished" to active "I banish you," but also the first person pronoun "my" applied to the very "air," thus showing how Coriolanus' world revolves around himself, and the riposte "here [may you] remain with your uncertainty," which reveals the gulf between the solitary martial hero's firmness of vision and the messy vicissitudes of communal life.

Coriolanus walks proudly away from Rome, soon to face the humiliation of being ordered around by mere servingmen. The very qualities that made him a great warrior—his singleness of purpose and lack of compromise—are those that make him a poor politician. The play is a tragedy because the man of war cannot keep the peace. It is also a work of deep irony. Coriolanus is the walking embodiment of masculinity. He feels a peculiarly intense bond with Aufidius, his opponent on the battlefield. The single erotic speech in the play is spoken by Aufidius when he welcomes the exiled Coriolanus to his home, an arrival that excites him more than his wife crossing his threshold on their wedding night. His nightly dream has been to wrestle with Coriolanus' body in hand-to-hand combat:

> We have been down together in my sleep,
> Unbuckling helms, fisting each other's throat,
> And waked half dead with nothing. . . .

Though Coriolanus does not respond to this extraordinary advance in verbal kind, he is manifestly a man who is at his most fulfilled when among other men. And yet the march of this supremely manly man comes to an abrupt halt in the face of his mother, Volumnia. "The ladies have prevailed": by a lovely irony, Rome is saved by the words of an old woman, not the deeds of a young man. No wonder

Caius Martius is so angry when Aufidius calls him "boy": Coriolanus is Peter Pan in full body armor, a boy who refuses to grow up.

PLUTARCH, VALOR, AND VIRTUE

Where did Shakespeare learn the Roman history that he so memorably dramatized in *Julius Caesar, Antony and Cleopatra,* and *Coriolanus?* Minor variants and improvisations apart, the answer is simple. While most of his plays involved him in the cutting and pasting of a whole range of literary and theatrical sources, in the Roman tragedies he kept his eye focused on the pages of a single great book.

That book was Plutarch's *Lives of the Noble Grecians and Romans.* Plutarch was a Greek, born in Boeotia in the first century AD. His book included forty-six biographies of the great figures of ancient history, arranged in pairs, half Greek and half Roman, with a brief "comparison" between each pair. The purpose of the "parallel" was to ask such questions as "who was the greater general, the Greek Alexander or the Roman Julius Caesar?" Shakespeare affectionately mocks the device of parallelism in *Henry V,* when Fluellen argues that Harry of Monmouth is like Alexander of Macedon because their respective birthplaces begin with an "M" and there's a river in each and "there is salmons in both." But the comedy here is at Fluellen's expense, not Plutarch's—and, like all Shakespeare's richest jokes, it has a serious point. As Alexander the Great killed his bosom-friend Cleitus in a drunken brawl, so King Harry in all sobriety caused his old chum Falstaff to die of a broken heart.

For Shakespeare, the historical parallel was a device of great power. The censorship of the stage exercised by court officialdom meant that it was exceedingly risky to dramatize contemporary affairs, so the best way of writing political drama was to take subjects from the past and leave it to the audience to see the parallel in the present. The uncertainty over the succession to the Virgin Queen meant that there were frequent whispers of conspiracy in the final years of Elizabeth's reign. It would hardly have been appropriate to write a play about a group of highly placed courtiers (the Earl of Essex and his circle, say) plotting to overthrow the monarchy. But a play about a group of highly placed Roman patricians (Brutus, Cassius, and company) plotting to assassinate Julius Caesar had the capacity to raise some awkward questions by means of the implicit parallel.

Plutarch's greatest importance for Shakespeare was his way of writing history through biography. He taught the playwright that the little human touch often says more than the large impersonal historical force. Plutarch explained his method in the *Life of Alexander*: "My intent is not to write histories, but only lives. For the noblest deeds do not always show men's virtues and vices; but oftentimes a light occasion, a word, or some sport, makes men's natural disposi-tions and manners appear more plain than the famous battles won wherein are slain ten thousand men, or the great armies, or cities won by siege or assault." So too in Shakespeare's Roman plays. It is the particular occasion—the single word, the moment of tenderness or jest—that humanizes the superpower politicians: Brutus and Cassius making up after their quarrel, the defeated Cleopatra remember-ing it is her birthday, Caius Martius exhausted from battle forgetting the name of the man who helped him in Corioles.

In his "Life of Caius Martius" Plutarch gives a brief character-sketch of the Roman general who, by virtue of his heroic endeavor behind the closed gates of Corioles, gained the surname Coriolanus: "For this Martius' natural wit and great heart did marvelously stir up his courage to do and attempt noble acts. But on the other side, for lack of education he was so choleric and impatient that he would yield to no living creature, which made him churlish, uncivil, and altogether unfit for any man's conversation." As the name Martius suggests, Coriolanus has all the martial virtues. His tragedy is that he has none of the civil ones. He devotes himself wholly to the code of valor (Latin *virtus*). Where Mark Antony is led astray from Roman values by his lover Cleopatra, Coriolanus is trained up in *virtus* by his mother, Volumnia. He has a suitably austere Roman wife, who usu-ally appears in company with a chaste companion (Valeria, the very opposite of Cleopatra's companion Charmian). And when his son, Young Martius, a chip off the old block, is praised for tearing the wings off a butterfly with his teeth, we gain a glimpse into the kind of upbringing that Coriolanus may be imagined to have had. "Anger's my meat," says Volumnia: perhaps in compensation for the premature disappearance of her husband, she has bred up an angry young man, ready to serve Rome on the battlefield where one senses she wishes she could go herself—as she does at the end of the play.

If *Antony and Cleopatra* is about the tragic consequences of the dissolution of Romanness, *Coriolanus* is about the equally tragic result of an unyielding adherence to it. "It is held," says Cominius,

> That valour is the chiefest virtue, and
> Most dignifies the haver: if it be,
> The man I speak of cannot in the world
> Be singly counterpoised. . . .

"If it be": Coriolanus' own mode of speaking, by contrast, is what he calls the "absolute shall." To leave room for an "if" would be to call his whole world-picture into question.

The play brings the absolute embodiment of *virtus* into hostile dialogue with other voices. As in *Julius Caesar*, the action begins not with the hero but with the people, to whom Plutarch (a believer in the theory that history is shaped by the deeds of great men alone) never gives a voice. In the very early period of the Roman republic, around the fifth century before Christ, Rome faced two threats: an external danger from neighboring territories (the Volscians, based in Antium and Corioles) and the internal danger of division between the patricians and the plebeians. The martial hero is supremely successful in dealing with the external threat through force, but his attempt to handle internal affairs in the same way leads to his banishment and eventual death. The opening scene reveals that the people do have a case: the First Citizen argues cogently against inequality, speaking "in hunger for bread, not in thirst for revenge." Diplomacy is the skill needed here; Coriolanus, who is always "himself alone" and who trusts in the deeds of the sword rather than the blandishments of the word, will have no truck with compromise. His pride and his desire to stand alone are only allayed when he faces his mother, wife, and son pleading for him to have mercy on the city. Volumnia appeals to the bond of family; after her eloquent entreaty, Coriolanus hovers for a moment in one of the most powerful silences in Shakespeare. He sets aside his code of manly strength, accepts the familial tie, and in so doing effectively signs his own death warrant. He has for the first time fully recognized the claims of other people, escaped the bond of absolute self. The knowledge of what he has done brings a kind of peace: "But let it come," he says of his inevitable end. He is speaking here in the voice of Stoic resignation.

FROM MOB TO MOTHER: THE CRITICS DEBATE

Shakespeare is traditionally praised for his disinterestedness, his ability to see both sides of a question, to enter into every character and give equal weight to every viewpoint, equal sympathy to every human dilemma. Samuel Taylor Coleridge, delivering a public lecture in the politically polarized wake of the French republican revolution and the subsequent restoration of monarchical values, said that *Coriolanus* "illustrates the wonderfully philosophic impartiality of Shakspere's politics." Coleridge knew that it would have been difficult for Shakespeare—with the king in his audience—to write with "philosophic impartiality" about the politics of his own time, so he turned instead to classical Rome: "The instruction of ancient history would seem more dispassionate." But then Coleridge told his audience that the play begins with "Shakspere's good-natured laugh at mobs."[1] For Coleridge, a sometime radical whose politics had lurched to the right by the time he delivered his lectures on Shakespeare, and for his predominantly genteel, middle-class audience, during an era of political uncertainty and unrest (the Regency period), "mobs" in the streets of London or Paris were something to be feared. It was comforting to imagine Shakespeare laughing at them, but remaining "good-natured" as he did so. But Coleridge's emphasis on the comedy—the joke about the "big toe" and so forth—meant that he didn't take the argument of the people entirely seriously. By not doing so, he was implying that Shakespeare did not, after all, give equal weight to the patrician and the plebeian sides of the question.

Hazlitt's essay on the play, with which this introduction began, must be seen in the context of Coleridge's move. Hazlitt, a committed radical democrat, did not regard the play's opening debate as a laughing matter. He recognized that food riots—whether in ancient Rome, in Shakespeare's time or his own—were a serious political matter, a matter of life and death. But he also recognized that the stage presence and verbal charisma of Coriolanus upset the political equilibrium:

> There is nothing heroical in a multitude of miserable rogues not wishing to be starved, or complaining that they are like to be so: but when a single man comes forward to brave their cries and to make them submit to the last indignities, from mere pride and self-will, our admiration of his prowess is immediately converted into contempt for their pusillanimity. The insolence of power is stronger than the plea of necessity.[2]

Hazlitt the political liberal finds himself at odds with Hazlitt the reader and writer who admires forceful poetic language more than anything else. *Coriolanus* troubled him with the thought that "the aristocracy of letters"—the best of literature and drama—might at some profound level be incompatible with political ideals of democracy and liberty. All men and women should be equal in the body politic but there is no equality within the body of great writing: Shakespeare stands like a king above his peers.

The influential late nineteenth-century critic Georg Brandes developed Hazlitt's ideas further. Perhaps literary greatness is inherently on the side of the "aristocratic" principle or at the very least of a form of individualism and inwardness that is at odds with "mass" feeling:

> Shakespeare's aversion to the mob was based upon his contempt for their discrimination, but it had its deepest roots in the purely physical repugnance of his artist nerves to their plebeian atmosphere. To him the Tribunes of the People were but political agitators of the lowest type, mere personifications of the envy of the masses, and representatives of their stupidity and their brute force of numbers. Ignoring every incident which shed favourable light upon the plebeians, he seized

upon every instance of popular folly which could be found in Plutarch's account of a later revolt, in order to incorporate it in his scornful delineation.[3]

Brandes's attention to the political implications of Shakespeare's subtle alterations of his source was further developed in twentieth-century criticism: "In Plutarch's version, the original revolt is occasioned by the Senate's support of the city's usurers, and the issue of the scarcity of grain does not come up until after Coriolanus's battles with the Volsces. Shakespeare pushes the issue of usury into the background . . . and brings the issue of grain to the fore."[4] Many critics have suggested that this emphasis was in part a response to the grain riots in the English Midlands—Shakespeare's home territory—in 1607.

, Brandes described *Coriolanus* as "the tragedy of an inviolably truthful personality in a world of small-minded folk; the tragedy of the punishment a reckless egoism incurs when it is betrayed into setting its own pride above duty to state and fatherland."[5] The question of the play's attitude to "state and fatherland" became a matter of intense debate in the first half of the twentieth century. Early in 1934, when the French Socialist government was close to collapse, a new translation of *Coriolanus* was staged at the Comédie Française in Paris. The production was perceived as an attack on democratic institutions. Rioting pro- and anti-government factions clashed in the auditorium. Shakespeare's translator, a Swiss, was branded a foreign Fascist. The prime minister fired the theater director and replaced him with the head of the security police, whose artistic credentials were somewhat questionable. What are we to conclude from this real life drama? That Coriolanus' contempt for the rabble makes Shakespeare himself into a proto-Fascist? How could it then have been that the following year the Maly Theatre company in Stalin's Moscow staged a production of the same play which sought to demonstrate that Coriolanus was an "enemy of the people" and that Shakespeare was therefore a true Socialist? Shakespeare was neither an absolutist nor a democrat, but the fact that both productions were possible is one of the major reasons why he continues to live through his work four centuries after his death.

There is something satisfying in the idea of a Shakespearean performance being condemned one night by fascists castigating it as communist propaganda and the next by communists castigating it as fascist propaganda. Bertolt Brecht, the twentieth-century theater's greatest political polemicist, was notably attracted to the play for precisely this reason. He saw it as his role to remake the drama in the light of contemporary politics. His adaptation of 1951–52 was shaped by his socialism and reacted against previous critics' glorification of the military hero: "He saw in it a drama of the people betrayed by their fascist leader."[6] Brecht individualized the citizens, made the tribunes more honorable than Shakespeare's, and turned the people into a united force. They are joined by some of the patricians in the defense of Rome.

The political problems of *Coriolanus* arise in part from the distance between Coriolanus' interaction with the citizens and his personal status as a specifically Roman hero. Roman concepts of honor and valor, as understood by Shakespeare and his contemporaries, ground Coriolanus' character:

Rome is an idea for Coriolanus, the idea of honor, and paradoxically that idea has led him to reject the state which has been its avatar. With increasing painfulness for the audience, Shakespeare explores the implications of this paradox as the play moves toward its bitter end. His honor drives the only honorable man in Rome to treachery, to the betrayal of the state with whom not only his fortunes but also his values are inextricably associated. The process means the destruction of the man.[7]

The debate over the nature of true "honour" is central to the drama: "Honor is . . . [Volumnia's] theme as it is her son's. But we have seen from the beginning that for Volumnia honor is the glory that Rome can confer on its loyal servants, and that honor can therefore employ policy, political expediency."[8]

Coriolanus' sense of personal honor is that it is a mixture of the inherent and the self-made, whereas some of the other characters and events in the play suggest that heroism is better regarded as a social construct, defined both by action and by society's recognition. "So our virtues / Lie in th'interpretation of the time," says Aufidius at the end of Act 4: "that, in one and a half lines," wrote the critic A. P. Rossiter, "gives the essence of the play. Run over the whole action, act by act, and each is seen as an 'estimate' or valuation of Martius."[9]

> To fulfil his distinction above other men he has to seek domin-ion over them; but he is bound to fail in this because the distinction is too great; he is too inhuman. Indeed the more godlike he seeks to be, the more *inhuman* he becomes. The play has very usefully been seen in relation to Aristotle's celebrated dictum: "He that is incapable of living in a society is a god or a beast" . . . The ambiguity of Aristotle's remark is nicely adjusted to the ambiguity . . . [in the] last tragedies, the moral ambiguity of heroes who are both godlike and *inhuman*.[10]

Coriolanus believes himself to be self-sufficient: "As he distrusts words in general and is preoccupied with the private meanings he invests them with, so he distrusts public estimations of himself and is preoccupied with his own inner integrity, his nobility."[11]

His self-centeredness means that it is hard for the actor playing him to win the sympathy of the audience. The most powerful tool for a Shakespearean tragic character's personal engagement with the spectator is strikingly lacking: "Coriolanus is Shakespeare's least inward tragic hero. He has but one soliloquy"[12] (critics actually differ on the number of Coriolanus' soliloquies, depending on editorial and staging choices, but he certainly speaks fewer than three). Cori-olanus' inward conflicts are veiled from us: "The change that came when he found himself alone and homeless in exile is not exhibited. The result is partly seen in the one soliloquy of this drama, but the process is hidden."[13] Whereas a super-articulate protagonist such as Hamlet is deeply sensitive to tone, verbal nuance, and connotation, for Coriolanus "language is not subject to modification by the requirements of different social situations, not flexible enough to respond in tone and style to the demands of decorum—if it is not a social instrument, neither is it an instrument with which to probe and express the workings of the consciousness."[14]

Coriolanus' belief in absolutes is his downfall: "The hero's virtue—his passionate sense of honor and allegiance to principles—is also his vice."[15] His betrayal "is bound up with his essential and crippling solitariness, and also with his failure ever to consider how much his heroism has truly been dedicated to Rome as a city, and how much to his own self-realization and personal fame."[16]

The individual character cannot be divorced from his communal context. Integrity is defined in the world of this play not just as truth to self but also as truth to Rome (or to the Volsces). For this reason,

> The "tragic flaw" analysis is far too simple. It will never do to say that Coriolanus's calamity is "caused" by his being too proud and unyielding and just that; for one of the play's central paradoxes is that though Caius Martius appears as a "character" almost unvaryingly the same, yet, for all his rigidity, he is pliant, unstable, trustless: traitor to Rome, false to the Volsces, then true to Rome and to home again, and twice traitor to himself.[17]

In contrast to Coriolanus,

> Aufidius is adaptable . . . he understands the importance of accommodating one's behaviour to the times. He has also divined (as, for that matter, did the Second Citizen in the opening scene) that his rival is fatally inflexible . . . In this judgement, Aufidius is almost, if not entirely, right. Coriolanus in exile is a man haunted by what seems to him the enormity of mutability and change. This is the burden of his soliloquy [in Act 4 Scene 4] . . . Only the embassy of women can shatter his convictions, force him into a new way of seeing . . . It is, of course, the moment when Coriolanus finally recognizes his common humanity, the strength of love and family ties. But the victory won here is not . . . as so often is assumed, that of a private over a public world. Shakespeare is at pains to assert

that, in republican Rome, the two are really inseparable. Hence the mute, but important presence of . . . Valeria . . . [who] is there to represent all the other women of Rome.[18]

Women are central to this play in a way that they were not in *Julius Caesar*, Shakespeare's earlier tragedy of Roman conduct and politics. "Subject from birth to the relentless pressure of his mother's affection, Coriolanus has grown into a man at once capable of the deepest feeling and unable to give it free expression . . . at once a hero, an inexorable fighting machine, and a childishly naïve and undeveloped human being."[19] Coriolanus' character and heroism are bound by concepts of masculinity that in turn are, paradoxically, reported to have been formed by his mother. Late twentieth-century commentators, especially feminists and psychoanalytically minded readers, reversed the tendency of earlier critics to idealize Volumnia, and explored how her vision of maternity and masculinity relates to theories of gender:

Woman, excluded from public life, is devalued save as the bearer of men-children; she must seek her primary emotional satisfaction through her son, who becomes a substitute for her absent husband, the vehicle through which she realizes herself . . . In this play, the father is absent and the mother's contribution is exposed and exaggerated.[20]

The juxtaposition of Volumnia the mother and Virgilia the wife offers a striking contrast:

Volumnia's intense adherence to the masculine code of honor is contrasted to Virgilia's feminine recoil from it. Virgilia fears wounds, blood, and death because they may deprive her of the husband she loves; Volumnia covets them as the signs and seals of honor that make her son a man, and her a man, in effect, through him. Coriolanus in himself does not exist for her; he is only a means for her to realize her own masculine ego ideal, a weapon she fashions for her own triumph.[21]

Though Volumnia defines herself primarily as a mother, her values are stereotypically "masculine." This paradox allows the post-Freudian critics to have a field day with the play's imagery:

> In thinking of the "valiantness" with which she suckled her sons as hers, Volumnia claims to possess the phallus, the prime signifier of masculinity in Rome, but identifies it with a signifier of femininity: mother's milk. Masculinity belongs first to the mother; only she can pass it on to a son. This construction contrasts with one common to many cultures, and certainly prevalent in early modern England: that the male child must be separated from the maternal environment at a certain age, and definitively located in a men's world in order to realize his masculinity.[22]

A psychoanalytic reading of *Coriolanus* claims that Coriolanus' strict adherence to masculine strategies is an attempt to separate himself from his mother. Thus for critic Janet Adelman masculinity in *Coriolanus* is "constructed in response to maternal power." In the absence of a father, "the hero attempts to recreate himself through his bloody heroics, in fantasy severing the connection with his mother even as he enacts the ruthless masculinity that is her bidding":

> Thrust prematurely from dependence on his mother, forced to feed himself on his own anger, Coriolanus refuses to acknowledge any neediness or dependency: for his entire sense of himself depends on his being able to see himself as a self-sufficient creature. The desperation behind his claim to self-sufficiency is revealed by his horror of praise. . . . Coriolanus's battlecry as he storms the gates [of Corioli] sexualizes the scene: "Come on; / If you'll stand fast, we'll beat them to their wives" . . . But the dramatic action itself presents the conquest of Corioli as an image not of rape but of triumphant rebirth: after Coriolanus enters the gates of the city, he is proclaimed dead; one of his comrades delivers a eulogy firmly in the past tense . . . then

Coriolanus miraculously re-emerges, covered with blood . . .
and is given a new name. For the assault on Corioli is both a
rape and a rebirth: the underlying fantasy is that intercourse is
a literal return to the womb, from which one is reborn, one's
own author. The fantasy of self-authorship is complete when
Coriolanus is given his new name, earned by his own actions.[23]

Concurrently, Coriolanus' escape from Volumnia and the estab-
lishment of his masculinity is defined "homosocially," through
combat—body contact—with other men. "Cominius reports that
Coriolanus entered his first battle a sexually indefinite thing, a boy or
an Amazon"; the battlefield is a place where he undergoes a rite of
passage into manhood. Psychologically, "The rigid masculinity that
Coriolanus finds in war becomes a defense against acknowledge-
ment of his neediness; he nearly succeeds in transforming himself
from a vulnerable human creature into a grotesquely invulnerable
and isolated thing."[24]

For Stanley Cavell, "Coriolanus's erotic attachment to battle and
to men who battle suggest a search for the father as much as an
escape from the mother."[25] Whether Coriolanus is in search of a
father or a lover, there is no doubt that his relationship with Aufidius
is charged with the electricity of desire.

The dominance of Volumnia's maternal presence is highlighted
by the language of the play: "The imagery of food and eating is perhaps the most extensive and important motif in the play. It calls
attention to the appetitive nature of the plebeians, while the negative
(images of temperance and austerity) represents an heroic aristocratic ideal."[26] Key speeches such as Menenius' fable of the belly in
the opening scene repay close attention to the language of digestion
employed:

The wording of the [belly] parable tends to the transformation
of a political commonplace, a theoretical vindication of natural "degree," into a criticism, not of this attitude or that, but
of Roman society itself. The impression of a general obstruc-
tion of all vital activity communicates itself through the
unhealthy stagnation of "idle and unactive," the coarseness of

"cupboarding." These effects are set against the very noticeable livening of the verse when Menenius turns to the "other instruments," the senses and active faculties of the body which represent, however, not the class he is defending but its enemies. These contrasted elements, thus concentrated, in a manner profoundly typical of the play, upon images of food and digestion, answer to the real state of the Roman polity. Stagnation and mutual distrust, mirroring the ruthlessness of contrary appetites for power, are the principal images by which we are introduced to the public issues of *Coriolanus*.[27]

Related to the images of food and the body are those of disease, as when Coriolanus describes the citizens as a pestilence, an infection that endangers the body politic. The tragic irony of his fate is that Rome comes to regard him as the plague that must be driven out. The disease imagery is turned against him: "By a reversal of roles he, and not the plebeians, is now the 'infection,' and the Tribunes have become physicians to the body politic."[28] So it is that "Coriolanus' death is at the same time tragic and ironic. It is tragic in the world created by Coriolanus; tragic according to his mad and absolute system of values. It is ironic in the real world."[29]

There is none of the sense of transcendence that occurs at the end of *Antony and Cleopatra*, nor any of the grim satisfaction of poetic justice which greets the end of the tyrant Macbeth. At the close, all that can be properly said is, in the words of an anonymous Volscian Lord, "Let's make the best of it."

ABOUT THE TEXT

Shakespeare endures through history. He illuminates later times as well as his own. He helps us to understand the human condition. But he cannot do this without a good text of the plays. Without editions there would be no Shakespeare. That is why every twenty years or so throughout the last three centuries there has been a major new edition of his complete works. One aspect of editing is the process of keeping the texts up to date—modernizing the spelling, punctuation, and typography (though not, of course, the actual words), providing explanatory notes in the light of changing educational practices (a generation ago, most of Shakespeare's classical and biblical allusions could be assumed to be generally understood, but now they can't).

Because Shakespeare did not personally oversee the publication of his plays, with some plays there are major editorial difficulties. Decisions have to be made as to the relative authority of the early printed editions, the pocket format "Quartos" published in Shakespeare's lifetime and the elaborately produced "First Folio" text of 1623, the original "Complete Works" prepared for the press after his death by Shakespeare's fellow actors, the people who knew the plays better than anyone else. *Coriolanus* exists only in a Folio text that is generally well printed. Its full, "literary" stage directions and spelling preferences suggest it was set from Shakespeare's authorial papers. The following notes highlight various aspects of the editorial process and indicate conventions used in the text of this edition:

Lists of Parts are supplied in the First Folio for only six plays, not including *Coriolanus*, so the list here is editorially supplied. Capitals indicate that part of the name used for speech headings in the script (thus "Caius MARTIUS, later CORIOLANUS").

Locations are provided by the Folio for only two plays, of which *Coriolanus* is not one. Eighteenth-century editors, working in an age of elaborately realistic stage sets, were the first to provide detailed locations ("*another part of the city*"). Given that Shakespeare wrote for a bare stage and often an imprecise sense of place, we have relegated locations to the explanatory notes at the foot of the page, where they are given at the beginning of each scene where the imaginary location is different from the one before. In the case of *Coriolanus* the action is divided between the city of Rome and the opposing cities (Corioles and Antium) or camps of the Volscians.

Act and Scene Divisions were provided in the Folio in a much more thoroughgoing way than in the Quartos. Sometimes, however, they were erroneous or omitted; corrections and additions supplied by editorial tradition are indicated by square brackets. Five-act division is based on a classical model, and act breaks provided the opportunity to replace the candles in the indoor Blackfriars playhouse which the King's Men used after 1608, but Shakespeare did not necessarily think in terms of a five-part structure of dramatic composition. The Folio convention is that a scene ends when the stage is empty. Nowadays, partly under the influence of film, we tend to consider a scene to be a dramatic unit that ends with either a change of imaginary location or a significant passage of time within the narrative. Shakespeare's fluidity of composition accords well with this convention, so in addition to act and scene numbers we provide a *running scene* count in the right margin at the beginning of each new scene, in the typeface used for editorial directions. Where there is a scene break caused by a momentary bare stage, but the location does not change and extra time does not pass, we use the convention *running scene continues*. There is inevitably a degree of editorial judgment in making such calls, but the system is very valuable in suggesting the pace of the plays.

Speakers' Names are often inconsistent in Folio. We have regularized speech headings, but retained an element of deliberate inconsistency in entry directions, in order to give the flavor of Folio.

Verse is indicated by lines that do not run to the right margin and by capitalization of each line. The Folio printers sometimes set verse as prose, and vice versa (either out of misunderstanding or for reasons of space). We have silently corrected in such cases, although in some instances there is ambiguity, in which case we have leaned toward the preservation of Folio layout. Folio sometimes uses contraction ("turnd" rather than "turned") to indicate whether or not the final "-ed" of a past participle is sounded, an area where there is variation for the sake of the five-beat iambic pentameter rhythm. We use the convention of a grave accent to indicate sounding (thus "turnèd" would be two syllables), but would urge actors not to overstress. In cases where one speaker ends with a verse half line and the next begins with the other half of the pentameter, editors since the late eighteenth century have indented the second line. We have abandoned this convention, since the Folio does not use it, nor did actors' cues in the Shakespearean theater. An exception is made when the second speaker actively interrupts or completes the first speaker's sentence.

Spelling is modernized, but older forms are very occasionally maintained where necessary for rhythm or aural effect.

Punctuation in Shakespeare's time was as much rhetorical as grammatical. "Colon" was originally a term for a unit of thought in an argument. The semicolon was a new unit of punctuation (some of the Quartos lack them altogether). We have modernized punctuation throughout, but have given more weight to Folio punctuation than many editors, since, though not Shakespearean, it reflects the usage of his period. In particular, we have used the colon far more than many editors: it is exceptionally useful as a way of indicating how many Shakespearean speeches unfold clause by clause in a developing argument that gives the illusion of enacting the process of thinking in the moment. We have also kept in mind the origin of punctuation in classical times as a way of assisting the actor and orator: the comma suggests the briefest of pauses for breath, the colon a middling one, and a full stop or period a longer pause. Semicolons, by contrast, belong to an era of punctuation that was only just coming in during Shakespeare's time and that is coming to an end now: we have accordingly only used them where they occur in our copy texts (and not always then). Dashes are sometimes used for parenthetical interjections where the Folio has brackets. They are also used for interruptions and changes in train of thought. Where a change of addressee occurs within a speech, we have used a dash preceded by a period (or occasionally another form of punctuation). Often the identity of the respective addressees is obvious from the context. When it is not, this has been indicated in a marginal stage direction.

Entrances and Exits are fairly thorough in Folio, which has accordingly been followed as faithfully as possible. Where characters are omitted or corrections are necessary, this is indicated by square brackets (e.g. "[*and Attendants*]"). *Exit* is sometimes silently normalized to *Exeunt* and *Manet* anglicized to "remains." We trust Folio positioning of entrances and exits to a greater degree than most editors.

Editorial Stage Directions such as stage business, asides, indications of addressee and of characters' position on the gallery stage are only used sparingly in Folio. Other editions mingle directions of this kind with original Folio and Quarto directions, sometimes marking them by means of square brackets. We have sought to distinguish what could be described as *directorial* interventions of this kind from Folio-style directions (either original or supplied) by placing them in the right margin in a different typeface. There is a degree of subjectivity about which directions are of which kind, but the procedure is intended as a reminder to the reader and the actor that Shakespearean stage directions are often dependent upon editorial inference alone and are not set in stone. We also depart from editorial tradition in sometimes admitting uncertainty and thus printing permissive stage directions, such as an ***Aside?*** (often a line may be equally effective as an aside or as a direct address—it is for each production or reading to make its own decision) or a ***may exit*** or a piece of business placed between arrows to indicate that it may occur at various different moments within a scene.

Line Numbers in the left margin are editorial, for reference and to key the explanatory and textual notes.

Explanatory Notes at the foot of each page explain allusions and gloss obsolete and difficult words, confusing phraseology, occasional major textual cruces, and so on. Particular attention is given to non-standard usage, bawdy innuendo, and technical terms (e.g. legal and military language). Where more than one sense is given, commas indicate shades of related meaning, slashes alternative or double meanings.

Textual Notes at the end of the play indicate major departures from the Folio. They take the following form: the reading of our text is given in bold and its source given after an equals sign, "F2" indicates a correction that derives from the Second Folio of 1632, "F3" a correction introduced in the Third Folio of 1664, "F4" from the Fourth Folio of 1685, and "Ed" one that derives from the subsequent editorial tradition. The rejected Folio ("F") reading is then given. Thus, for example, "**5.6.131 Fluttered** = F3. F = Flatter'd" indicates that at Act 5 Scene 6 line 131, we have accepted the Third Folio's correction "Fluttered" which makes sense of Coriolanus' imagery in the lines, "That, like an eagle in a dovecote, I / Fluttered your Volscians in Corioles."

KEY FACTS

MAJOR PARTS: (*with percentage of lines/number of speeches/scenes on stage*) Caius Martius/Coriolanus (23%/189/18), Menenius Agrippa (15%/162/13), Volumnia (8%/57/6), Sicinius Velutus (8%/117/10), Cominius (8%/67/11), Tullus Aufidius (7%/45/8), Junius Brutus (7%/91/9), Titus Lartius (2%/23/6), First Citizen (2%/33/4), Third Servingman (1%/20/1), Third Citizen (1%/18/3), Valeria (1%/14/2).

LINGUISTIC MEDIUM: 80% verse, 20% prose.

DATE: 1608? Probably uses Camden's *Remaines* (1605); a phrase is parodied in Ben Jonson's *Epicoene* (late 1609). Allusion to "coal of fire upon the ice" in Act 1 Scene 1 sometimes taken to refer to the great frost of winter 1607/08, when the Thames was frozen and people with "pans of coals to warm your fingers" were stationed on the middle of the river; the issue of grain shortage and hoarding with which the action begins has been related to an insurrection in the English midlands in 1607–08. Theaters were closed because of the plague for the majority of the time in these years, so the play may belong to the open period of April–July 1608.

SOURCES: Closely based on "The Life of Caius Martius Coriolanus" in Sir Thomas North's English translation of Plutarch's *Lives of the Most Noble Grecians and Romanes* (Shakespeare probably used the 1595 edition). Menenius' fable of the belly in the first scene is the only occasion on which an additional source seems to have been used: the wording suggests the influence of both Livy's *Romane Historie* (trans. Philemon Holland, 1600) and William Camden's *Remaines of a greater worke concerning Britaine* (1605).

TEXT: 1623 Folio, apparently set from Shakespeare's manuscript or a scribal transcript of it, is the only early edition; irregular lineation is the main problem in the printing.

THE TRAGEDY OF CORIOLANUS

LIST OF PARTS

Caius MARTIUS, later CORIOLANUS

VOLUMNIA, Coriolanus' mother

VIRGILIA, his wife

YOUNG MARTIUS, his son

VALERIA, friend of Virgilia

GENTLEWOMAN, attending on
    Virgilia

MENENIUS Agrippa, Coriolanus'
    elderly friend

Titus LARTIUS }
COMINIUS } Roman generals

SICINIUS Velutus }
JUNIUS BRUTUS } Roman tribunes

NICANOR, a Roman traitor

Two MESSENGERS

LIEUTENANT

Two SOLDIERS

Two OFFICERS

Five CITIZENS

Three ROMANS

A HERALD

An AEDILE

A PATRICIAN

Two SENATORS

Tullus AUFIDIUS, Volscian general

LIEUTENANT to Aufidius

ADRIAN, a Volscian

Three SERVINGMEN

Three CONSPIRATORS

Two WATCHMEN

Three LORDS

Usher, Valeria's Gentlewoman,
    Captains, Soldiers, Drummer,
    Trumpeter, Scout, Nobles,
    Attendants

Act 1 Scene 1

*Enter a company of mutinous Citizens, with staves, clubs and other
weapons*

FIRST CITIZEN   Before we proceed any further, hear me speak.

ALL   Speak, speak.

FIRST CITIZEN   You are all resolved rather to die than to famish?

ALL   Resolved, resolved.

5   FIRST CITIZEN   First, you know Caius Martius is chief enemy to
the people.

ALL   We know't, we know't.

FIRST CITIZEN   Let us kill him, and we'll have corn at our own
price. Is't a verdict?

10   ALL   No more talking on't: let it be done: away, away.

SECOND CITIZEN   One word, good citizens.

FIRST CITIZEN   We are accounted poor citizens, the patricians
good: what authority surfeits on would relieve us. If they
would yield us but the superfluity while it were wholesome,

15   we might guess they relieved us humanely: but they think
we are too dear: the leanness that afflicts us, the object of our
misery, is as an inventory to particularize their abundance:
our sufferance is a gain to them. Let us revenge this with our
pikes, ere we become rakes. For the gods know, I speak this in

20   hunger for bread, not in thirst for revenge.

SECOND CITIZEN   Would you proceed especially against Caius
Martius?

ALL   Against him first: he's a very dog to the commonalty.

1.1 *Location: Rome (a public place)*   **3 famish** starve   **9 verdict** agreed decision
10 on't i.e. about it   **12 poor** impoverished (playing on the sense of "bad, unworthy")
patricians members of the noble families of Rome from whom senators and consuls were
chosen   **13 good** wealthy, well-to-do (playing on the sense of "worthy")   **authority** those in
power, i.e. the patricians   **surfeits on** is overfed on, overindulges in   **14 but the superfluity**
merely the excess   **wholesome** nutritious, good, restorative   **15 guess** believe, judge
16 dear costly   **object** sight   **17 inventory . . . abundance** detailed account that enables them
to itemize their own wealth through contrast   **18 sufferance** suffering   **19 pikes** long-
handled weapon topped with a spearhead   **ere** before   **rakes** i.e. very thin   **23 dog** i.e. cruel,
pitiless   **24 commonalty** common people

25   SECOND CITIZEN   Consider you what services he has done for his country?

FIRST CITIZEN   Very well, and could be content to give him good report for't, but that he pays himself with being proud.

ALL   Nay, but speak not maliciously.

30   FIRST CITIZEN   I say unto you, what he hath done famously, he did it to that end: though soft-conscienced men can be content to say it was for his country, he did it to please his mother and to be partly proud, which he is, even to the altitude of his virtue.

35   SECOND CITIZEN   What he cannot help in his nature, you account a vice in him. You must in no way say he is covetous.

FIRST CITIZEN   If I must not, I need not be barren of accusations: he hath faults, with surplus, to tire in repetition.

Shouts within

What shouts are these? The other side o'th'city is risen: why
40   stay we prating here? To th'Capitol!

ALL   Come, come.

FIRST CITIZEN   Soft, who comes here?

Enter Menenius Agrippa

SECOND CITIZEN   Worthy Menenius Agrippa, one that hath always loved the people.

45   FIRST CITIZEN   He's one honest enough: would all the rest were so!

MENENIUS   What work's, my countrymen, in hand?

     Where go you

With bats and clubs? The matter, speak, I pray you.

SECOND CITIZEN   Our business is not unknown to th'senate: they have had inkling this fortnight what we intend to do, which
50   now we'll show 'em in deeds. They say poor suitors have strong breaths: they shall know we have strong arms too.

---

30 **famously** gloriously, in a manner that gained him fame   31 **to that end** i.e. in order to achieve fame   **soft-conscienced** weak-minded   33 **to . . . proud** i.e. partly out of pride **even . . . virtue** i.e. he is just as proud as he is courageous   37 **If** even if   38 **tire in repetition** exhaust the speaker in recounting them   39 **risen** in revolt   40 **prating** chattering **th'Capitol** Capitoline Hill, site of the temple of Jupiter; used in the play as the location of the senate house   42 **Soft** wait a moment   47 **bats** cudgels   **matter** matter in hand/reason 50 **suitors** petitioners   51 **strong** strong-smelling (sense then shifts to "powerful")

MENENIUS   Why, masters, my good friends, mine honest
    neighbours,
    Will you undo yourselves?

SECOND CITIZEN   We cannot, sir, we are undone already.

55 MENENIUS   I tell you, friends, most charitable care
    Have the patricians of you. For your wants,
    Your suffering in this dearth, you may as well
    Strike at the heaven with your staves as lift them
    Against the Roman state, whose course will on
60   The way it takes, cracking ten thousand curbs
    Of more strong link asunder than can ever
    Appear in your impediment. For the dearth,
    The gods, not the patricians, make it, and
    Your knees to them, not arms, must help. Alack,
65   You are transported by calamity
    Thither where more attends you, and you slander
    The helms o'th'state, who care for you like fathers,
    When you curse them as enemies.

SECOND CITIZEN   Care for us? True, indeed, they ne'er cared for us
70   yet. Suffer us to famish, and their store-houses crammed
    with grain: make edicts for usury, to support usurers: repeal
    daily any wholesome act established against the rich, and
    provide more piercing statutes daily, to chain up and restrain
    the poor. If the wars eat us not up, they will: and there's all
75   the love they bear us.

MENENIUS   Either you must
    Confess yourselves wondrous malicious,
    Or be accused of folly. I shall tell you
    A pretty tale: it may be you have heard it,

---

52 **masters** sirs   53 **undo** ruin   56 **For** as for   57 **dearth** scarcity, famine   58 **staves** staffs
used as weapons   59 **on** continue on   60 **curbs** restraints (literally, chain passed under a
horse's jaw)   62 **your impediment** any obstacle you can present   64 **knees** i.e. in prayer
arms weapons (playing on the sense of "limbs")   65 **transported** carried away   66 **attends**
awaits   67 **helms** helmsmen, i.e. guides (possibly plays on the sense of "protective helmets")
69 **True, indeed** either spoken ironically or "indeed, as a matter of fact"   70 **Suffer** allow (plays
on the sense of "inflict pain on")   71 **for** i.e. allowing   **usury** money lending (often at very
high rates of interest)   **usurers** moneylenders   73 **piercing** oppressive, severe   77 **wondrous**
extraordinarily   79 **pretty** apt

80 But since it serves my purpose, I will venture
To stale't a little more.
SECOND CITIZEN   Well, I'll hear it, sir: yet you must not think to
fob off our disgrace with a tale: but, an't please you, deliver.
MENENIUS   There was a time when all the body's members
85 Rebelled against the belly, thus accused it:
That only like a gulf it did remain
I'th'midst o'th'body, idle and unactive,
Still cupboarding the viand, never bearing
Like labour with the rest, where th'other instruments
90 Did see and hear, devise, instruct, walk, feel,
And, mutually participate, did minister
Unto the appetite and affection common
Of the whole body. The belly answered—
SECOND CITIZEN   Well, sir, what answer made the belly?
95 MENENIUS   Sir, I shall tell you: with a kind of smile,
Which ne'er came from the lungs, but even thus —
For look you, I may make the belly smile
As well as speak — it tauntingly replied
To th'discontented members, the mutinous parts
100 That envied his receipt: even so most fitly
As you malign our senators for that
They are not such as you.
SECOND CITIZEN   Your belly's answer: what?
The kingly crownèd head, the vigilant eye,
105 The counsellor heart, the arm our soldier,
Our steed the leg, the tongue our trumpeter,
With other muniments and petty helps
In this our fabric, if that they—

---

81 stale't make it stale, wear it out   **83 disgrace** misfortune/injury   **an't** if it   **deliver** tell
(the tale)   **88 cupboarding** hoarding   **viand** food   **89 Like** equal   **instruments** functioning
body parts, organs   **90 devise** think   **91 participate** participating   **92 affection** desires,
inclination   **96 ne'er . . . lungs** i.e. was not hearty and genuine   **thus** Menenius imitates the
smile, either with his mouth or with his belly (perhaps by belching)   **100 his receipt** what he
received   **even . . . fitly** just as aptly, fittingly (said in irony)   **101 for that** because
107 muniments provisions/defenses, fortifications   **108 fabric** building, structure (i.e. body)

MENENIUS   What then?
Fore me, this fellow speaks! What then? What then?

110   SECOND CITIZEN   Should by the cormorant belly be restrained,
Who is the sink o'th'body—

MENENIUS   Well, what then?

SECOND CITIZEN   The former agents, if they did complain,
What could the belly answer?

115   MENENIUS   I will tell you,
If you'll bestow a small — of what you have little —
Patience awhile, you'st hear the belly's answer.

SECOND CITIZEN   You're long about it.

MENENIUS   Note me this, good friend:

120   Your most grave belly was deliberate,
Not rash like his accusers, and thus answered:
'True is it, my incorporate friends,' quoth he,
'That I receive the general food at first
Which you do live upon: and fit it is,

125   Because I am the storehouse and the shop
Of the whole body. But, if you do remember,
I send it through the rivers of your blood
Even to the court, the heart, to th'seat o'th'brain,
And through the cranks and offices of man,

130   The strongest nerves and small inferior veins
From me receive that natural competency
Whereby they live. And though that all at once' —
You, my good friends, this says the belly, mark me—

SECOND CITIZEN   Ay, sir, well, well.

135   MENENIUS   'Though all at once cannot
See what I do deliver out to each,
Yet I can make my audit up, that all

---

109 Fore me before me (oath)   **speaks** i.e. talks a lot   **110 cormorant** greedy (like the seabird)
111 sink sewer   **113 former** previously named   **116 small** i.e. small quantity   **117 you'st** you
shall   **120 Your** i.e. this   **grave** serious, dignified   **122 incorporate** united in one body
123 general belonging to everyone   **128 court** plays on the Latin *cor* ("heart") and on "core"
("inmost part")   **129 cranks** winding passages   **offices** parts of the house used by servants
(kitchen etc.)   **130 nerves** sinews   **131 competency** means of life   **133 mark** pay attention,
listen to   **137 make . . . up** compile my account, balance my records

From me do back receive the flour of all,
And leave me but the bran.' What say you to't?

140 SECOND CITIZEN   It was an answer: how apply you this?

MENENIUS   The senators of Rome are this good belly,
And you the mutinous members: for examine
Their counsels and their cares, digest things rightly
Touching the weal o'th'common, you shall find

145 No public benefit which you receive
But it proceeds or comes from them to you
And no way from yourselves. What do you think,
You, the great toe of this assembly?

SECOND CITIZEN   I the great toe? Why the great toe?

150 MENENIUS   For that, being one o'th'lowest, basest, poorest
Of this most wise rebellion, thou goest foremost:
Thou rascal, that art worst in blood to run,
Lead'st first to win some vantage.
But make you ready your stiff bats and clubs:

155 Rome and her rats are at the point of battle:
The one side must have bale.

Enter Caius Martius

Hail, noble Martius.

MARTIUS   Thanks. What's the matter, you dissentious rogues,
That, rubbing the poor itch of your opinion,
Make yourselves scabs?

160 SECOND CITIZEN   We have ever your good word.

MARTIUS   He that will give good words to thee will flatter
Beneath abhorring. What would you have, you curs,
That like nor peace nor war? The one affrights you,
The other makes you proud. He that trusts to you,

165 Where he should find you lions, finds you hares:

---

138 flour i.e. finest quality meal of wheat or other grain, plays on "flower" (the best part)
139 bran husks (separated from flour after grinding), i.e. inedible part   **143 digest** interpret,
understand (plays on the bodily sense)   **144 weal o'th'common** public welfare   **152 rascal**
rogue/one of low birth/(hunting) dog   **worst in blood** least lively, in poorest condition
(hunting term)/most ill-bred   **153 vantage** (individual) advantage   **156 The one side** one
side or the other   **bale** misfortune   **157 dissentious** quarrelsome, rebellious   **159 scabs**
sores/contemptible rogues   **160 ever** always   **162 abhorring** contempt   **curs** dogs   **163 nor**
neither   **The one** i.e. war   **164 proud** arrogant, self-important   **165 hares** i.e. timid

Where foxes, geese: you are no surer, no,
Than is the coal of fire upon the ice,
Or hailstone in the sun. Your virtue is
To make him worthy whose offence subdues him
170   And curse that justice did it. Who deserves greatness
Deserves your hate, and your affections are
A sick man's appetite, who desires most that
Which would increase his evil. He that depends
Upon your favours swims with fins of lead,
175   And hews down oaks with rushes. Hang ye! Trust ye?
With every minute you do change a mind,
And call him noble that was now your hate,
Him vile that was your garland. What's the matter,
That in these several places of the city
180   You cry against the noble senate, who,
Under the gods, keep you in awe, which else
Would feed on one another?— What's their   *To Menenius*
   seeking?

MENENIUS   For corn at their own rates, whereof they say
The city is well stored.

185 MARTIUS   Hang 'em! They say?
They'll sit by th'fire, and presume to know
What's done i'th'Capitol: who's like to rise,
Who thrives and who declines: side factions and give out
Conjectural marriages, making parties strong
190   And feebling such as stand not in their liking
Below their cobbled shoes. They say there's grain enough?
Would the nobility lay aside their ruth,
And let me use my sword, I'd make a quarry

---

166 foxes i.e. clever, cunning   **geese** i.e. foolish   **surer** more reliable   **168 virtue** particular
ability   **169 make . . . it** honor a man whose wrongdoing is punished, and curse the justice
that did so   **170 Who** whoever   **171 Deserves** earns, acquires   **affections** desires,
inclinations   **173 evil** sickness   **175 rushes** flimsy reeds   **177 now** just now, recently
178 garland hero (deserving of a wreath of victory)   **179 several** various   **181 which else**
who otherwise   **182 seeking** request/demand   **188 side** takes sides in   **give out** report
189 marriages political alliances   **190 feebling** weakening   **191 cobbled** patched, roughly
mended   **192 ruth** compassion, pity   **193 quarry** pile of dead bodies (hunting term)

With thousands of these quartered slaves, as high
195   As I could pick my lance.

MENENIUS   Nay, these are almost thoroughly persuaded:
For though abundantly they lack discretion,
Yet are they passing cowardly. But I beseech you,
What says the other troop?

200   MARTIUS   They are dissolved: hang 'em:
They said they were an-hungry, sighed forth proverbs
That hunger broke stone walls, that dogs must eat,
That meat was made for mouths, that the gods sent not
Corn for the rich men only: with these shreds
205   They vented their complainings, which being answered,
And a petition granted them, a strange one —
To break the heart of generosity,
And make bold power look pale — they threw their caps
As they would hang them on the horns o'th'moon,
210   Shouting their emulation.

MENENIUS   What is granted them?

MARTIUS   Five tribunes to defend their vulgar wisdoms,
Of their own choice. One's Junius Brutus,
Sicinius Velutus, and I know not. 'Sdeath,
215   The rabble should have first unroofed the city,
Ere so prevailed with me: it will in time
Win upon power and throw forth greater themes
For insurrection's arguing.

MENENIUS   This is strange.

220   MARTIUS   Go get you home, you fragments.   *To the Citizens*

Enter a Messenger hastily

---

194 **quartered** mutilated, cut into quarters   195 **pick** pitch, throw   198 **passing** surpassingly, excessively   201 **an-hungry** hungry (Martius mocks the people's unsophisticated speech)
202 **dogs** even dogs   203 **meat** food   204 **shreds** scraps (of reasoning)   207 **generosity** the nobles   209 **As** as if   210 **Shouting their emulation** each competing to shout the loudest/shouting in ambitious triumph   212 **tribunes** officials appointed to protect the interests and rights of the people   **vulgar** common, public, plebeian   214 **'Sdeath** by God's death (common oath)   217 **Win upon power** gain the advantage over those in power
themes subjects/arguments   218 **For insurrection's arguing** to justify rebellion
220 **fragments** insignificant beings (literally, scraps of food)

MESSENGER   Where's Caius Martius?

MARTIUS   Here: what's the matter?

MESSENGER   The news is, sir, the Volsces are in arms.

MARTIUS   I am glad on't: then we shall ha' means to vent

225   Our musty superfluity. See, our best elders.

Enter Sicinius Velutus, Junius Brutus, Cominius, Titus Lartius, with
other Senators

FIRST SENATOR   Martius, 'tis true that you have lately told us:

The Volsces are in arms.

MARTIUS   They have a leader,

Tullus Aufidius, that will put you to't:

230   I sin in envying his nobility,

And were I anything but what I am,

I would wish me only he.

COMINIUS   You have fought together!

MARTIUS   Were half to half the world by th'ears and he

235   Upon my party, I'd revolt to make

Only my wars with him. He is a lion

That I am proud to hunt.

FIRST SENATOR   Then, worthy Martius,

Attend upon Cominius to these wars.

240   COMINIUS   It is your former promise.   *To Martius*

MARTIUS   Sir, it is,

And I am constant: Titus Lartius, thou

Shalt see me once more strike at Tullus' face.

What, art thou stiff? Stand'st out?

245   LARTIUS   No, Caius Martius,

I'll lean upon one crutch and fight with t'other,

Ere stay behind this business.

MENENIUS   O, true-bred!

---

224 vent get rid of/excrete or urinate   **225 musty superfluity** moldy excess, i.e. the
troublesome citizens (imaged as stale goods or as bodily waste matter)   **226 that** what
229 to't i.e. to the test   **233 together** i.e. against each other   **234 by th'ears** fighting
235 party side   **236 with** i.e. against   **239 Attend upon** serve under, follow   **242 constant**
unchanging, true to my word   **244 stiff** reluctant/stiff with age/rendered incapable by injury
Stand'st out? Will you not fight?   **247 Ere** in preference to

FIRST SENATOR   Your company to th'Capitol, where I know
250   Our greatest friends attend us.

LARTIUS   Lead you on.—   *To Cominius*
    Follow Cominius, we must follow you,   *To Martius*
    Right worthy your priority.

COMINIUS   Noble Martius.

255 FIRST SENATOR   Hence to your homes, be gone.   *To the Citizens*

MARTIUS   Nay, let them follow:
    The Volsces have much corn: take these rats thither
    To gnaw their garners. Worshipful mutineers,
    Your valour puts well forth: pray follow.   *Exeunt*

Citizens steal away. Sicinius and Brutus remain

260 SICINIUS   Was ever man so proud as is this Martius?

BRUTUS   He has no equal.

SICINIUS   When we were chosen tribunes for the people—

BRUTUS   Marked you his lip and eyes?

SICINIUS   Nay, but his taunts.

265 BRUTUS   Being moved, he will not spare to gird the gods.

SICINIUS   Bemock the modest moon.

BRUTUS   The present wars devour him: he is grown
    Too proud to be so valiant.

SICINIUS   Such a nature,
270   Tickled with good success, disdains the shadow
    Which he treads on at noon: but I do wonder
    His insolence can brook to be commanded
    Under Cominius.

BRUTUS   Fame, at the which he aims,
275   In whom already he's well graced, cannot
    Better be held nor more attained than by
    A place below the first: for what miscarries

---

249 **Your** i.e. may I have your   250 **attend** await   253 **Right . . . priority** you deserve to go first
258 **garners** granaries, storehouses   **Worshipful** esteemed (sarcastic)   259 **puts well forth**
develops well, is promising (mocking)   265 **moved** roused, angered   **spare to gird** refrain
from mocking   266 **modest** chaste (the **moon** was associated with Diana, Roman goddess of
chastity)   267 **The** may the   270 **Tickled with** pleased by/excited by/provoked, urged on by
271 **noon** suggestive of the height of success, when shadows are smallest (but later grow)
272 **insolence** haughty pride   **brook** bear   277 **miscarries** fails

Shall be the general's fault, though he perform
To th'utmost of a man, and giddy censure
280　Will then cry out of Martius 'O, if he
Had borne the business!'

SICINIUS　　Besides, if things go well,
Opinion that so sticks on Martius shall
Of his demerits rob Cominius.

285　BRUTUS　　Come:
Half all Cominius' honours are to Martius,
Though Martius earned them not: and all his faults
To Martius shall be honours, though indeed
In aught he merit not.

290　SICINIUS　　Let's hence, and hear
How the dispatch is made, and in what fashion,
More than his singularity, he goes
Upon this present action.

BRUTUS　　Let's along.　　　　　　　　　　　　　　*Exeunt*

[Act 1 Scene 2]　　　　　　　　　　　　　*running scene 2*

Enter Tullus Aufidius with Senators of Corioles

FIRST SENATOR　　So, your opinion is, Aufidius,
That they of Rome are entered in our counsels
And know how we proceed.

AUFIDIUS　　Is it not yours?
5　Whatever have been thought on in this state,
That could be brought to bodily act ere Rome
Had circumvention? 'Tis not four days gone
Since I heard thence: these are the words: I think
I have the letter here: yes, here it is.　　*He reads the letter*
10　'They have pressed a power, but it is not known

---

279 **giddy censure** fickle (public) opinion　283 **Opinion** the reputation/public opinion
284 **demerits** deserts　286 **are** belong　289 **aught** anything　291 **dispatch** settlement of
affairs　292 **More . . . singularity** his individual qualities aside/with even greater self-
importance　293 **action** military enterprise　294 **along** go　**1.2 Location: Corioli (also
known as Corioles)**　2 **entered in** acquainted with　**counsels** opinions/plans/secrets　6 **ere**
before　7 **circumvention** a chance to outwit (the plan)　10 **pressed a power** raised an army

Whether for east or west: the dearth is great,
The people mutinous: and it is rumoured,
Cominius, Martius your old enemy,
Who is of Rome worse hated than of you,
15 And Titus Lartius, a most valiant Roman,
These three lead on this preparation
Whither 'tis bent: most likely 'tis for you:
Consider of it.'

FIRST SENATOR   Our army's in the field:
20 We never yet made doubt but Rome was ready
To answer us.

AUFIDIUS   Nor did you think it folly
To keep your great pretences veiled, till when
They needs must show themselves, which in the hatching,
25 It seemed, appeared to Rome. By the discovery,
We shall be shortened in our aim, which was
To take in many towns ere, almost, Rome
Should know we were afoot.

SECOND SENATOR   Noble Aufidius,
30 Take your commission, hie you to your bands:
Let us alone to guard Corioles.
If they set down before's, for the remove
Bring up your army: but, I think, you'll find
They've not prepared for us.

35 AUFIDIUS   O, doubt not that:
I speak from certainties. Nay, more,
Some parcels of their power are forth already,
And only hitherward. I leave your honours.
If we and Caius Martius chance to meet,
40 'Tis sworn between us we shall ever strike
Till one can do no more.

ALL   The gods assist you!

14 of by   16 preparation equipped military force   17 Whither wherever   bent directed
19 field battlefield   20 made doubt but doubted that   23 pretences plans   24 needs
necessarily   26 shortened curtailed   27 take in capture   30 hie hurry   bands troops
32 set down before's besiege us   remove removal, lifting (of the siege)   37 parcels parts,
sections   power army   forth out, on the move   38 only hitherward march only in our
direction   40 ever ceaselessly, constantly

AUFIDIUS   And keep your honours safe.

FIRST SENATOR   Farewell.

45   SECOND SENATOR   Farewell.

ALL ·   Farewell.   *Exeunt*

[Act 1 Scene 3]   *running scene 3*

Enter Volumnia and Virgilia, mother and wife to Martius: they set
them down on two low stools and sew

VOLUMNIA   I pray you, daughter, sing, or express yourself in a
more comfortable sort: if my son were my husband, I should
freelier rejoice in that absence wherein he won honour than
in the embracements of his bed where he would show most
5   love. When yet he was but tender-bodied and the only son of
my womb, when youth with comeliness plucked all gaze his
way, when for a day of kings' entreaties a mother should not
sell him an hour from her beholding, I, considering how
honour would become such a person, that it was no better
10   than, picture-like, to hang by th'wall if renown made it not
stir, was pleased to let him seek danger where he was like to
find fame: to a cruel war I sent him, from whence he
returned, his brows bound with oak. I tell thee, daughter, I
sprang not more in joy at first hearing he was a man-child
15   than now in first seeing he had proved himself a man.

VIRGILIA   But had he died in the business, madam, how then?

VOLUMNIA   Then his good report should have been my son: I
therein would have found issue. Hear me profess sincerely:
had I a dozen sons, each in my love alike, and none less dear
20   than thine and my good Martius, I had rather had eleven die
nobly for their country than one voluptuously surfeit out of
action.

1.3 **Location:** *Martius' house, Rome*   2 **comfortable** cheerful   **sort** manner   3 **freelier**
more freely   5 **tender-bodied** young   6 **comeliness** good looks   9 **become** befit, suit
person character/physical appearance   10 **picture-like . . . th'wall** i.e. purely ornamental
renown (desire for) honor   11 **like** likely   13 **oak** a garland of oak leaves, signifying that he
had saved the life of a fellow Roman citizen   15 **now** i.e. at that time   18 **issue** offspring
21 **voluptuously surfeit** live in luxurious, sensual excess

Enter a Gentlewoman

GENTLEWOMAN   Madam, the lady Valeria is come to visit you.

To Volumnia

VIRGILIA   Beseech you give me leave to retire myself. *To Volumnia*

25   VOLUMNIA   Indeed, you shall not.
Methinks I hear hither your husband's drum:
See him pluck Aufidius down by th'hair,
As children from a bear, the Volsces shunning him:
Methinks I see him stamp thus, and call thus,
30   'Come on, you cowards, you were got in fear,
Though you were born in Rome'; his bloody brow
With his mailed hand then wiping, forth he goes,
Like to a harvest-man that's tasked to mow
Or all or lose his hire.

35   VIRGILIA   His bloody brow? O Jupiter, no blood!

VOLUMNIA   Away, you fool! It more becomes a man
Than gilt his trophy. The breasts of Hecuba
When she did suckle Hector looked not lovelier
Than Hector's forehead when it spit forth blood
40   At Grecian sword, contemning.— Tell Valeria, *To the Gentlewoman*
We are fit to bid her welcome.   *Exit Gentlewoman*

VIRGILIA   Heavens bless my lord from fell Aufidius!

VOLUMNIA   He'll beat Aufidius' head below his knee
And tread upon his neck.

Enter Valeria with an Usher and a Gentlewoman

45   VALERIA   My ladies both, good day to you.

VOLUMNIA   Sweet madam.

VIRGILIA   I am glad to see your ladyship.

VALERIA   How do you both? You are manifest housekeepers.
What are you sewing here? A fine spot, in good faith. How
50   does your little son?

---

24 give . . . myself permit me to withdraw   **26 hither** from here/coming this way   **27 See** i.e.
I imagine I see   **30 got** begot, conceived   **32 mailed** armored   **33 tasked** employed   **mow** Or
either mow   **34 hire** fee   **35 Jupiter** Roman supreme god   **37 gilt his trophy** than a covering
of gold befits the monument to his victory   **Hecuba** Queen of Troy and mother of **Hector**,
who led the Trojan army   **40 contemning** in scorn   **41 fit** ready, in a proper state   **42 bless**
i.e. protect   **fell** fierce, cruel   *Usher* male attendant who walked before a person of rank
48 manifest housekeepers clearly engaged in domestic affairs   **49 spot** piece of embroidery

VIRGILIA   I thank your ladyship: well, good madam.

VOLUMNIA   He had rather see the swords and hear a drum than look upon his schoolmaster.

VALERIA   O'my word, the father's son: I'll swear 'tis a very
55   pretty boy. O'my troth, I looked upon him o'Wednesday half an hour together: he's such a confirmed countenance. I saw him run after a gilded butterfly, and when he caught it, he let it go again, and after it again, and over and over he comes, and up again, catched it again: or whether his fall enraged
60   him, or how 'twas, he did so set his teeth and tear it. O, I warrant how he mammocked it!

VOLUMNIA   One on's father's moods.

VALERIA   Indeed, la, 'tis a noble child.

VIRGILIA   A crack, madam.

65 **VALERIA**   Come, lay aside your stitchery, I must have you play the idle housewife with me this afternoon.

VIRGILIA   No, good madam, I will not out of doors.

VALERIA   Not out of doors?

VOLUMNIA   She shall, she shall.

70 **VIRGILIA**   Indeed, no, by your patience: I'll not over the threshold till my lord return from the wars.

VALERIA   Fie, you confine yourself most unreasonably: come, you must go visit the good lady that lies in.

VIRGILIA   I will wish her speedy strength, and visit her with
75   my prayers: but I cannot go thither.

VOLUMNIA   Why, I pray you?

VIRGILIA   'Tis not to save labour, nor that I want love.

VALERIA   You would be another Penelope: yet they say all the yarn she spun in Ulysses' absence did but fill Ithaca full of

---

54 **O'my** on my   55 **troth** faith   **half . . . together** for a full half hour   56 **he's** he has **confirmed** determined   58 **after** i.e. ran after   59 **or whether** whether   60 **set** clench 61 **warrant** assure you   **mammocked** tore to pieces   62 **on's** of his   63 **la** exclamation used for emphasis   64 **crack** little rascal   66 **housewife** may play on the sense of "hussy, worthless woman"   67 **out** go out   72 **Fie** expression of reproach   73 **lies in** is due to have a baby soon 77 **want** lack   78 **Penelope** faithful wife of **Ulysses**, king of **Ithaca**; while he was away fighting in the Trojan wars, she deterred her suitors by insisting that she had to finish weaving her father-in-law's shroud, which she then unpicked every night

80   moths. Come, I would your cambric were sensible as your
      finger, that you might leave pricking it for pity. Come, you
      shall go with us.

VIRGILIA   No, good madam, pardon me, indeed I will not forth.

VALERIA   In truth, la, go with me, and I'll tell you excellent
85   news of your husband.

VIRGILIA   O, good madam, there can be none yet.

VALERIA   Verily I do not jest with you: there came news from
      him last night.

VIRGILIA   Indeed, madam?

90   VALERIA   In earnest, it's true: I heard a senator speak it. Thus
      it is: the Volsces have an army forth, against whom Cominius
      the general is gone, with one part of our Roman power. Your
      lord and Titus Lartius are set down before their city Corioles:
      they nothing doubt prevailing and to make it brief wars. This
95   is true, on mine honour: and so, I pray, go with us.

VIRGILIA   Give me excuse, good madam: I will obey you in
      everything hereafter.

VOLUMNIA   Let her alone, lady: as she is now, she will but
      disease our better mirth.

100   VALERIA   In troth, I think she would. Fare you well, then.
      Come, good sweet lady. Prithee, Virgilia, turn thy solemness
      out o'door, and go along with us.

VIRGILIA   No, at a word, madam: indeed, I must not. I wish
      you much mirth.

105   VALERIA   Well then, farewell.   *Exeunt Ladies*

---

80 would wish   cambric fine linen (originally from Cambray in Flanders)   sensible
capable of feeling, sensitive   81 leave cease   87 Verily truly   94 nothing doubt prevailing
have no doubt they will succeed   96 Give me excuse excuse me, i.e. permit me to stay
99 disease . . . mirth spoil our good cheer   100 troth truth   103 at a word once and for all, in
a word

[Act 1 Scene 4]   *running scene 4*

Enter Martius, Titus Lartius, with Drum [, Trumpeter] and Colours,
with Captains and Soldiers [with scaling ladders], as before the city
Corioles: to them a Messenger

	MARTIUS	Yonder comes news: a wager they have met.
	LARTIUS	My horse to yours, no.
	MARTIUS	'Tis done.
	LARTIUS	Agreed.
5	MARTIUS	Say, has our general met the enemy? *To the Messenger*
	MESSENGER	They lie in view, but have not spoke as yet.
	LARTIUS	So, the good horse is mine.
	MARTIUS	I'll buy him of you.
	LARTIUS	No, I'll nor sell nor give him: lend you him I will
10		For half a hundred years.— Summon the town. *To Trumpeter*
	MARTIUS	How far off lie these armies?
	MESSENGER	Within this mile and half.
	MARTIUS	Then shall we hear their 'larum, and they ours.

      Now, Mars, I prithee make us quick in work,
15   That we with smoking swords may march from hence
      To help our fielded friends.— Come, blow thy blast.   *To Trumpeter*

They sound a parley: enter two Senators with others on the walls of
Corioles

      Tullus Aufidius, is he within your walls?

FIRST SENATOR   No, nor a man that fears you less than he,
      That's lesser than a little.

                        Hark, our drums   *Drum afar off*
20   Are bringing forth our youth: we'll break our walls
      Rather than they shall pound us up: our gates,

1.4 Location: outside Corioles; the rest of the scenes in Act 1 take place at varying
distances from the city   Drum a drummer   **Colours** ensigns, bearers of military banners or
flags   **to them** i.e. to them comes   **1 met** i.e. in battle   **2 My . . . no** i.e. I bet my horse against
yours that they haven't   **6 spoke** encountered one another, fought   **9 nor** neither
13 'larum alarum, i.e. call to arms   **14 Mars** Roman god of war   **15 smoking** i.e. steaming
(after immersion in hot blood)   **16 fielded** engaged on the battlefield   **parley** trumpet
summons to negotiation between enemy forces   **on the walls** i.e. the upper staging level or
gallery, conventionally used to represent city walls   **18 nor . . . he** i.e. there are no men within
the walls who fear you   **21 pound us up** confine us (like animals)

Which yet seem shut, we have but pinned with rushes:
They'll open of themselves.

                        Hark you, far off   *Alarum far off*

There is Aufidius. List what work he makes

25   Amongst your cloven army.

MARTIUS   O, they are at it!

LARTIUS   Their noise be our instruction. Ladders, ho!   *They*

Enter the army of the Volsces   *prepare their ladders to assault the walls*

MARTIUS   They fear us not, but issue forth their city.

Now put your shields before your hearts, and fight

30   With hearts more proof than shields. Advance, brave Titus:

They do disdain us much beyond our thoughts,

Which makes me sweat with wrath. Come on, my fellows:

He that retires, I'll take him for a Volsce,

And he shall feel mine edge.

Alarum: the Romans are beat back to their trenches [and exeunt,
followed by the Volsces]. Enter Martius cursing

35   MARTIUS   All the contagion of the south light on you,

You shames of Rome! You herd of— boils and plagues

Plaster you o'er, that you may be abhorred

Further than seen, and one infect another

Against the wind a mile: you souls of geese

40   That bear the shapes of men, how have you run

From slaves that apes would beat! Pluto and hell:

All hurt behind, backs red, and faces pale

With flight and agued fear! Mend and charge home,

Or, by the fires of heaven, I'll leave the foe

45   And make my wars on you: look to't. Come on:

---

22 **pinned with rushes** i.e. bolted weakly, as if with mere reeds   24 **List** listen (to)   25 **cloven** split in two, divided   27 **Their** let their   **our instruction** our example, a lesson to us   30 **proof** impenetrable   31 **beyond our thoughts** more than we had imagined   34 **edge** sword edge   35 **south** south wind, thought to carry disease   38 **Further than seen** even before you are seen (because of your diseased stench)   39 **Against . . . mile** so contagiously that the infection will carry a whole mile against a contrary wind   **souls of geese** i.e. cowards and fools 41 **Pluto** Roman god of the underworld   42 **behind** in the back, i.e. as they fled in cowardice 43 **agued** trembling (an ague was a fever characterized by shaking)   **Mend** improve   **home** toward the target, i.e. the enemy

If you'll stand fast, we'll beat them to their wives,
As they us to our trenches followed.

Another alarum, and Martius follows [the Volsces] to [the] gates

So, now the gates are ope: now prove good seconds:
'Tis for the followers fortune widens them,
50   Not for the fliers: mark me, and do the like.

[He] enter[s] the gates

FIRST SOLDIER   Foolhardiness: not I.

SECOND SOLDIER   Nor I.

[The gates close and Martius] is shut in

FIRST SOLDIER   See, they have shut him in.   *Alarum continues*

ALL   To th'pot, I warrant him.

Enter Titus Lartius

55   LARTIUS   What is become of Martius?

ALL   Slain, sir, doubtless.

FIRST SOLDIER   Following the fliers at the very heels,
With them he enters, who upon the sudden
Clapped to their gates: he is himself alone,
60   To answer all the city.

LARTIUS   O noble fellow!
Who sensibly outdares his senseless sword,
And when it bows, stand'st up. Thou art left, Martius:
A carbuncle entire, as big as thou art,
65   Were not so rich a jewel. Thou wast a soldier
Even to Cato's wish, not fierce and terrible
Only in strokes: but with thy grim looks, and
The thunder-like percussion of thy sounds,
Thou mad'st thine enemies shake, as if the world
70   Were feverous and did tremble.

Enter Martius, bleeding, assaulted by the enemy

FIRST SOLDIER   Look, sir.

---

46 beat drive with blows   **48 ope** open   **seconds** supporters   **49 followers** pursuers
them i.e. the gates   **50 fliers** those who retreat   **54 th'pot** the cooking pot, i.e. death
59 Clapped to shut   **60 answer** face/encounter in a fight   **62 sensibly** capable of feeling pain
outdares dares more than   **63 bows** bends   **stand'st** he stands   **left** i.e. alone in the city
64 carbuncle entire flawless red precious stone   **66 Cato** Marcus Cato, known as the
"Censor," an advocate of Rome's military virtues (an anachronism: Cato lived 234–149 BC)

LARTIUS   O, 'tis Martius!
Let's fetch him off, or make remain alike.
They fight, and all enter the city

[Act 1 Scene 5]   *running scene 4 continues*

Enter certain Romans with spoils

FIRST ROMAN   This will I carry to Rome.

SECOND ROMAN   And I this.

THIRD ROMAN   A murrain on't, I took this for silver.   *Exeunt*

Alarum continues still afar off
Enter Martius and Titus [Lartius] with a Trumpet

MARTIUS   See here these movers that do prize their honours
5   At a cracked drachma: cushions, leaden spoons,
Irons of a doit, doublets that hangmen would
Bury with those that wore them, these base slaves,
Ere yet the fight be done, pack up: down with them!
And hark, what noise the general makes: to him.
10   There is the man of my soul's hate, Aufidius,
Piercing our Romans: then, valiant Titus, take
Convenient numbers to make good the city,
Whilst I, with those that have the spirit, will haste
To help Cominius.
15   LARTIUS   Worthy sir, thou bleed'st:
Thy exercise hath been too violent
For a second course of fight.

MARTIUS   Sir, praise me not:
My work hath yet not warmed me. Fare you well:
20   The blood I drop is rather physical
Than dangerous to me: to Aufidius thus
I will appear, and fight.

---

73 fetch him off rescue him   **make remain** stay (with him)   **1.5   3 murrain** plague (literally, disease affecting cattle and sheep)   *Trumpet* trumpeter   **4 prize** value   **5 drachma** silver coin (here deemed of little value)   **6 Irons** iron weapons, swords   **of a doit** i.e. worth very little
doit Dutch coin worth only half an English farthing   **doublets** close-fitting jackets   **hangmen** hangmen were entitled to keep the clothing of those they put to death   **9 the general** i.e. Cominius   **12 Convenient** appropriate   **make good** secure   **20 physical** medicinal, restorative (a reference to the common medical treatment of bloodletting)

LARTIUS   Now the fair goddess, Fortune,
Fall deep in love with thee, and her great charms
25   Misguide thy opposers' swords! Bold gentleman,
Prosperity be thy page.

MARTIUS   Thy friend no less
Than those she placeth highest. So farewell.

LARTIUS   Thou worthiest Martius!   [*Exit Martius*]
30   Go sound thy trumpet in the market-place:
Call thither all the officers o'th'town,
Where they shall know our mind. Away.   *Exeunt*

[Act 1 Scene 6]   *running scene 4 continues*

Enter Cominius, as it were in retire, with Soldiers

COMINIUS   Breathe you, my friends: well fought: we are come off
Like Romans, neither foolish in our stands,
Nor cowardly in retire: believe me, sirs,
We shall be charged again. Whiles we have struck,
5   By interims and conveying gusts we have heard
The charges of our friends. The Roman gods
Lead their successes as we wish our own,
That both our powers, with smiling fronts encount'ring,
May give you thankful sacrifice.

Enter a Messenger

Thy news?

10   MESSENGER   The citizens of Corioles have issued,
And given to Lartius and to Martius battle:
I saw our party to their trenches driven,
And then I came away.

COMINIUS   Though thou speak'st truth,
15   Methinks thou speak'st not well. How long is't since?

---

24 **charms** magic spells   25 **opposers'** opponents'   26 **Prosperity . . . page** i.e. may success attend on you   27 **Thy . . . highest** i.e. may prosperity be no less a friend to you   **1.6** *retire* retreat   1 **Breathe you** catch your breath, rest   2 **stands** resistance/holding of a military position   4 **struck** been fighting, given blows   5 **By . . . gusts** at intervals and blown in on the wind   6 **The** may the   8 **fronts** faces/front ranks (of the army)   10 **issued** come forth

MESSENGER   Above an hour, my lord.

COMINIUS   'Tis not a mile: briefly we heard their drums.
How couldst thou in a mile confound an hour,
And bring thy news so late?

20   MESSENGER   Spies of the Volsces
Held me in chase, that I was forced to wheel
Three or four miles about, else had I, sir,
Half an hour since brought my report.

Enter Martius [bleeding]

COMINIUS   Who's yonder,

25   That does appear as he were flayed? O gods,
He has the stamp of Martius, and I have
Before-time seen him thus.

MARTIUS   Come I too late?

COMINIUS   The shepherd knows not thunder from a tabor

30   More than I know the sound of Martius' tongue
From every meaner man.

MARTIUS   Come I too late?

COMINIUS   Ay, if you come not in the blood of others,
But mantled in your own.

35   MARTIUS   O, let me clip ye
In arms as sound as when I wooed in heart,
As merry as when our nuptial day was done,
And tapers burned to bedward.   *He embraces Cominius*

COMINIUS   Flower of warriors, how is't with Titus Lartius?

40   MARTIUS   As with a man busied about decrees:
Condemning some to death, and some to exile,
Ransoming him, or pitying, threat'ning th'other;
Holding Corioles in the name of Rome,
Even like a fawning greyhound in the leash,

45   To let him slip at will.

---

17 briefly not long ago   **18 confound** waste   **21 that** so that   **25 as** as if   **26 stamp** imprint, i.e. form, bearing   **27 Before-time** formerly   **29 tabor** small drum used for reveling
31 meaner humbler, lower-ranking/less worthy   **35 clip** clasp, embrace   **38 tapers** candles
to bedward to indicate bedtime, to show the way to bed   **40 busied about decrees** busy with legal judgments   **45 slip** be unleashed

COMINIUS   Where is that slave
Which told me they had beat you to your trenches?
Where is he? Call him hither.

MARTIUS   Let him alone:
50   He did inform the truth: but for our gentlemen,
The common file — a plague — tribunes for them! —
The mouse ne'er shunned the cat as they did budge
From rascals worse than they.

COMINIUS   But how prevailed you?

55   MARTIUS   Will the time serve to tell? I do not think.
Where is the enemy? Are you lords o'th'field?
If not, why cease you till you are so?

COMINIUS   Martius, we have at disadvantage fought
And did retire to win our purpose.

60   MARTIUS   How lies their battle? Know you on which side
They have placed their men of trust?

COMINIUS   As I guess, Martius,
Their bands i'th'vanguard are the Antiates,
Of their best trust: o'er them Aufidius,
65   Their very heart of hope.

MARTIUS   I do beseech you,
By all the battles wherein we have fought,
By th'blood we have shed together, by th'vows
We have made to endure friends, that you directly
70   Set me against Aufidius and his Antiates,
And that you not delay the present, but,
Filling the air with swords advanced and darts,
We prove this very hour.

COMINIUS   Though I could wish
75   You were conducted to a gentle bath

---

51 common file ordinary soldiers   **52 budge** flinch   **55 think** think so   **59 to . . . purpose**
i.e. draw breath, regroup (in order to win)   **60 lies their battle** are their troops drawn up
63 bands i'th'vanguard troops in the foremost part of the army (spelled "vaward" in
Shakespearean English)   **Antiates** people from Antium, now Anzio, in southern Italy
64 Of . . . trust their most reliable men   **69 endure** remain   **72 advanced** upraised   **darts**
small spears/arrows   **73 prove** test

And balms applied to you, yet dare I never
Deny your asking: take your choice of those
That best can aid your action.

MARTIUS   Those are they
80 That most are willing: if any such be here,
As it were sin to doubt, that love this painting
Wherein you see me smeared, if any fear
Lesser his person than an ill report:
If any think brave death outweighs bad life,
85 And that his country's dearer than himself,
Let him alone, or so many so minded,
Wave thus to express his disposition,
And follow Martius.

They all shout and wave their swords, take him up in their arms, and
cast up their caps

O, me alone, make you a sword of me?
90 If these shows be not outward, which of you
But is four Volsces? None of you but is
Able to bear against the great Aufidius
A shield as hard as his. A certain number,
Though thanks to all, must I select from all.
95 The rest shall bear the business in some other fight,
As cause will be obeyed. Please you to march,
And I shall quickly draw out my command,
Which men are best inclined.

COMINIUS   March on, my fellows:
100 Make good this ostentation, and you shall
Divide in all with us.   *Exeunt*

---

76 balms healing ointments   **81 painting** i.e. blood   **83 Lesser . . . report** less for his personal
safety than for his reputation   **84 brave** noble, splendid/courageous   **86 him alone** only that
man   **89 O . . . me?** Do you choose me as your sword? (where **O, me alone** is an exclamation
of surprise)/Do you select only me as your weapon? (perhaps referring to the fact that the
soldiers have raised him aloft like a sword)   **90 outward** superficial, for the sake of appearance
91 But is is not worth   **96 cause . . . obeyed** circumstance dictates   **100 Make . . .**
ostentation i.e. match this impressive display with action   **101 Divide in all** have a portion of
all (the booty)

[Act 1 Scene 7]   *running scene 4 continues*

Titus Lartius, having set a guard upon Corioles, going with Drum and
Trumpet toward Cominius and Caius Martius, enters with a
Lieutenant, other Soldiers and a Scout

LARTIUS   So, let the ports be guarded: keep your duties

                                                     To the Lieutenant

As I have set them down. If I do send, dispatch
Those centuries to our aid: the rest will serve
For a short holding: if we lose the field,
5   We cannot keep the town.
LIEUTENANT   Fear not our care, sir.
LARTIUS   Hence, and shut your gates upon's:
Our guider, come; to th'Roman camp conduct us.   *Exeunt*

[Act 1 Scene 8]   *running scene 4 continues*

Alarum, as in battle. Enter Martius and Aufidius at several doors

MARTIUS   I'll fight with none but thee, for I do hate thee
Worse than a promise-breaker.
AUFIDIUS   We hate alike:
Not Afric owns a serpent I abhor
5   More than thy fame and envy. Fix thy foot.
MARTIUS   Let the first budger die the other's slave,
And the gods doom him after.
AUFIDIUS   If I fly, Martius, holla me like a hare.
MARTIUS   Within these three hours, Tullus,
10   Alone I fought in your Corioles' walls,
And made what work I pleased: 'tis not my blood
Wherein thou see'st me masked: for thy revenge
Wrench up thy power to th'highest.

1.7 1 ports gates   **3 centuries** companies of one hundred soldiers   **4 holding** i.e. of the city
6 Fear not do not doubt/do not worry about   **care** diligence/responsibility   **1.8 *several***
separate   **4 Not Afric owns** Africa does not possess   **5 fame and envy** great reputation and
personal malice/envied reputation/hated reputation   **Fix thy foot** stand firm (in preparation
for hand-to-hand combat)   **6 budger** one who flinches   **8 holla** shout at (as, while hunting,
one would cry out after a fleeing **hare**)   **13 Wrench up** strain, summon

AUFIDIUS   Wert thou the Hector

15   That was the whip of your bragged progeny,

        Thou shouldst not scape me here.

Here they fight, and certain Volsces come in the aid of Aufidius.

Martius fights till they be driven in breathless

        Officious, and not valiant, you have shamed me

        In your condemnèd seconds.   [*Exit*]

[Act 1 Scene 9]   *running scene 4 continues*

Alarum. Flourish. A retreat is sounded. Enter at one door Cominius
with the Romans: at another door Martius, with his arm in a scarf

COMINIUS   If I should tell thee o'er this thy day's work,

        Thou't not believe thy deeds: but I'll report it

        Where senators shall mingle tears with smiles,

        Where great patricians shall attend and shrug,

5   I'th'end admire: where ladies shall be frighted,

        And, gladly quaked, hear more: where the dull tribunes,

        That with the fusty plebeians, hate thine honours,

        Shall say against their hearts, 'We thank the gods

        Our Rome hath such a soldier.'

10   Yet cam'st thou to a morsel of this feast,

        Having fully dined before.

Enter Titus [Lartius] with his power, from the pursuit

LARTIUS   O general,

        Here is the steed, we the caparison:

        Hadst thou beheld—

15   MARTIUS   Pray now, no more: my mother,

        Who has a charter to extol her blood,

---

15 bragged progeny the (Trojan) ancestry you boast of   **16 scape** escape from   **18 In . . .
seconds** with your damned supporters   **1.9 *Flourish*** trumpet fanfare (usually signaling the
arrival or departure of a person in authority)   ***retreat*** trumpet call instructing soldiers to
retreat   ***scarf*** sling/bandage   **1 tell thee o'er** recount to you   **4 attend** listen   **shrug** i.e. in
disbelief   **5 I'th'end admire** and eventually marvel   **6 gladly quaked** willingly frightened,
eager and trembling   **dull** sluggish/stupid   **7 fusty** stale, moldy   **8 hearts** wills, inclinations
10 cam'st . . . before i.e. this was a trifling challenge for you, in comparison with the battle you
fought at Corioles   **13 caparison** mere trappings   **16 charter . . . blood** right to praise her
offspring

When she does praise me, grieves me. I have done
As you have done: that's what I can, induced
As you have been, that's for my country:
20   He that has but effected his good will
Hath overta'en mine act.

COMINIUS   You shall not be the grave of your deserving:
Rome must know the value of her own:
'Twere a concealment worse than a theft,
25   No less than a traducement,
To hide your doings, and to silence that
Which, to the spire and top of praises vouched,
Would seem but modest: therefore, I beseech you
In sign of what you are, not to reward
30   What you have done, before our army hear me.

MARTIUS   I have some wounds upon me, and they smart
To hear themselves remembered.

COMINIUS   Should they not,
Well might they fester gainst ingratitude,
35   And tent themselves with death. Of all the horses,
Whereof we have ta'en good and good store, of all
The treasure in this field achieved and city,
We render you the tenth, to be ta'en forth,
Before the common distribution,
40   At your only choice.

MARTIUS   I thank you, general:
But cannot make my heart consent to take
A bribe to pay my sword: I do refuse it,
And stand upon my common part with those
45   That have beheld the doing.

---

18 induced prevailed upon   **20 effected** carried out   **21 overta'en** outdone
22 be . . . deserving i.e. bury your worthiness   **25 a traducement** slander   **27 to . . . vouched**
i.e. affirmed in the highest possible terms   **29 In sign** as a token   **33 not** i.e. not hear
themselves remembered   **34 gainst** in the face of   **35 tent** probe, clean surgically (i.e. cure)
36 good . . . store fine ones and plenty of them   **37 in . . . city** gained in the field and in the
city   **38 the** i.e. one   **40 At . . . choice** entirely as you choose   **44 stand** insist   **common part**
ordinary share   **45 beheld the doing** seen the action

A long flourish. They all cry 'Martius, Martius!' *cast up their caps and*
lances: Cominius and Lartius stand bare

    May these same instruments, which you profane,
    Never sound more: when drums and trumpets shall
    I'th'field prove flatterers, let courts and cities be
    Made all of false-faced soothing: when steel grows
50   Soft as the parasite's silk, let him be made
    An overture for th'wars: no more, I say,
    For that I have not washed my nose that bled,
    Or foiled some debile wretch, which, without note,
    Here's many else have done, you shout me forth
55   In acclamations hyperbolical,
    As if I loved my little should be dieted
    In praises sauced with lies.
COMINIUS   Too modest are you:
    More cruel to your good report than grateful
60   To us that give you truly: by your patience,
    If gainst yourself you be incensed, we'll put you,
    Like one that means his proper harm, in manacles,
    Then reason safely with you: therefore be it known,
    As to us, to all the world, that Caius Martius
65   Wears this war's garland: in token of the which,
    My noble steed, known to the camp, I give him,
    With all his trim belonging: and from this time,
    For what he did before Corioles, call him,
    With all th'applause and clamour of the host,
70   Martius Caius Coriolanus. Bear th'addition nobly ever!

---

bare bareheaded, a sign of respect   **49 soothing** flattery   **50 parasite** sycophantic, sponging
courtier (playing on the sense of "silkworm")   **him** i.e. the **parasite** (though functioning as
"it," **him** could refer to **steel** or **silk**)   **51 overture** announcer, a herald/leader, opener of the
attack (some editors emend to "ovator," i.e. one who receives an ovation or a processional
entrance into Rome for a military commander)   **52 For that** because   **53 debile** feeble   **note**
attention, notice being taken   **54 shout me forth** proclaim my virtues/hail me   **56 little** small
achievements   **dieted In** fed on   **57 sauced** seasoned, flavored   **60 give** portray, report
by your patience with your permission   **62 means** intends   **proper** own   **65 garland** wreath
of victory   **67 his trim belonging** the equipment (**trim**) that goes with him   **69 host** army
70 th'addition the title/mark of distinction

Flourish. Trumpets sound, and Drums

ALL   Martius Caius Coriolanus!

CORIOLANUS I will go wash: *To Cominius*
     And when my face is fair, you shall perceive
     Whether I blush or no: howbeit, I thank you:
75   I mean to stride your steed, and at all times
     To undercrest your good addition
     To th'fairness of my power.

COMINIUS   So, to our tent,
     Where, ere we do repose us, we will write
80   To Rome of our success. You, Titus Lartius,
     Must to Corioles back: send us to Rome
     The best, with whom we may articulate,
     For their own good and ours.

LARTIUS   I shall, my lord.

85   CORIOLANUS The gods begin to mock me: I, that now
     Refused most princely gifts, am bound to beg
     Of my lord general.

COMINIUS   Take't, 'tis yours: what is't?

CORIOLANUS I sometime lay here in Corioles
90   At a poor man's house: he used me kindly:
     He cried to me: I saw him prisoner:
     But then Aufidius was within my view,
     And wrath o'erwhelmed my pity: I request you
     To give my poor host freedom.

95   COMINIUS   O, well begged!
     Were he the butcher of my son, he should
     Be free as is the wind. Deliver him, Titus.

LARTIUS   Martius, his name?

CORIOLANUS By Jupiter, forgot:
100 I am weary: yea, my memory is tired:
     Have we no wine here?

---

73 fair clean   **74 howbeit** nevertheless   **75 stride** sit astride   **76 undercrest** bear (as if on a crest)   **77 th'fairness . . . power** the best of my ability   **82 best** leading citizens, most high-ranking men (of Corioles)   **articulate** negotiate a treaty   **89 sometime** at one time, formerly **lay** lodged   **90 used** treated   **91 cried** called out   **97 Deliver** release

COMINIUS   Go we to our tent:
The blood upon your visage dries: 'tis time
It should be looked to: come.   *Exeunt*

[Act 1 Scene 10]

*A flourish. Cornets. Enter Tullus Aufidius, bloody, with two or three
Soldiers*

AUFIDIUS   The town is ta'en.
FIRST SOLDIER   'Twill be delivered back on good condition.
AUFIDIUS   Condition?
I would I were a Roman, for I cannot,
5   Being a Volsce, be that I am. Condition?
What good condition can a treaty find
I'th'part that is at mercy? Five times, Martius,
I have fought with thee: so often hast thou beat me,
And wouldst do so, I think, should we encounter
10   As often as we eat. By th'elements,
If e'er again I meet him beard to beard,
He's mine, or I am his: mine emulation
Hath not that honour in't it had: for where
I thought to crush him in an equal force,
15   True sword to sword, I'll potch at him some way
Or wrath or craft may get him.
FIRST SOLDIER   He's the devil.
AUFIDIUS   Bolder, though not so subtle: my valour's poisoned
With only suff'ring stain by him: for him
20   Shall fly out of itself: nor sleep nor sanctuary,
Being naked, sick, nor fane nor Capitol,
The prayers of priests, nor times of sacrifice,

---

103 **visage** face   **1.10 1 ta'en** captured   **2 good condition** favorable terms   **5 that** what
6 condition quality   **7 I'th'part . . . mercy** for the side that is at the mercy of the victors
9 encounter meet in combat   **12 emulation** rivalry   **13 where** whereas   **15 potch** poke,
thrust   **16 Or** either   **craft** skill/cunning   **18 subtle** cunning, treacherous   **19 stain**
disgrace/eclipse   **20 Shall . . . itself** shall my valor fly from its own nature   **21 naked**
defenseless   **fane** temple

Embarquements all of fury, shall lift up
Their rotten privilege and custom gainst
25   My hate to Martius. Where I find him, were it
At home, upon my brother's guard, even there,
Against the hospitable canon, would I
Wash my fierce hand in's heart. Go you to th'city:
Learn how 'tis held, and what they are that must
30   Be hostages for Rome.

FIRST SOLDIER   Will not you go?

AUFIDIUS   I am attended at the cypress grove. I pray you —
'Tis south the city mills — bring me word thither
How the world goes, that to the pace of it
35   I may spur on my journey.

FIRST SOLDIER   I shall, sir.   [*Exeunt*]

Act 2 [Scene 1]   *running scene 5*

Enter Menenius with the two Tribunes of the people, Sicinius and
Brutus

MENENIUS   The augurer tells me we shall have news tonight.

BRUTUS   Good or bad?

MENENIUS   Not according to the prayer of the people, for they
love not Martius.

5   SICINIUS   Nature teaches beasts to know their friends.

MENENIUS   Pray you, who does the wolf love?

SICINIUS   The lamb.

MENENIUS   Ay, to devour him, as the hungry plebeians would
the noble Martius.

10   BRUTUS   He's a lamb indeed that baas like a bear.

MENENIUS   He's a bear indeed that lives like a lamb. You two are
old men: tell me one thing that I shall ask you.

---

23 Embarquements prohibitions   **24 rotten** corrupt, decayed   **26 upon** under   **guard**
protection   **27 hospitable canon** law of hospitality   **29 what** who   **32 attended** awaited
33 south south of   **2.1** *Location: Rome*   **1 augurer** Roman religious official who foretold
the future through studying celestial phenomena, the behavior and entrails of birds and other
sacrificial creatures   **3 Not . . . people** not what the people wish for   **5 beasts** i.e. even beasts
10 baas bleats

SICINIUS and BRUTUS   Well, sir.

MENENIUS   In what enormity is Martius poor in that you two
15   have not in abundance?

BRUTUS   He's poor in no one fault, but stored with all.

SICINIUS   Especially in pride.

BRUTUS   And topping all others in boasting.

MENENIUS   This is strange now: do you two know how you are
20   censured here in the city, I mean of us o'th'right-hand file?
Do you?

SICINIUS and BRUTUS   Why? How are we censured?

MENENIUS   Because you talk of pride now: will you not be
angry?

25   SICINIUS and BRUTUS   Well, well, sir, well.

MENENIUS   Why, 'tis no great matter: for a very little thief of
occasion will rob you of a great deal of patience: give your
dispositions the reins, and be angry at your pleasures, at the
least, if you take it as a pleasure to you in being so: you blame
30   Martius for being proud.

BRUTUS   We do it not alone, sir.

MENENIUS   I know you can do very little alone, for your helps
are many, or else your actions would grow wondrous single:
your abilities are too infant-like for doing much alone. You
35   talk of pride: O, that you could turn your eyes toward the
napes of your necks, and make but an interior survey of
your good selves! O, that you could!

BRUTUS   What then, sir?

MENENIUS   Why, then you should discover a brace of
40   unmeriting, proud, violent, testy magistrates, alias fools, as
any in Rome.

SICINIUS   Menenius, you are known well enough too.

MENENIUS   I am known to be a humorous patrician, and one

---

14 enormity vice, wickedness   **16 stored** well supplied   **20 censured** judged, thought of
o'th'right-hand file by honorable and noble men (who were, in battle, traditionally placed on
the right-hand side of a troop formation)   **26 'tis . . . matter** i.e. if you do get angry
a . . . occasion i.e. the slightest opportunity, serving as a thief   **28 at your pleasures** as you
choose   **33 single** solitary/feeble   **35 toward . . . necks** i.e. inward   **39 brace** pair   **40 testy**
irritable   **43 humorous** temperamental (governed by the four bodily humors thought to
control disposition and mood)

that loves a cup of hot wine with not a drop of allaying Tiber
45 in't: said to be something imperfect in favouring the first
complaint, hasty and tinder-like upon too trivial motion: one
that converses more with the buttock of the night than with
the forehead of the morning. What I think, I utter, and spend
my malice in my breath. Meeting two such wealsmen as you
50 are — I cannot call you Lycurguses — if the drink you give
me touch my palate adversely, I make a crooked face at it. I
can say your worships have delivered the matter well, when I
find the ass in compound with the major part of your
syllables. And though I must be content to bear with those
55 that say you are reverend grave men, yet they lie deadly that
tell you have good faces: if you see this in the map of my
microcosm, follows it that I am known well enough too?
What harm can your bisson conspectuities glean out of this
character, if I be known well enough too?

60 BRUTUS   Come, sir, come, we know you well enough.

MENENIUS   You know neither me, yourselves nor anything: you
are ambitious for poor knaves' caps and legs: you wear out a
good wholesome forenoon in hearing a cause between an
orange-wife and a faucet-seller, and then rejourn the
65 controversy of threepence to a second day of audience.
When you are hearing a matter between party and party, if

---

44 **hot** spiced/warm   **allaying** moderating, cooling   **Tiber** Rome's river, i.e. water
45 **imperfect** faulty (in character)   46 **complaint** i.e. complainant in a legal case   **tinder-like**
hot-tempered, easily incensed   **motion** cause   47 **converses** associates, is familiar
buttock . . . night i.e. late nights   48 **spend** expend, use up   49 **breath** utterance, words
(i.e. he does not bear grudges)   **wealsmen** public servants   50 **Lycurguses** i.e. wise men;
Lycurgus was a legendary Spartan legislator, noted for his wisdom   51 **I . . . it** i.e. my grimace
will reveal what I think   52 **delivered** expressed, reported   53 **the . . . syllables** i.e.
foolishness in most of what you say   **compound** union, association   55 **deadly** excessively
56 **tell** say/report   **good** honest/handsome   **this** i.e. all that I have just admitted about myself
the . . . microcosm i.e. my face (which charts the nature of the body, often viewed as a "little
world")   58 **bisson** bleary-eyed   **conspectuities** faculties of sight/insights   59 **character**
personality sketch/physical appearance   62 **caps** i.e. doffing of caps in deference   **legs**
i.e. bows   63 **wholesome forenoon** potentially profitable morning   64 **orange-wife** woman
who sells oranges; perhaps suggesting a dispute between a prostitute and her client; prostitutes
often posed as orange-sellers in the public theaters   **faucet-seller** seller of taps for wine or beer
barrels   **rejourn** postpone, adjourn   65 **controversy** dispute   **audience** hearing   66 **party
and party** i.e. two sides in a legal dispute

you chance to be pinched with the colic, you make faces like mummers, set up the bloody flag against all patience, and in roaring for a chamber-pot, dismiss the controversy bleeding,
70 the more entangled by your hearing: all the peace you make in their cause is calling both the parties knaves. You are a pair of strange ones.

BRUTUS   Come, come, you are well understood to be a perfecter giber for the table than a necessary bencher in the
75 Capitol.

MENENIUS   Our very priests must become mockers, if they shall encounter such ridiculous subjects as you are. When you speak best unto the purpose, it is not worth the wagging of your beards, and your beards deserve not so honourable a
80 grave as to stuff a botcher's cushion, or to be entombed in an ass's pack-saddle: yet you must be saying, 'Martius is proud', who, in a cheap estimation, is worth all your predecessors since Deucalion, though peradventure some of the best of 'em were hereditary hangmen. Good e'en to your worships:
85 more of your conversation would infect my brain, being the herdsmen of the beastly plebeians. I will be bold to take my leave of you.

Brutus and Sicinius [stand] aside
Enter Volumnia, Virgilia and Valeria

How now, my as fair as noble ladies: and the moon, were she earthly, no nobler: whither do you follow your eyes so fast?
90 VOLUMNIA   Honourable Menenius, my boy Martius approaches: for the love of Juno, let's go.

MENENIUS   Ha? Martius coming home?

---

67 pinched tormented   **68 mummers** actors in a mime   **set . . . flag** i.e. declare war
69 bleeding unhealed, unresolved   **74 giber** joker   **table** dinner table   **bencher** magistrate
77 subjects citizens/topics   **When** even when   **80 botcher** one who mends old clothes
82 in a cheap even at the lowest   **83 Deucalion** in Greek mythology, the son of Prometheus; he and his wife were the only survivors of Zeus' great flood   **peradventure** perhaps/probably
84 e'en evening, i.e. farewell   **88 the moon** governed by Diana, Roman goddess of chastity
89 follow your eyes i.e. go eagerly   **91 Juno** supreme Roman goddess and wife of Jupiter

VOLUMNIA		Ay, worthy Menenius, and with most prosperous approbation.

95 MENENIUS Take my cap, Jupiter, and I thank thee. Hoo, Martius coming home? *He throws up his cap*

VIRGILIA *and* VALERIA Nay, 'tis true.

VOLUMNIA Look, here's a letter from him: the state hath another, his wife another, and, I think, there's one at home
100 for you.

MENENIUS I will make my very house reel tonight: a letter for me?

VIRGILIA Yes, certain, there's a letter for you: I saw't.

MENENIUS A letter for me? It gives me an estate of seven years'
105 health, in which time I will make a lip at the physician: the most sovereign prescription in Galen is but empiricutic, and to this preservative, of no better report than a horse-drench. Is he not wounded? He was wont to come home wounded.

VIRGILIA O, no, no, no.

110 VOLUMNIA O, he is wounded, I thank the gods for't.

MENENIUS So do I too, if it be not too much: brings a victory in his pocket? The wounds become him.

VOLUMNIA On's brows: Menenius, he comes the third time home with the oaken garland.

115 MENENIUS Has he disciplined Aufidius soundly?

VOLUMNIA Titus Lartius writes they fought together, but Aufidius got off.

MENENIUS And 'twas time for him too, I'll warrant him that: an he had stayed by him, I would not have been so 'fidiussed
120 for all the chests in Corioles, and the gold that's in them. Is the senate possessed of this?

---

93 **most prosperous approbation** great proof of success/great success and acclaim
104 **estate** endowment   105 **make . . . at** mock dismissively   106 **sovereign** efficacious, excellent   **Galen** famous Greek physician (an anachronism; Galen lived in the second century) **empiricutic** empirical/fraudulent   107 **to** compared with   **report** reputation   **horse-drench** dose of horse medicine   108 **wont** accustomed   111 **a** he   113 **brows** i.e. in the form of a victor's garland   115 **disciplined** beaten, punished   119 **an** if   **'fidiussed** i.e. treated as Aufidius was; Menenius playfully coins a word from Aufidius' name   121 **possessed** aware, informed

VOLUMNIA   Good ladies, let's go. Yes, yes, yes: the senate has
letters from the general, wherein he gives my son the whole
name of the war: he hath in this action outdone his former
125   deeds doubly.

VALERIA   In troth, there's wondrous things spoke of him.

MENENIUS   Wondrous: ay, I warrant you, and not without his
true purchasing.

VIRGILIA   The gods grant them true.

130   VOLUMNIA   True? Pow waw!

MENENIUS   True? I'll be sworn they are true. Where   *To the Tribunes*
is he wounded?— God save your good worships! Martius is
coming home: he has more cause to be proud.— Where is he
wounded?

135   VOLUMNIA   I'th'shoulder, and i'th'left arm: there will be large
cicatrices to show the people, when he shall stand for his
place: he received in the repulse of Tarquin seven hurts
i'th'body.

MENENIUS   One i'th'neck, and two i'th'thigh: there's nine that I
140   know.

VOLUMNIA   He had, before this last expedition, twenty-five
wounds upon him.

MENENIUS   Now it's twenty-seven: every gash was an enemy's
grave.

A shout and flourish

145   Hark, the trumpets.

VOLUMNIA   These are the ushers of Martius: before him he
carries noise, and behind him he leaves tears:
Death, that dark spirit, in's nervy arm doth lie,
Which being advanced, declines, and then men die.

---

124 name of honor, credit for   **action** military enterprise   **128 purchasing** deserving,
winning   **130 Pow waw!** expression of dismissive scorn (i.e. "Of course they're true!")
136 cicatrices scars   **137 place** i.e. as a consul   **repulse** driving back/defeat   **Tarquin** the
last king of Rome, defeated in about 496 BC   **139 One . . . nine** either an error arising from
the desire to outdo Volumnia, or Menenius begins adding up aloud, then does not bother to
enumerate the other six wounds as he makes a mental leap to the total   **148 nervy** sinewy,
muscular   **149 advanced** raised up   **declines** descends

A sennet. Trumpets sound. Enter Cominius the general, and Titus Lartius: between them Coriolanus, crowned with an oaken garland with Captains and Soldiers, and a Herald

150 HERALD   Know, Rome, that all alone Martius did fight
Within Corioles' gates: where he hath won,
With fame, a name to 'Martius Caius':
These in honour follows 'Coriolanus'.
Welcome to Rome, renownèd Coriolanus!

Sound [a] flourish

155 ALL   Welcome to Rome, renownèd Coriolanus!

CORIOLANUS   No more of this, it does offend my heart:
Pray now, no more.

COMINIUS   Look, sir, your mother.

CORIOLANUS   O, you have, I know, petitioned all the gods
160   For my prosperity.   *Kneels*

VOLUMNIA   Nay, my good soldier, up: *He rises*
My gentle Martius, worthy Caius,
And by deed-achieving honour newly named:
What is it? 'Coriolanus' must I call thee?
165   But O, thy wife!

CORIOLANUS   My gracious silence, hail.   *To Virgilia*
Wouldst thou have laughed had I come coffined home,
That weep'st to see me triumph? Ah, my dear,
Such eyes the widows in Corioles wear,
170   And mothers that lack sons.

MENENIUS   Now the gods crown thee!

CORIOLANUS   And live you yet? O my sweet lady, pardon.   *To Valeria*

VOLUMNIA   I know not where to turn. O, welcome home:
And welcome, general, and you're welcome all.

175 MENENIUS   A hundred thousand welcomes: I could weep
And I could laugh, I am light and heavy: welcome:

---

sennet trumpet call signaling a procession   **152 to** in addition to   **153 These . . . follows** these names, as a mark of honor, are to be followed by   **160 prosperity** good fortune, success   **162 gentle** noble, honorable   **163 deed-achieving honour** honor won by actions   **166 gracious** delightful/virtuous/full of divine grace   **176 light** joyful (playing on the sense of "not weighty" to provide antithesis with the literal sense of **heavy** here signifying "sad")

A curse begin at very root on's heart
That is not glad to see thee. You are three
That Rome should dote on: yet, by the faith of men,

180 We have some old crab-trees here at home that will not
Be grafted to your relish. Yet welcome, warriors:
We call a nettle but a nettle and
The faults of fools but folly.

COMINIUS   Ever right.

185 **CORIOLANUS**   Menenius, ever, ever.

HERALD   Give way there, and go on.

CORIOLANUS   Your hand, and yours.   *To Volumnia and Virgilia*
Ere in our own house I do shade my head,
The good patricians must be visited,

190 From whom I have received not only greetings,
But with them change of honours.

VOLUMNIA   I have lived
To see inherited my very wishes,
And the buildings of my fancy: only

195 There's one thing wanting, which I doubt not but
Our Rome will cast upon thee.

CORIOLANUS   Know, good mother,
I had rather be their servant in my way,
Than sway with them in theirs.

200 **COMINIUS**   On, to the Capitol.

Flourish. Cornets. Exeunt in state, as before
Enter Brutus and Sicinius

BRUTUS   All tongues speak of him, and the blearèd sights
Are spectacled to see him. Your prattling nurse
Into a rapture lets her baby cry

---

177 on's of his   **180 crab-trees** crab-apple trees, i.e. the bitter tribunes   **181 grafted** altered,
made to grow (literally, grafted to a superior tree)   **relish** taste   **182 We . . . folly** i.e. some
painful or foolish things must be accepted for what they are and cannot be called otherwise
186 Give make   **188 shade** conceal   **191 change of honours** new honors (i.e. his new name)
193 inherited realized, acquired   **194 fancy** imagination   **195 wanting** lacking   **196 cast**
bestow   **199 sway** rule   *state* ceremony, formal procession   **201 blearèd** dim, bleary
202 spectacled made clear, given glasses   **prattling** gossiping, chattering   **203 rapture** fit

While she chats him: the kitchen malkin pins
205   Her richest lockram 'bout her reechy neck,
Clamb'ring the walls to eye him: stalls, bulks, windows
Are smothered up, leads filled, and ridges horsed
With variable complexions, all agreeing
In earnestness to see him: seld-shown flamens
210   Do press among the popular throngs and puff
To win a vulgar station: our veiled dames
Commit the war of white and damask in
Their nicely gauded cheeks to th'wanton spoil
Of Phoebus' burning kisses: such a pother
215   As if that whatsoever god who leads him
Were slily crept into his human powers,
And gave him graceful posture.

SICINIUS   On the sudden, I warrant him consul.

BRUTUS   Then our office may, during his power, go sleep.

220 SICINIUS   He cannot temp'rately transport his honours
From where he should begin and end, but will
Lose those he hath won.

BRUTUS   In that there's comfort.

SICINIUS   Doubt not
225   The commoners, for whom we stand, but they
Upon their ancient malice will forget
With the least cause these his new honours, which

---

204 **chats** chats about   **malkin** girl, wench   205 **lockram** linen   **reechy** dirty (picks up aurally on **richest**)   206 **stalls** display tables in front of shops   **bulks** frameworks projecting from the fronts of shops, used to display goods   207 **leads** lead-covered flat roofs   **ridges** roof ridges   **horsed** straddled   208 **variable complexions** various types of person   **agreeing** in agreement/alike, equal   209 **seld-shown** seldom-seen   **flamens** priests   210 **popular** plebeian   **puff** become out of breath   211 **vulgar station** place among the crowd   212 **Commit . . . kisses** i.e. they raise their veils and risk getting sunburn   **damask** pink   213 **nicely gauded** skillfully made-up   **th'wanton spoil** the unrestrained destruction/lascivious plundering   214 **Phoebus** the sun god   **pother** fuss, commotion   215 **that . . . him** whichever god it is that leads Coriolanus   216 **his human powers** i.e. Coriolanus' body   **powers** faculties   217 **graceful posture** divine bearing   218 **On the sudden** suddenly/immediately   **warrant** guarantee/predict   219 **office** task, function   **power** authority, i.e. term of office   220 **He . . . end** he cannot carry his honors steadily from their beginning to their proper conclusion, i.e. he cannot long maintain his new honors   225 **for . . . stand** whom we represent   226 **Upon** because of   **ancient** long-standing   227 **which** i.e. which cause

That he will give them make I as little question
As he is proud to do't.

230   BRUTUS   I heard him swear,
Were he to stand for consul, never would he
Appear i'th'market-place nor on him put
The napless vesture of humility,
Nor, showing, as the manner is, his wounds

235   To th'people, beg their stinking breaths.

SICINIUS   'Tis right.

BRUTUS   It was his word: O, he would miss it rather
Than carry it but by the suit of the gentry to him,
And the desire of the nobles.

240   SICINIUS   I wish no better
Than have him hold that purpose and to put it
In execution.

BRUTUS   'Tis most like he will.

SICINIUS   It shall be to him then, as our good wills:

245   A sure destruction.

BRUTUS   So it must fall out
To him or our authorities for an end.
We must suggest the people in what hatred
He still hath held them: that to's power he would

250   Have made them mules, silenced their pleaders,
And dispropertied their freedoms, holding them,
In human action and capacity,
Of no more soul nor fitness for the world
Than camels in their war, who have their provand

255   Only for bearing burdens, and sore blows
For sinking under them.

---

229 As as that   **233 napless vesture** threadbare garment   **235 breaths** i.e. voices of support
237 miss it i.e. not be appointed consul   **238 carry it but** i.e. obtain it other than   **243 like**
likely   **244 good wills** interest wishes   **246 So . . . end** matters shall end either with his
destruction or that of us and our authority (many editors emend **authorities** to "authority's")
248 suggest hint, insinuate to   **249 still** always   **250 mules** i.e. subservient beasts of burden
pleaders i.e. the tribunes   **251 dispropertied** deprived, dispossessed (them of)   **252 capacity**
capability, understanding   **254 provand** provender, food

SICINIUS   This, as you say, suggested
            At some time when his soaring insolence
            Shall teach the people — which time shall not want,
260   If he be put upon't, and that's as easy
            As to set dogs on sheep — will be his fire
            To kindle their dry stubble, and their blaze
            Shall darken him for ever.

Enter a Messenger

BRUTUS   What's the matter?
265 MESSENGER You are sent for to the Capitol: 'tis thought
            That Martius shall be consul: I have seen
            The dumb men throng to see him and the blind
            To hear him speak: matrons flung gloves,
            Ladies and maids their scarves and handkerchiefs,
270   Upon him as he passed: the nobles bended
            As to Jove's statue, and the commons made
            A shower and thunder with their caps and shouts:
            I never saw the like.

BRUTUS   Let's to the Capitol,
275   And carry with us ears and eyes for th'time,
            But hearts for the event.

SICINIUS   Have with you.   *Exeunt*

[Act 2 Scene 2]   *running scene 6*

Enter two Officers, to lay cushions, as it were, in the Capitol

FIRST OFFICER   Come, come, they are almost here: how many
            stand for consulships?

SECOND OFFICER   Three, they say: but 'tis thought of everyone
            Coriolanus will carry it.

---

259 **want** be lacking   260 **put upon't** encouraged, incited to it   263 **darken** obscure/taint
268 **matrons** married women   270 **bended** i.e. bowed   271 **Jove** Roman supreme god (also
known as Jupiter)   275 **carry . . . th'time** i.e. let us be vigilant for the present   276 **hearts** i.e.
valor/commitment/hidden desires   **event** future outcome   277 **Have with you** I'll join
you/let's go   **2.2 Location: Rome (the Capitol)**   3 **of** by

5   FIRST OFFICER   That's a brave fellow: but he's vengeance proud,
and loves not the common people.

SECOND OFFICER   Faith, there hath been many great men that
have flattered the people, who ne'er loved them: and there be
many that they have loved, they know not wherefore: so that
10   if they love they know not why, they hate upon no better a
ground. Therefore, for Coriolanus neither to care whether
they love or hate him manifests the true knowledge he has in
their disposition, and out of his noble carelessness lets them
plainly see't.

15   FIRST OFFICER   If he did not care whether he had their love or no,
he waved indifferently 'twixt doing them neither good nor
harm: but he seeks their hate with greater devotion than
they can render it him, and leaves nothing undone that may
fully discover him their opposite. Now to seem to affect the
20   malice and displeasure of the people is as bad as that which
he dislikes, to flatter them for their love.

SECOND OFFICER   He hath deserved worthily of his country, and
his ascent is not by such easy degrees as those who, having
been supple and courteous to the people, bonneted, without
25   any further deed to have them at all into their estimation and
report: but he hath so planted his honours in their eyes and
his actions in their hearts that for their tongues to be silent
and not confess so much were a kind of ingrateful injury: to
report otherwise were a malice that, giving itself the lie,
30   would pluck reproof and rebuke from every ear that heard it.

FIRST OFFICER   No more of him: he's a worthy man: make way,
they are coming.

A sennet. Enter the Patricians, and the Tribunes of the people [Sicinius
and Brutus], Lictors before them: Coriolanus, Menenius, Cominius the

---

5 **brave** splendid   **vengeance** exceedingly   **8 them** refers either to the **people** or to the **great
man**   9 **they** i.e. the people   **wherefore** why   12 **in** of   16 **waved** would waver   19 **discover
him** reveal him to be   **opposite** enemy   **affect** seek out/like, enjoy   23 **degrees** steps
24 **supple** compliant, obsequious   **bonneted** removed their hats (a mark of respect)
without . . . report and gained others' esteem and a good reputation without doing anything
else   29 **giving . . . lie** being manifestly untrue   *Lictors* officers attending magistrates

consul. Sicinius and Brutus take their places by themselves: Coriolanus
stands

MENENIUS   Having determined of the Volsces and
To send for Titus Lartius, it remains
35   As the main point of this our after-meeting,
To gratify his noble service that
Hath thus stood for his country. Therefore please you,
Most reverend and grave elders, to desire
The present consul and last general
40   In our well-found successes to report
A little of that worthy work performed
By Martius Caius Coriolanus, whom
We met here both to thank and to remember
With honours like himself.
45   FIRST SENATOR   Speak, good Cominius:
Leave nothing out for length, and make us think
Rather our state's defective for requital
Than we to stretch it out.— Masters o'th'people,   *To the Tribunes*
We do request your kindest ears: and after
50   Your loving motion toward the common body,
To yield what passes here.
SICINIUS   We are convented upon a pleasing treaty, and have
hearts inclinable to honour and advance the theme of our
assembly.
55   BRUTUS   Which the rather we shall be blest to do if he
remember a kinder value of the people than he hath hereto
prized them at.
MENENIUS   That's off, that's off. I would you rather had been
silent: please you to hear Cominius speak?

---

33 **determined of** made a decision about   35 **after-meeting** follow-up meeting   36 **gratify**
reward   37 **stood for** defended   38 **grave** dignified, respected   40 **well-found** commendable/
found to be good   44 **like himself** appropriate to him, as worthy as he is   46 **length** fear of
taking too long   47 **for requital** in its ability to recompense (such deeds)   49 **after** afterward,
then   50 **motion** encouragement, prompting   **body** i.e. people   51 **yield** consent to
52 **convented** assembled   **upon** i.e. to consider   **treaty** proposition   53 **theme** subject
55 **blest** happy   56 **kinder value** more generous estimation   **hereto** previously   58 **off** beside
the point

60 BRUTUS   Most willingly: but yet my caution was more
        pertinent than the rebuke you give it.

    MENENIUS   He loves your people, but tie him not to be their
        bedfellow. Worthy Cominius, speak.

    Coriolanus rises, and offers to go away
        Nay, keep your place.   *To Coriolanus*

65 FIRST SENATOR   Sit, Coriolanus: never shame to hear
        What you have nobly done.

    CORIOLANUS   Your honour's pardon:
        I had rather have my wounds to heal again
        Than hear say how I got them.

70 BRUTUS   Sir, I hope my words disbenched you not?

    CORIOLANUS   No, sir: yet oft,
        When blows have made me stay, I fled from words.
        You soothed not, therefore hurt not: but your people,
        I love them as they weigh—

75 MENENIUS   Pray now, sit down.

    CORIOLANUS   I had rather have one scratch my head i'th'sun
        When the alarum were struck than idly sit
        To hear my nothings monstered.   *Exit Coriolanus*

    MENENIUS   Masters of the people,
80   Your multiplying spawn how can he flatter —
        That's thousand to one good one — when you now see
        He had rather venture all his limbs for honour
        Than one on's ears to hear it? Proceed, Cominius.

    COMINIUS   I shall lack voice: the deeds of Coriolanus
85   Should not be uttered feebly: it is held
        That valour is the chiefest virtue, and
        Most dignifies the haver: if it be,
        The man I speak of cannot in the world
        Be singly counterpoised. At sixteen years,

---

offers attempts   **70 disbenched** unseated   **73 soothed** flattered   **74 as they weigh**
according to their worth   **76 have . . . struck** i.e. remain idle when the call to battle goes out
78 monstered made into unnatural marvels   **80 multiplying spawn** rapidly breeding
commoners   **81 That's . . . one** i.e. for one good Coriolanus there are a thousand inadequate
commoners/for every worthy commoner there are a thousand bad ones   **83 one on's** for one
of his   **89 singly counterpoised** matched by any other individual

90 When Tarquin made a head for Rome, he fought
    Beyond the mark of others: our then dictator,
    Whom with all praise I point at, saw him fight,
    When with his Amazonian chin he drove
    The bristled lips before him: he bestrid
95 An o'erpressed Roman, and i'th'consul's view
    Slew three opposers: Tarquin's self he met,
    And struck him on his knee: in that day's feats,
    When he might act the woman in the scene,
    He proved best man i'th'field and for his meed
100 Was brow-bound with the oak. His pupil age
    Man-entered thus, he waxèd like a sea,
    And in the brunt of seventeen battles since
    He lurched all swords of the garland: for this last,
    Before and in Corioles, let me say
105 I cannot speak him home: he stopped the fliers,
    And by his rare example made the coward
    Turn terror into sport: as weeds before
    A vessel under sail, so men obeyed
    And fell below his stem: his sword, death's stamp,
110 Where it did mark, it took: from face to foot
    He was a thing of blood, whose every motion
    Was timed with dying cries: alone he entered
    The mortal gate of th'city, which he, painted
    With shunless destiny, aidless came off,

90 made . . . for raised troops to attack   **91 mark** range, capacity   **dictator** leader   **92 point at** allude to   **93 Amazonian** beardless, like the Amazons, a race of female warriors   **94 bestrid** stood over to defend   **95 o'erpressed** overpowered   **view** sight   **97 on** onto   **98 might . . . scene** i.e. might have wept or been afraid (**act** and **scene** set up the image of a boy player)   **99 meed** reward   **100 brow-bound . . . oak** given a wreath of oak leaves to wear on his head (signifying that he had saved the life of a fellow Roman)   **pupil . . . thus** his youth being thus initiated into manhood/his apprenticeship thus begun in the manner of a fully grown man   **101 waxèd** grew   **102 brunt** shock, violence   **103 lurched . . . garland** robbed all fellow soldiers of the victory garland   **for** as for   **105 speak him home** find words to describe him adequately   **fliers** those fleeing   **106 rare** marvelous/exceptional   **109 stem** prow   **stamp** tool with which to imprint a design   **110 took** made a lasting impression (i.e. killed)   **112 timed** accompanied regularly   **113 mortal** fatal (either threatening death to Coriolanus or bringing death to the city)   **which** from which   **painted . . . destiny** i.e. stained with the blood of the dead   **114 shunless** inescapable   **came off** came away, emerged

115   And with a sudden reinforcement struck
    Corioles like a planet: now all's his:
    When by and by the din of war gan pierce
    His ready sense: then straight his doubled spirit
    Requickened what in flesh was fatigate,
120   And to the battle came he, where he did
    Run reeking o'er the lives of men, as if
    'Twere a perpetual spoil: and till we called
    Both field and city ours, he never stood
    To ease his breast with panting.

125 **MENENIUS**   Worthy man.

FIRST SENATOR   He cannot but with measure fit the honours
which we devise him.

COMINIUS   Our spoils he kicked at,
And looked upon things precious as they were
130 The common muck of the world: he covets less
Than misery itself would give, rewards
His deeds with doing them, and is content
To spend the time to end it.

MENENIUS   He's right noble: let him be called for.

135 **FIRST SENATOR**   Call Coriolanus.

OFFICER   He doth appear.

Enter Coriolanus

MENENIUS   The senate, Coriolanus, are well pleased to make
thee consul.

CORIOLANUS   I do owe them still my life and services.

140 **MENENIUS**   It then remains that you do speak to the people.

CORIOLANUS   I do beseech you,
Let me o'erleap that custom, for I cannot

---

115 **reinforcement** fresh attack   **struck** astrological term referring to the power of a **planet** to emit a deadly influence   **117 gan** began to   **118 ready sense** alert sense of hearing   **straight** straight away   **doubled** redoubled in strength   **119 requickened** revived, reanimated **fatigate** weary, fatigued   **121 reeking** steaming (with the fresh blood of enemies)   **122 spoil** slaughter, destruction   **126 with measure** fittingly, with due proportion   **128 kicked at** rejected, spurned   **129 as** as if   **131 misery** complete poverty   **132 with doing them** i.e. by taking satisfaction from performing them   **133 To . . . it** that time well spent is an end in itself/in seeking death   **139 still** always

Put on the gown, stand naked, and entreat them,
For my wounds' sake, to give their sufferage:
145   Please you that I may pass this doing.

SICINIUS   Sir, the people must have their voices:
Neither will they bate one jot of ceremony.

MENENIUS   Put them not to't:
Pray you, go fit you to the custom and
150   Take to you, as your predecessors have,
Your honour with your form.

CORIOLANUS   It is a part that I shall blush in acting,
And might well be taken from the people.

BRUTUS   Mark you that?   *To Sicinius*

155   CORIOLANUS   To brag unto them, 'Thus I did, and thus':
Show them th'unaching scars which I should hide,
As if I had received them for the hire
Of their breath only!

MENENIUS   Do not stand upon't:
160   We recommend to you, tribunes of the people,
Our purpose to them, and to our noble consul
Wish we all joy and honour.

SENATORS   To Coriolanus come all joy and honour!

Flourish [of] cornets. Then exeunt [all but] Sicinius and Brutus

BRUTUS   You see how he intends to use the people.

165   SICINIUS   May they perceive's intent! He will require them
As if he did contemn what he requested
Should be in them to give.

BRUTUS   Come, we'll inform them
Of our proceedings here: on th'market-place
170   I know they do attend us.   [*Exeunt*]

---

143 naked exposed (to the view of the people)/vulnerable/wearing nothing beneath the **gown** (to permit a better view of war wounds)   **144 sufferage** vote, approval   **145 pass** avoid, bypass   **146 voices** votes   **147 bate** omit   **148 Put** force   **151 your form** the formality that befits your status   **157 hire** payment   **159 stand upon't** make an issue of it   **160 recommend** commit, entrust   **161 purpose to them** intentions regarding the people   **164 use** treat **165 require** ask   **166 contemn . . . give** despise the fact that what he requested should be in their power to give   **170 attend** await

[Act 2 Scene 3]   *running scene 7*

Enter seven or eight Citizens

FIRST CITIZEN   Once, if he do require our voices, we ought not to
     deny him.

SECOND CITIZEN   We may, sir, if we will.

THIRD CITIZEN   We have power in ourselves to do it, but it is a
5   power that we have no power to do: for, if he show us his
     wounds and tell us his deeds, we are to put our tongues into
     those wounds and speak for them: so, if he tell us his noble
     deeds, we must also tell him our noble acceptance of them.
     Ingratitude is monstrous, and for the multitude to be
10   ingrateful, were to make a monster of the multitude: of the
     which we, being members, should bring ourselves to be
     monstrous members.

FIRST CITIZEN   And to make us no better thought of, a little help
     will serve: for once we stood up about the corn, he himself
15   stuck not to call us the many-headed multitude.

THIRD CITIZEN   We have been called so of many, not that our
     heads are some brown, some black, some abram, some bald,
     but that our wits are so diversely coloured: and truly I think
     if all our wits were to issue out of one skull, they would fly
20   east, west, north, south, and their consent of one direct way
     should be at once to all the points o'th'compass.

SECOND CITIZEN   Think you so? Which way do you judge my wit
     would fly?

THIRD CITIZEN   Nay, your wit will not so soon out as another
25   man's will: 'tis strongly wedged up in a blockhead: but if it
     were at liberty, 'twould sure southward.

SECOND CITIZEN   Why that way?

2.3 *Location: Rome (marketplace)*   **1 Once** once and for all   **5 power . . . do** a legal
prerogative that we have no moral right to exercise   **9 monstrous** unnatural   **13 a . . . serve**
will require little effort   **14 once** once when   **15 stuck** hesitated   **16 of** by   **that** because
17 abram auburn, here meaning "blond"   **20 consent of** agreement on   **24 wit . . . will**
perhaps playing on sexual connotations of both words to signify "penis"   **out** emerge, come
out   **26 southward** the south wind was thought to carry disease and storms/the lower
regions, i.e. genitals

THIRD CITIZEN   To lose itself in a fog, where being three parts
melted away with rotten dews, the fourth would return for
30   conscience' sake, to help to get thee a wife.

SECOND CITIZEN   You are never without your tricks: you may,
you may.

THIRD CITIZEN   Are you all resolved to give your voices? But that's
no matter, the greater part carries it. I say, if he would incline
35   to the people, there was never a worthier man.

Enter Coriolanus in a gown of humility, with Menenius

Here he comes, and in the gown of humility: mark his
behaviour. We are not to stay all together, but to come by
him where he stands, by ones, by twos, and by threes. He's to
make his requests by particulars, wherein every one of us
40   has a single honour, in giving him our own voices with our
own tongues: therefore follow me, and I'll direct you how
you shall go by him.

ALL   Content, content.   [*Exeunt Citizens*]

MENENIUS   O sir, you are not right: have you not known
45   The worthiest men have done't?

CORIOLANUS   What must I say?
'I pray, sir'? Plague upon't, I cannot bring
My tongue to such a pace: 'Look, sir, my wounds:
I got them in my country's service when
50   Some certain of your brethren roared and ran
From th'noise of our own drums.'

MENENIUS   O me, the gods! You must not speak of that:
You must desire them to think upon you.

CORIOLANUS   Think upon me? Hang 'em:
55   I would they would forget me, like the virtues
Which our divines lose by 'em.

MENENIUS   You'll mar all:

---

29 rotten corrupting, unwholesome—playing on "affected by venereal disease"; **conscience**
and **tricks** also have potential sexual meanings   **31 you may** i.e. go on, say what you like
34 greater part majority   **incline** be well-disposed   **39 by particulars** to individuals, one by
one   **40 single honour** individual privilege, right   **48 pace** obedient, measured movement
55 would wish   **virtues** i.e. exhortations to virtue   **56 divines** priests   **lose by** waste on

I'll leave you: pray you, speak to 'em, I pray you,
In wholesome manner.   *Exit*

60   CORIOLANUS Bid them wash their faces
And keep their teeth clean.

Enter three of the Citizens

So, here comes a brace.
You know the cause, sir, of my standing here.

THIRD CITIZEN We do, sir: tell us what hath brought you to't.

CORIOLANUS Mine own desert.

65   SECOND CITIZEN Your own desert?

CORIOLANUS Ay, but not mine own desire.

THIRD CITIZEN How not your own desire?

CORIOLANUS No, sir, 'twas never my desire yet to trouble the poor
with begging.

70   THIRD CITIZEN You must think, if we give you anything, we hope
to gain by you.

CORIOLANUS Well then, I pray, your price o'th'consulship?

FIRST CITIZEN The price is to ask it kindly.

CORIOLANUS Kindly, sir, I pray let me ha't: I have wounds to show
75   you, which shall be yours in private: your good voice, sir:
what say you?

SECOND CITIZEN You shall ha't, worthy sir.

CORIOLANUS A match, sir. There's in all two worthy voices
begged: I have your alms: adieu.

80   THIRD CITIZEN But this is something odd.

SECOND CITIZEN An 'twere to give again — but 'tis no matter.

                                                    Exeunt [Citizens]

Enter two other Citizens

CORIOLANUS Pray you now, if it may stand with the tune of your
voices that I may be consul, I have here the customary gown.

FOURTH CITIZEN You have deserved nobly of your country, and
85   you have not deserved nobly.

---

59 wholesome profitable/beneficial   **61 brace** pair (originally used of dogs); an inconsistency,
as *three* citizens have entered; similarly, the subsequent acknowledgment of **two worthy
voices** seems to neglect the third citizen   **73 kindly** pleasantly   **75 yours** i.e. yours to view
78 A match agreed   **80 something** somewhat   **81 An 'twere** if it were   **82 stand** agree

CORIOLANUS Your enigma?

FOURTH CITIZEN   You have been a scourge to her enemies, you
have been a rod to her friends: you have not indeed loved the
common people.

90   CORIOLANUS You should account me the more virtuous that I
have not been common in my love: I will, sir, flatter my sworn
brother the people to earn a dearer estimation of them: 'tis a
condition they account gentle: and since the wisdom of their
choice is rather to have my hat than my heart, I will practise

95   the insinuating nod, and be off to them most counterfeitly:
that is, sir, I will counterfeit the bewitchment of some popular
man and give it bountiful to the desirers. Therefore, beseech
you, I may be consul.

FIFTH CITIZEN   We hope to find you our friend, and therefore give

100   you our voices heartily.

FOURTH CITIZEN   You have received many wounds for your
country.

CORIOLANUS I will not seal your knowledge with showing them. I
will make much of your voices, and so trouble you no

105   further.

BOTH CITIZENS   The gods give you joy, sir, heartily.

[*Exeunt Citizens*]

CORIOLANUS Most sweet voices:
Better it is to die, better to starve,
Than crave the hire which first we do deserve.

110   Why in this wolvish tongue should I stand here,
To beg of Hob and Dick that does appear

---

86 **enigma** riddle   87 **scourge** punishing whip   88 **rod** punishment cane   91 **common**
promiscuous, indiscriminate   **sworn brother** loyal friend bound by oath   92 **a . . . them** a
more valuable place in their esteem   93 **condition** attribute, habit   **gentle** noble   94 **have
my hat** i.e. have me remove my hat as a mark of respect and deference   95 **insinuating**
ingratiating   **be off** remove my hat   **counterfeitly** falsely, insincerely   96 **counterfeit the
bewitchment** copy the bewitching charm   **popular man** man who curries favor with the
people/man of the people   97 **bountiful** bountifully   103 **seal** confirm   109 **crave** beg   **hire**
payment, reward   110 **in . . . tongue** i.e. uttering such deceptions (many editors emend to
"toge," i.e. "toga," the gown of humility Coriolanus wears)   111 **Hob . . . appear** any fellow
who turns up (**Hob and Dick** were typical names for common men or rustics)

Their needless vouches? Custom calls me to't.
What custom wills, in all things should we do't?
The dust on antique time would lie unswept,
115   And mountainous error be too highly heaped
For truth to o'erpeer. Rather than fool it so,
Let the high office and the honour go
To one that would do thus. I am half through:
The one part suffered, the other will I do.

Enter three Citizens more

120   Here come more voices.
Your voices! For your voices I have fought,
Watched for your voices: for your voices bear
Of wounds two dozen odd: battles thrice six
I have seen and heard of: for your voices have
125   Done many things, some less, some more: your voices!
Indeed I would be consul.

SIXTH CITIZEN He has done nobly, and cannot go without any
honest man's voice.

SEVENTH CITIZEN Therefore let him be consul: the gods give him
130   joy, and make him good friend to the people.

ALL CITIZENS Amen, amen. God save thee, noble consul.

CORIOLANUS Worthy voices!   *[Exeunt Citizens]*

Enter Menenius, with Brutus and Sicinius

MENENIUS You have stood your limitation, and the tribunes
Endue you with the people's voice: remains
135   That in th'official marks invested, you
Anon do meet the senate.

CORIOLANUS Is this done?

SICINIUS The custom of request you have discharged:
The people do admit you, and are summoned
140   To meet anon, upon your approbation.

---

112 **needless** unnecessary   **vouches** formal confirmations   114 **antique time** ancient
customs   116 **o'erpeer** peer over, rise above   118 **do thus** behave in such a foolish manner
120 **voices** votes   122 **Watched** kept guard   124 **heard of** heard, i.e. experienced firsthand
133 **limitation** allotted time   134 **Endue** endow   **remains** it only remains   135 **marks**
insignia of office   136 **Anon** shortly   138 **request** i.e. asking for the people's approval
140 **upon your approbation** to confirm their approval of you

CORIOLANUS   Where? At the senate house?

SICINIUS   There, Coriolanus.

CORIOLANUS   May I change these garments?

SICINIUS   You may, sir.

145   CORIOLANUS   That I'll straight do, and, knowing myself again,
Repair to th'senate house.

MENENIUS   I'll keep you company.— Will you along?

To the Tribunes

BRUTUS   We stay here for the people.

SICINIUS   Fare you well.   *Exeunt Coriolanus and Menenius*

150   He has it now, and by his looks methinks
'Tis warm at's heart.

BRUTUS   With a proud heart he wore his humble weeds.
Will you dismiss the people?

Enter the Plebeians [Citizens]

SICINIUS   How now, my masters, have you chose this man?

155   FIRST CITIZEN   He has our voices, sir.

BRUTUS   We pray the gods he may deserve your loves.

SECOND CITIZEN   Amen, sir: to my poor unworthy notice,
He mocked us when he begged our voices.

THIRD CITIZEN   Certainly: he flouted us downright.

160   FIRST CITIZEN   No, 'tis his kind of speech: he did not mock us.

SECOND CITIZEN   Not one amongst us, save yourself, but says
He used us scornfully: he should have showed us
His marks of merit, wounds received for's country.

SICINIUS   Why, so he did, I am sure.

165   ALL CITIZENS   No, no: no man saw 'em.

THIRD CITIZEN   He said he had wounds, which he could show in
private;
And with his hat, thus waving it in scorn,
'I would be consul', says he: 'Agèd custom,
But by your voices, will not so permit me.

170   Your voices therefore.' When we granted that,
Here was 'I thank you for your voices: thank you:

---

146 **Repair** make my way   152 **weeds** clothes   154 **my masters** sirs   157 **notice** observation
159 **flouted** insulted, mocked   160 **kind of speech** way of speaking

Your most sweet voices: now you have left your voices,
I have no further with you.' Was not this mockery?

SICINIUS   Why either were you ignorant to see't,
175   Or, seeing it, of such childish friendliness
To yield your voices?

BRUTUS   Could you not have told him   *To the Citizens*
As you were lessoned: when he had no power,
But was a petty servant to the state,
180   He was your enemy, ever spake against
Your liberties and the charters that you bear
I'th'body of the weal: and now arriving
A place of potency and sway o'th'state,
If he should still malignantly remain
185   Fast foe to th'plebeii, your voices might
Be curses to yourselves. You should have said
That as his worthy deeds did claim no less
Than what he stood for, so his gracious nature
Would think upon you for your voices, and
190   Translate his malice towards you into love,
Standing your friendly lord.

SICINIUS   Thus to have said,   *To the Citizens*
As you were fore-advised, had touched his spirit
And tried his inclination: from him plucked
195   Either his gracious promise, which you might,
As cause had called you up, have held him to:
Or else it would have galled his surly nature,
Which easily endures not article
Tying him to aught: so putting him to rage,
200   You should have ta'en th'advantage of his choler
And passed him unelected.

---

173 **further with** further need of   174 **ignorant** too dull   178 **lessoned** instructed   180 **ever**
always   181 **charters . . . weal** privileges that you hold in the commonwealth   182 **arriving**
reaching   183 **sway o'th'state** state authority   185 **th'plebeii** the plebeians   188 **what . . .**
for i.e. the position of consul   189 **think upon** esteem   190 **Translate** transform
191 **Standing . . . lord** supporting you as a patron, acting on your behalf   193 **had touched**
would have tested (as the quality of gold was tested by rubbing it on a touchstone)   196 **cause**
occasion   **called you up** prompted you   197 **galled** irritated, inflamed   198 **article**
condition, stipulation   199 **aught** anything   200 **choler** anger

BRUTUS   Did you perceive   *To the Citizens*
He did solicit you in free contempt
When he did need your loves? And do you think
205   That his contempt shall not be bruising to you
When he hath power to crush? Why, had your bodies
No heart among you? Or had you tongues to cry
Against the rectorship of judgement?

SICINIUS   Have you, ere now, denied the asker,   *To the Citizens*
210   And now again, of him that did not ask but mock,
Bestow your sued-for tongues?

THIRD CITIZEN   He's not confirmed: we may deny him yet.

SECOND CITIZEN   And will deny him:
I'll have five hundred voices of that sound.

215   FIRST CITIZEN   I twice five hundred and their friends to piece 'em.

BRUTUS   Get you hence instantly, and tell those friends
They have chose a consul that will from them take
Their liberties: make them of no more voice
Than dogs that are as often beat for barking
220   As therefor kept to do so.

SICINIUS   Let them assemble, and on a safer judgement
To the Citizens
All revoke your ignorant election: enforce his pride,
And his old hate unto you: besides, forget not
With what contempt he wore the humble weed,
225   How in his suit he scorned you: but your loves,
Thinking upon his services, took from you
Th'apprehension of his present portance,
Which most gibingly, ungravely, he did fashion
After the inveterate hate he bears you.

230   BRUTUS   Lay a fault on us, your tribunes,   *To the Citizens*

---

203 **free** frank, undisguised   207 **heart** courage, spirit   **cry** protest, rebel   208 **rectorship**
rule   209 **ere . . . asker** on previous occasions refused to vote for one who asked you
211 **sued-for** begged for/formally entreated   215 **piece** add to, augment   220 **therefor** for
that purpose, i.e. barking   221 **safer** more sensible   222 **enforce** emphasize   225 **suit**
petition (may play on the sense of "clothing")   227 **Th'apprehension** the understanding
portance behavior, demeanor   228 **gibingly** tauntingly   **ungravely** derisively, disrespectfully
229 **After** according to   **inveterate** long-standing   230 **Lay . . . on** blame

That we laboured, no impediment between,
But that you must cast your election on him.

SICINIUS   Say you chose him more after our commandment

To the Citizens

Than as guided by your own true affections, and that
235   Your minds, preoccupied with what you rather must do
Than what you should, made you against the grain
To voice him consul. Lay the fault on us.

BRUTUS   Ay, spare us not: say we read lectures to you,

To the Citizens

How youngly he began to serve his country,
240   How long continued, and what stock he springs of,
The noble house o'th'Martians, from whence came
That Ancus Martius, Numa's daughter's son,
Who after great Hostilius here was king:
Of the same house Publius and Quintus were,
245   That our best water brought by conduits hither:
And Censorinus that was so surnamed,
And nobly named so, twice being censor,
Was his great ancestor.

SICINIUS   One thus descended,
250   That hath beside well in his person wrought
To be set high in place, we did commend
To your remembrances: but you have found,
Scaling his present bearing with his past,
That he's your fixèd enemy, and revoke
255   Your sudden approbation.

---

231 no impediment between allowing nothing to stand in the way   **234 affections** wishes, preferences   **236 against the grain** perversely, against your true inclinations   **237 voice** vote   **238 read lectures to** instructed   **239 youngly** early in life   **242 Ancus Martius** traditionally, the fourth king of Rome   **Numa** Numa Pompilius, second king of Rome   **243 Hostilius** Tullus Hostilius, third king of Rome   **244 Publius** unknown ancestor of Coriolanus   **Quintus . . . conduits** an anachronism: Quintus Martius Rex was involved in building the Aqua Martia aqueduct in Rome in the second century BC   **245 conduits** aqueducts   **246 Censorinus** another anachronism: Caius Martius Rutilius was given the title "Censorinus" in the third century BC   **247 censor** magistrate in charge of the census of citizens   **250 That . . . wrought** who has, in addition, well deserved through his own actions   **253 Scaling** weighing up   **255 sudden** hasty

BRUTUS   Say, you ne'er had done't —
Harp on that still — but by our putting on:
And presently, when you have drawn your number,
Repair to th'Capitol.

260   ALL   We will so: almost all repent in their election.

Exeunt Plebeians [Citizens]

BRUTUS   Let them go on:
This mutiny were better put in hazard,
Than stay, past doubt, for greater:
If, as his nature is, he fall in rage

265   With their refusal, both observe and answer
The vantage of his anger.

SICINIUS   To th'Capitol, come:
We will be there before the stream o'th'people,
And this shall seem, as partly 'tis, their own,

270   Which we have goaded onward.   *Exeunt*

Act 3 [Scene 1]   *running scene 8*

Cornets. Enter Coriolanus, Menenius, all the gentry, Cominius, Titus Lartius, and other Senators

CORIOLANUS   Tullus Aufidius then had made new head?

LARTIUS   He had, my lord, and that it was which caused
Our swifter composition.

CORIOLANUS   So then the Volsces stand but as at first,

5   Ready, when time shall prompt them, to make road
Upon's again.

COMINIUS   They are worn, lord consul, so,
That we shall hardly in our ages see
Their banners wave again.

---

257 **putting on** encouragement, urging   258 **presently . . . number** as soon as you have gathered your crowd of supporters   259 **Repair** make your way   262 **put in hazard** risked
263 **Than . . . greater** than to await the greater revolt that would doubtless occur
265 **answer . . . of** respond to the advantages offered by   269 **own** i.e. own doing
3.1 *Location: Rome (a street—the procession is on its way to the marketplace)*
1 **made new head** raised a new army   3 **composition** coming to terms   5 **road** inroads, incursions   7 **worn** weakened, exhausted   8 **ages** lifetimes

10	CORIOLANUS	Saw you Aufidius? *To Lartius*
	LARTIUS	On safeguard he came to me, and did curse
		Against the Volsces, for they had so vilely
		Yielded the town: he is retired to Antium.
	CORIOLANUS	Spoke he of me?
15	LARTIUS	He did, my lord.
	CORIOLANUS	How? What?
	LARTIUS	How often he had met you sword to sword:
		That of all things upon the earth, he hated
		Your person most: that he would pawn his fortunes
20		To hopeless restitution, so he might
		Be called your vanquisher.
	CORIOLANUS	At Antium lives he?
	LARTIUS	At Antium.
	CORIOLANUS	I wish I had a cause to seek him there,
25		To oppose his hatred fully. Welcome home.

Enter Sicinius and Brutus

		Behold, these are the tribunes of the people,
		The tongues o'th'common mouth. I do despise them,
		For they do prank them in authority,
		Against all noble sufferance.
30	SICINIUS	Pass no further.
	CORIOLANUS	Ha? What is that?
	BRUTUS	It will be dangerous to go on. No further.
	CORIOLANUS	What makes this change?
	MENENIUS	The matter?
35	COMINIUS	Hath he not passed the noble and the common?
	BRUTUS	Cominius, no.
	CORIOLANUS	Have I had children's voices?
	FIRST SENATOR	Tribunes, give way: he shall to th'market-place.
	BRUTUS	The people are incensed against him.

---

11 On safeguard under safe conduct   **12 for** because   **vilely** contemptibly, shamefully
13 retired withdrawn   **Antium** town situated on the coast, about thirty-five miles south of
Rome; now Anzio   **20 To hopeless restitution** beyond hope of recovery   **so** provided that
28 prank them dress themselves up   **29 Against . . . sufferance** beyond what the nobility can
endure   **35 passed . . . common** been approved by the nobility and the common people

40 SICINIUS   Stop, or all will fall in broil.

CORIOLANUS   Are these your herd?

Must these have voices, that can yield them now
And straight disclaim their tongues? What are your offices?
You being their mouths, why rule you not their teeth?

45 Have you not set them on?

MENENIUS   Be calm, be calm.

CORIOLANUS   It is a purposed thing, and grows by plot,
To curb the will of the nobility:
Suffer't, and live with such as cannot rule

50 Nor ever will be ruled.

BRUTUS   Call't not a plot:
The people cry you mocked them, and of late,
When corn was given them gratis, you repined,
Scandalled the suppliants for the people, called them

55 Time-pleasers, flatterers, foes to nobleness.

CORIOLANUS   Why, this was known before.

BRUTUS   Not to them all.

CORIOLANUS   Have you informed them sithence?

BRUTUS   How? I inform them?

60 CORIOLANUS   You are like to do such business.

BRUTUS   Not unlike each way to better yours.

CORIOLANUS   Why then should I be consul? By yond clouds,
Let me deserve so ill as you, and make me
Your fellow tribune.

65 SICINIUS   You show too much of that
For which the people stir: if you will pass
To where you are bound, you must inquire your way,
Which you are out of, with a gentler spirit,

---

40 **broil** turmoil, fighting   42 **voices** votes   43 **straight** immediately (afterward)   **offices**
roles, responsibilities   44 **rule . . . teeth** i.e. can you not control their vicious snapping   45 **set
them on** encouraged them (suggesting the incitement of dogs in bear-baiting)   47 **purposed**
planned   49 **Suffer't, and live** if you put up with it, you will have to live   52 **of late** recently
53 **gratis** free   **repined** complained   54 **Scandalled** scorned, slandered   55 **Time-pleasers**
followers of fashion/opportunists   58 **sithence** since   60 **like** likely   61 **Not . . . yours**
i.e. I am likely to better you in any case   62 **yond** yonder, those   65 **that** that quality
68 **are out of** have strayed from

Or never be so noble as a consul,
70   Nor yoke with him for tribune.

MENENIUS   Let's be calm.

COMINIUS   The people are abused: set on. This palt'ring
Becomes not Rome: nor has Coriolanus
Deserved this so dishonoured rub, laid falsely
75   I'th'plain way of his merit.

CORIOLANUS   Tell me of corn?
This was my speech, and I will speak't again—

MENENIUS   Not now, not now.

FIRST SENATOR   Not in this heat, sir, now.

80   CORIOLANUS   Now, as I live, I will.
My nobler friends, I crave their pardons:
For the mutable, rank-scented meinie,
Let them regard me, as I do not flatter,
And therein behold themselves: I say again,
85   In soothing them, we nourish gainst our senate
The cockle of rebellion, insolence, sedition,
Which we ourselves have ploughed for, sowed and
    scattered,
By mingling them with us, the honoured number,
Who lack not virtue, no, nor power, but that
90   Which they have given to beggars.

MENENIUS   Well, no more.

FIRST SENATOR   No more words, we beseech you.

CORIOLANUS   How? No more?
As for my country I have shed my blood,
95   Not fearing outward force: so shall my lungs
Coin words till their decay against those measles

---

70 yoke associate yourself   **72 abused** deceived   **palt'ring** evasiveness, trickery
74 dishonoured dishonorable   **rub** obstacle (bowling term)   **laid falsely** placed treacherously
75 I'th'plain in the level, smooth   **82 For** as for   **meinie** common people, rabble (pronounced
"many" or "meeny")   **83 regard** take note of, observe   **84 behold themselves** i.e. reflected in
the unflattering truths Coriolanus will utter   **85 soothing** flattering   **86 cockle** weed
sedition revolt   **88 honoured** honorable   **96 Coin** create   **their** i.e. the lungs'   **measles** red
spots of disease; possibly also "lepers"

Which we disdain should tetter us, yet sought
The very way to catch them.

BRUTUS   You speak o'th'people as if you were a god
100   To punish, not a man of their infirmity.

SICINIUS   'Twere well we let the people know't.

MENENIUS   What, what, his choler?

CORIOLANUS   Choler? Were I as patient as the midnight sleep,
By Jove, 'twould be my mind.

105   SICINIUS   It is a mind that shall remain a poison
Where it is, not poison any further.

CORIOLANUS   Shall remain?
Hear you this Triton of the minnows? Mark you
His absolute 'shall'?

110   COMINIUS   'Twas from the canon.

CORIOLANUS   'Shall'? O good but most unwise patricians: why,
You grave but reckless senators, have you thus
Given Hydra here to choose an officer,
That with his peremptory 'shall', being but
115   The horn and noise o'th'monster's, wants not spirit
To say he'll turn your current in a ditch,
And make your channel his? If he have power
Then vail your ignorance: if none, awake
Your dangerous lenity. If you are learned,
120   Be not as common fools: if you are not,
Let them have cushions by you. You are plebeians,
If they be senators: and they are no less,
When, both your voices blended, the great'st taste

---

97 tetter cover with pustules   yet sought although we have sought   100 infirmity (human)
weakness   102 choler bile, i.e. anger; one of the four humors of early physiology, causing
irascibility of temper   103 patient calm   104 mind opinion   108 Triton minor Greek sea god
minnows small fish, i.e. common people   110 from the canon out of order, exceeding a
tribune's authority   113 Given allowed   Hydra in Greek mythology, a monster that grew two
heads for every one that was cut off   114 peremptory imperious   115 horn and noise noisy
horn   wants lacks   116 turn divert   current flow of water   118 vail your ignorance yield in
ignorant submission   vail to lower a flag or weapon in submission   awake . . . lenity rouse
yourselves from this dangerous mildness   121 cushions i.e. seats in the senate   by with, next
to/courtesy of   123 both your voices i.e. those of senators and plebeians   the . . . theirs the
blend of voices tastes most strongly of the plebeians/the plebeians most enjoy the prevalent
taste (i.e. their own)

Most palates theirs. They choose their magistrate,
125　And such a one as he, who puts his 'shall',
His popular 'shall', against a graver bench
Than ever frowned in Greece. By Jove himself,
It makes the consuls base: and my soul aches
To know, when two authorities are up,
130　Neither supreme, how soon confusion
May enter 'twixt the gap of both, and take
The one by th'other.

COMINIUS　　Well, on to th'market-place.

CORIOLANUS　Whoever gave that counsel to give forth
135　The corn o'th'storehouse gratis, as 'twas used
Sometime in Greece—

MENENIUS　　Well, well, no more of that.

CORIOLANUS　Though there the people had more absolute power,
I say, they nourished disobedience, fed
140　The ruin of the state.

BRUTUS　　　Why shall the people give
One that speaks thus their voice?

CORIOLANUS　I'll give my reasons,
More worthier than their voices. They know the corn
145　Was not our recompense, resting well assured
They ne'er did service for't: being pressed to th'war,
Even when the navel of the state was touched,
They would not thread the gates: this kind of service
Did not deserve corn gratis. Being i'th'war,
150　Their mutinies and revolts, wherein they showed
Most valour, spoke not for them. Th'accusation
Which they have often made against the senate,
All cause unborn, could never be the native

---

126 **popular** i.e. on behalf of the people　**graver** more revered　**bench** governing
body/judicial court　**129 up** active, exerting power　**130 confusion** destruction/chaos
131 of both between the two　**take** conquer/destroy　**132 by** by using　**135 used Sometime**
formerly customary　**141 give . . . voice** give their vote to one who speaks thus　**145 our**
recompense reward from us　**146 pressed** impressed, conscripted　**147 navel** i.e. very center
touched threatened, affected　**148 thread** pass through　**151 spoke not for** didn't
recommend　**153 All cause unborn** without any justification　**native** origin

Of our so frank donation. Well, what then?
155 How shall this bosom multiplied digest
The senate's courtesy? Let deeds express
What's like to be their words: 'We did request it,
We are the greater poll, and in true fear
They gave us our demands.' Thus we debase
160 The nature of our seats, and make the rabble
Call our cares fears, which will in time
Break ope the locks o'th'senate, and bring in
The crows to peck the eagles.

MENENIUS   Come, enough.

165 BRUTUS   Enough with over-measure.

CORIOLANUS   No, take more.
What may be sworn by, both divine and human,
Seal what I end withal. This double worship,
Where one part does disdain with cause, the other
170 Insult without all reason: where gentry, title, wisdom,
Cannot conclude but by the yea and no
Of general ignorance, it must omit
Real necessities, and give way the while
To unstable slightness. Purpose so barred, it follows,
175 Nothing is done to purpose. Therefore, beseech you —
You that will be less fearful than discreet,
That love the fundamental part of state
More than you doubt the change on't, that prefer

---

154 frank generous, free   **155 bosom multiplied** (creature of) many stomachs   **digest**
comprehend/digest bodily   **157 like** likely   **158 greater poll** majority   **poll** number of people
(literally, heads)   **161 cares** concerns (for state welfare)   **163 crows** plays on the sense of
"crowbars" (with which to **break** the **locks o'th'senate**)   **eagles** i.e. superior birds; a symbol of
Roman power   **165 over-measure** excess   **168 Seal** (may it) confirm   **withal** with   **double
worship** divided authority   **170 Insult** behave insolently   **without all** without any/beyond all
gentry social rank, being a gentleman   **171 conclude** come to a decision   **172 general**
common, popular   **omit** neglect   **173 the while** in the meantime   **174 slightness** triviality
Purpose so barred proper planning being thus prevented   **175 to purpose** effectively
176 fearful timid, cowardly   **discreet** discerning, prudent   **177 love . . . on't** love the
foundations of sound government more than you fear making the changes that are necessary
to preserve it (i.e. getting rid of the tribunes)

A noble life before a long, and wish
180 To jump a body with a dangerous physic
That's sure of death without it — at once pluck out
The multitudinous tongue: let them not lick
The sweet which is their poison. Your dishonour
Mangles true judgement, and bereaves the state
185 Of that integrity which should become't,
Not having the power to do the good it would,
For th'ill which doth control't.

BRUTUS   He's said enough.

SICINIUS   He's spoken like a traitor, and shall answer
190 As traitors do.

CORIOLANUS Thou wretch, despite o'erwhelm thee!
What should the people do with these bald tribunes?
On whom depending, their obedience fails
To th'greater bench? In a rebellion,
195 When what's not meet, but what must be, was law,
Then were they chosen: in a better hour,
Let what is meet be said it must be meet,
And throw their power i'th'dust.

BRUTUS   Manifest treason.

200 **SICINIUS**   This a consul? No.

BRUTUS   The aediles, ho!

Enter an Aedile

Let him be apprehended.

SICINIUS   Go, call the people:—   [*Exit Aedile*]
                            in whose name myself *To Coriolanus*
Attach thee as a traitorous innovator,

---

180 **jump** risk (treating)   **physic** medicine   182 **multitudinous tongue** voice of the multitude, i.e. the tribunes   183 **sweet** i.e. power   **dishonour** current shameful situation   184 **bereaves** deprives   185 **integrity** unity   187 **For th'ill** because of the evil (i.e. the tribunes and the people they represent)   189 **answer** pay for it   191 **despite** contempt   192 **bald** lacking both hair and wisdom   194 **th'greater bench** the more important governing body, i.e. the senate 195 **what's . . . law** when force and circumstance, rather than what was right, prevailed 197 **what . . . meet** what is right and proper be openly acknowledged as the correct thing to do 201 **aediles** public officers, assistants to the tribunes   202 **apprehended** arrested   204 **Attach** arrest   **innovator** revolutionary

205   A foe to th'public weal. Obey, I charge thee,
      And follow to thine answer.

CORIOLANUS Hence, old goat!

ALL PATRICIANS   We'll surety him.

COMINIUS Agèd sir, hands off.   *To Sicinius*

210 CORIOLANUS Hence, rotten thing, or I shall shake thy bones

                                                        To Sicinius

      Out of thy garments.

SICINIUS   Help, ye citizens!

Enter a rabble of Plebeians [Citizens] with the Aediles

MENENIUS   On both sides more respect.

SICINIUS   Here's he that would take from you all your power.

215 BRUTUS   Seize him, aediles!

ALL CITIZENS Down with him, down with him!

SECOND SENATOR   Weapons, weapons, weapons!

They all bustle about Coriolanus

      Tribunes! Patricians! Citizens! What, ho!
      Sicinius! Brutus! Coriolanus! Citizens!

220 ALL   Peace, peace, peace! Stay, hold, peace!

MENENIUS   What is about to be? I am out of breath:
      Confusion's near: I cannot speak. You, tribunes
      To th'people, Coriolanus, patience!
      Speak, good Sicinius.

225 SICINIUS   Hear me, people, peace.

ALL CITIZENS Let's hear our tribune: peace! Speak, speak, speak!

SICINIUS   You are at point to lose your liberties:
      Martius would have all from you: Martius,
      Whom late you have named for consul.

230 MENENIUS   Fie, fie, fie, this is the way to kindle, not to quench.

FIRST SENATOR   To unbuild the city and to lay all flat.

SICINIUS   What is the city but the people?

ALL CITIZENS True, the people are the city.

---

205 **th'public weal** the commonwealth   206 **answer** interrogation, trial/punishment
208 **surety** stand bail for   222 **Confusion** destruction/disorder/overthrow   227 **at . . . lose** on
the point of losing

BRUTUS   By the consent of all, we were established the people's
235   magistrates.

ALL CITIZENS You so remain.

MENENIUS   And so are like to do.

CORIOLANUS That is the way to lay the city flat,
To bring the roof to the foundation,
240   And bury all, which yet distinctly ranges,
In heaps and piles of ruin.

SICINIUS   This deserves death.

BRUTUS   Or let us stand to our authority,
Or let us lose it: we do here pronounce,
245   Upon the part o'th'people, in whose power
We were elected theirs, Martius is worthy
Of present death.

SICINIUS   Therefore lay hold of him:
Bear him to th'rock Tarpeian, and from thence
250   Into destruction cast him.

BRUTUS   Aediles, seize him.

ALL CITIZENS Yield, Martius, yield.

MENENIUS   Hear me one word: beseech you, tribunes,
Hear me but a word.

255   **AEDILES**   Peace, peace!

MENENIUS   Be that you seem, truly your country's friend,
And temp'rately proceed to what you would
Thus violently redress.

BRUTUS   Sir, those cold ways,
260   That seem like prudent helps, are very poisonous
Where the disease is violent. Lay hands upon him,
And bear him to the rock.

Coriolanus draws his sword

CORIOLANUS No, I'll die here:
There's some among you have beheld me fighting:
265   Come, try upon yourselves what you have seen me.

240 **distinctly ranges** is laid out in a clear and orderly manner 243 **Or** either   **stand to** uphold 245 **part** behalf 247 **present** immediate 249 **th'rock Tarpeian** the precipice on the Capitoline Hill, from which criminals were thrown to their deaths 256 **that** what
257 **temp'rately** calmly 259 **cold** calm, unimpassioned 265 **seen me** seen me do

MENENIUS   Down with that sword: tribunes, withdraw a while.

BRUTUS   Lay hands upon him.

COMINIUS   Help Martius, help! You that be noble, help him,
young and old.

270   ALL CITIZENS Down with him, down with him.   *Exeunt*

In this mutiny, the Tribunes, the Aediles and the people are beat in

MENENIUS   Go, get you to your house: be gone, away!
All will be naught else.

SECOND SENATOR   Get you gone.

CORIOLANUS Stand fast: we have as many friends as enemies.

275   MENENIUS   Shall it be put to that?

FIRST SENATOR   The gods forbid!
I prithee, noble friend, home to thy house:
Leave us to cure this cause.

MENENIUS   For 'tis a sore upon us,

280   You cannot tent yourself: be gone, beseech you.

COMINIUS   Come, sir, along with us.

CORIOLANUS I would they were barbarians, as they are,
Though in Rome littered: not Romans, as they are not,
Though calved i'th'porch o'th'Capitol.

285   MENENIUS   Be gone:
Put not your worthy rage into your tongue:
One time will owe another.

CORIOLANUS On fair ground I could beat forty of them.

MENENIUS   I could myself take up a brace o'th'best of them,

290   yea, the two tribunes.

COMINIUS   But now 'tis odds beyond arithmetic,
And manhood is called foolery when it stands
Against a falling fabric. Will you hence,
Before the tag return, whose rage doth rend

---

beat in beaten offstage   **272 naught** lost, brought to nothing   **else** otherwise   **278 cause**
disease   **280 tent** probe and clean (a wound) surgically, i.e. cure   **283 littered** born (like
calved, used of animals)   **287 One . . . another** another time will compensate for this one
289 up on   **brace** pair   **291 'tis . . . arithmetic** i.e. we are incalculably outnumbered
292 manhood manliness/valor   **foolery** folly   **293 fabric** building   **294 tag** rabble   **rend**
tear apart, lay waste

295   Like interrupted waters and o'erbear
       What they are used to bear?

MENENIUS   Pray you be gone: *To Coriolanus*
       I'll try whether my old wit be in request
       With those that have but little: this must be patched
300   With cloth of any colour.

COMINIUS   Nay, come away.   *Exeunt Coriolanus and Cominius*

A PATRICIAN   This man has marred his fortune.

MENENIUS   His nature is too noble for the world:
       He would not flatter Neptune for his trident,
305   Or Jove for's power to thunder: his heart's his mouth:
       What his breast forges, that his tongue must vent,
       And, being angry, does forget that ever
       He heard the name of death.   *A noise within*
                          Here's goodly work.

A PATRICIAN   I would they were abed.

310   MENENIUS   I would they were in Tiber. What the vengeance!
       Could he not speak 'em fair?

Enter Brutus and Sicinius with the rabble again

SICINIUS   Where is this viper
       That would depopulate the city and
       Be every man himself?

315   MENENIUS   You worthy tribunes—

SICINIUS   He shall be thrown down the Tarpeian rock
       With rigorous hands; he hath resisted law,
       And therefore law shall scorn him further trial
       Than the severity of the public power
320   Which he so sets at naught.

FIRST CITIZEN   He shall well know the noble tribunes are
       The people's mouths, and we their hands.

---

295 interrupted obstructed   **o'erbear . . . bear** overwhelm what usually contains them (i.e. river banks)   **298 in request With** required by   **299 patched . . . colour** i.e. mended by any means possible   **304 Neptune** Roman god of the sea, who traditionally carried a **trident** (three-pronged spear)   **305 thunder** Jove's weapon was the thunderbolt   **his . . . mouth** i.e. he speaks what he feels   **310 Tiber** Rome's river   **What the vengeance!** intensifying phrase, similar to "What the hell!"   **311 'em fair** to them courteously   **317 rigorous** harsh, severe   **318 scorn** disdain to offer   **320 sets** values

	ALL CITIZENS	He shall, sure on't.
	MENENIUS	Sir, sir—
325	SICINIUS	Peace!
	MENENIUS	Do not cry havoc where you should but hunt

ALL CITIZENS He shall, sure on't.

MENENIUS Sir, sir—

325 **SICINIUS** Peace!

MENENIUS Do not cry havoc where you should but hunt
With modest warrant.

SICINIUS Sir, how com'st that you have holp
To make this rescue?

330 **MENENIUS** Hear me speak: as I do know
The consul's worthiness, so can I name his faults.

SICINIUS Consul? What consul?

MENENIUS The consul Coriolanus.

BRUTUS He consul?

335 **ALL CITIZENS** No, no, no, no, no.

MENENIUS If, by the tribunes' leave, and yours, good people,
I may be heard, I would crave a word or two,
The which shall turn you to no further harm
Than so much loss of time.

340 **SICINIUS** Speak briefly then,
For we are peremptory to dispatch
This viperous traitor: to eject him hence
Were but our danger, and to keep him here
Our certain death: therefore it is decreed

345 He dies tonight.

MENENIUS Now the good gods forbid
That our renownèd Rome, whose gratitude
Towards her deservèd children is enrolled
In Jove's own book, like an unnatural dam

350 Should now eat up her own!

SICINIUS He's a disease that must be cut away.

MENENIUS O, he's a limb that has but a disease:
Mortal to cut it off: to cure it, easy.

---

323 **sure on't** be sure of it   326 **cry havoc** call for slaughter and general devastation
327 **modest warrant** limited license   328 **holp** helped   329 **rescue** forcible removal of a
prisoner from custody (legal term)   336 **leave** permission   341 **peremptory** resolved
342 **eject him hence** exile him   348 **deservèd** deserving   **enrolled** recorded   349 **dam**
mother   353 **Mortal** fatal

What has he done to Rome that's worthy death?
355   Killing our enemies, the blood he hath lost —
Which I dare vouch is more than that he hath
By many an ounce — he dropped it for his country:
And what is left, to lose it by his country,
Were to us all that do't and suffer it,
360   A brand to th'end o'th'world.

SICINIUS   This is clean cam.

BRUTUS   Merely awry:
When he did love his country, it honoured him.

MENENIUS   The service of the foot,
365   Being once gangrened, is not then respected
For what before it was.

BRUTUS   We'll hear no more:
Pursue him to his house, and pluck him thence,
Lest his infection, being of catching nature,
370   Spread further.

MENENIUS   One word more, one word:
This tiger-footed rage, when it shall find
The harm of unscanned swiftness, will too late
Tie leaden pounds to's heels. Proceed by process,
375   Lest parties, as he is beloved, break out,
And sack great Rome with Romans.

BRUTUS   If it were so?

SICINIUS   What do ye talk?   *To Menenius*
Have we not had a taste of his obedience?
380   Our aediles smote, ourselves resisted? Come.

MENENIUS   Consider this: he has been bred i'th'wars
Since a could draw a sword, and is ill-schooled
In bolted language: meal and bran together
He throws without distinction. Give me leave,
385   I'll go to him, and undertake to bring him

---

358 by at the hands of   **359 suffer** permit   **360 brand** mark of disgrace   **361 clean cam**
utterly misleading   **cam** crooked, awry   **362 Merely** totally   **373 unscanned** thoughtless
374 to's to its   **process** proper legal procedure   **375 parties** sides, factions   **378 What** why
380 smote struck   **382 a** he   **383 bolted** sifted (i.e. refined, considered)   **meal and bran** flour
and worthless husks

Where he shall answer by a lawful form,
In peace, to his utmost peril.

FIRST SENATOR   Noble tribunes,
It is the humane way: the other course
390 Will prove too bloody, and the end of it
Unknown to the beginning.

SICINIUS   Noble Menenius,
Be you then as the people's officer:
Masters, lay down your weapons.

395 **BRUTUS**   Go not home.

SICINIUS   Meet on the market-place: we'll attend you there,
Where, if you bring not Martius, we'll proceed
In our first way.

MENENIUS   I'll bring him to you.
400 Let me desire your company: he must come,   *To the Senators*
Or what is worst will follow.

FIRST SENATOR   Pray you, let's to him.   *Exeunt*

[Act 3 Scene 2]   *running scene 9*

Enter Coriolanus with Nobles

CORIOLANUS Let them pull all about mine ears, present me
Death on the wheel, or at wild horses' heels,
Or pile ten hills on the Tarpeian rock,
That the precipitation might down stretch
5 Below the beam of sight, yet will I still
Be thus to them.

Enter Volumnia

A PATRICIAN   You do the nobler.

CORIOLANUS   I muse my mother

---

386 **Where . . . peril** where he, his life at stake, shall answer for his behavior through the
calm process of a trial   391 **Unknown . . . beginning** unpredictable   396 **attend** await
3.2 Location: Rome (Coriolanus' house)   1 pull . . . ears i.e. destroy everything, crush me
present me put me forward for   **2 wheel** torture wheel to which the victim was tied and their
bones broken before they died   **at . . . heels** a form of death in which the victim's limbs were
tied to horses that then ran in different directions   **4 precipitation** steep drop   **5 beam** the
eyes were thought to emit beams that enabled vision   **8 muse** wonder (that)

Does not approve me further, who was wont
10 To call them woollen vassals, things created
To buy and sell with groats, to show bare heads
In congregations, to yawn, be still and wonder,
When one but of my ordinance stood up
To speak of peace or war.— I talk of you: *To Volumnia*
15 Why did you wish me milder? Would you have me
False to my nature? Rather say I play
The man I am.

VOLUMNIA   O, sir, sir, sir,
I would have had you put your power well on,
20 Before you had worn it out.

CORIOLANUS   Let go.

VOLUMNIA   You might have been enough the man you are,
With striving less to be so: lesser had been
The things of your dispositions, if
25 You had not showed them how ye were disposed
Ere they lacked power to cross you.

CORIOLANUS   Let them hang.

VOLUMNIA   Ay, and burn too.

Enter Menenius with the Senators

MENENIUS   Come, come, you have been too rough, something
too rough:
30 You must return and mend it.

FIRST SENATOR   There's no remedy:
Unless by not so doing, our good city
Cleave in the midst and perish.

VOLUMNIA   Pray, be counselled: *To Coriolanus*
35 I have a heart as little apt as yours,

---

9 approve support, praise   **wont** accustomed   **10 woollen** i.e. coarsely clothed   **vassals**
servants/slaves   **11 groats** coins worth four old pence (suggesting the people are mere petty
traders)   **show bare heads** i.e. remove their hats as a mark of deference   **12 congregations**
gatherings   **yawn** gape   **13 ordinance** rank, standing   **19 put . . . on** i.e. fully gained and
exercised your new authority   **21 Let go** enough   **23 lesser . . . dispositions** the people
would have understood less of your plans/moods (sense is awkward, so many editors emend
"things," e.g. to "thwartings")   **26 Ere . . . you** i.e. before they could prevent you actually
becoming consul   **cross** thwart   **29 something** somewhat   **33 Cleave . . . midst** split down
the middle   **35 apt** compliant, submissive

But yet a brain that leads my use of anger
To better vantage.

MENENIUS   Well said, noble woman:
Before he should thus stoop to th'herd, but that
40   The violent fit o'th'time craves it as physic
For the whole state, I would put mine armour on,
Which I can scarcely bear.

CORIOLANUS   What must I do?

MENENIUS   Return to th'tribunes.

45   CORIOLANUS   Well, what then? What then?

MENENIUS   Repent what you have spoke.

CORIOLANUS   For them? I cannot do it to the gods:
Must I then do't to them?

VOLUMNIA   You are too absolute,
50   Though therein you can never be too noble,
But when extremities speak. I have heard you say,
Honour and policy, like unsevered friends,
I'th'war do grow together: grant that, and tell me
In peace what each of them by th'other lose,
55   That they combine not there.

CORIOLANUS   Tush, tush!

MENENIUS   A good demand.

VOLUMNIA   If it be honour in your wars to seem
The same you are not, which for your best ends
60   You adopt your policy, how is it less or worse
That it shall hold companionship in peace
With honour, as in war, since that to both
It stands in like request?

CORIOLANUS   Why force you this?

---

37 vantage advantage, benefit   **39 but** were it not   **40 fit** attack of illness/seizure   **physic** medicine   **49 absolute** inflexible   **50 therein . . . speak** i.e. being uncompromising is a noble stance, except in cases of extreme urgency   **52 policy** strategy/cunning   **unsevered** inseparable, united   **57 demand** question   **58 seem . . . not** dissimulate, pretend to be what you are not   **60 adopt** adopt as   **less** i.e. less honorable   **61 That . . . request** for policy to be honorable in peacetime as well as in war, given that both situations require it equally   **64 force** urge

65	VOLUMNIA	Because that now it lies you on to speak to th'people,
		Not by your own instruction, nor by th'matter
		Which your heart prompts you, but with such words
		That are but roted in your tongue, though but
		Bastards and syllables of no allowance
70		To your bosom's truth. Now this no more
		Dishonours you at all than to take in
		A town with gentle words, which else would put you
		To your fortune and the hazard of much blood.
		I would dissemble with my nature where
75		My fortunes and my friends at stake required
		I should do so in honour. I am in this
		Your wife, your son, these senators, the nobles:
		And you will rather show our general louts
		How you can frown than spend a fawn upon 'em,
80		For the inheritance of their loves, and safeguard
		Of what that want might ruin.
	MENENIUS	Noble lady!—
		Come, go with us: speak fair: you may salve so, *To Coriolanus*
		Not what is dangerous present, but the loss
85		Of what is past.
	VOLUMNIA	I prithee now, my son,
		Go to them, with this bonnet in thy hand,
		And thus far having stretched it — here be with them —
		Thy knee bussing the stones: for in such business
90		Action is eloquence, and the eyes of th'ignorant
		More learnèd than the ears — waving thy head,

---

65 lies you on is incumbent upon you   **66 instruction** conviction, prompting   **68 but roted** merely learned by heart   **69 Bastards** i.e. illegitimate, not genuine   **of . . . To** unacknowledged by   **71 take in** capture   **72 gentle** honorable/soft, kind   **else** otherwise   **put . . . blood** put your chances to the test and risk much bloodshed   **74 dissemble with** disguise   **where . . . honour** in a case where, my fortunes and friends being at risk, honor required me to do so   **76 I . . . this** i.e. my views represent those of   **78 general** common   **79 a fawn** flattery   **80 inheritance** acquisition   **81 want** lack (i.e. of their loves/of flattery)   **83 salve** heal, remedy   **84 Not** not only   **87 bonnet** hat   **88 stretched it** held it out to them   **here . . . them** go this far in humoring them/on this point, give them what they want   **89 bussing** kissing   **91 learnèd** i.e. responsive   **waving** shaking or bowing (in repentance and humility)

With often thus correcting thy stout heart,
Now humble as the ripest mulberry
That will not hold the handling: or say to them,
95   Thou art their soldier, and being bred in broils
Hast not the soft way which, thou dost confess,
Were fit for thee to use as they to claim,
In asking their good loves, but thou wilt frame
Thyself, forsooth, hereafter theirs so far
100   As thou hast power and person.

MENENIUS   This but done,
Even as she speaks, why, their hearts were yours:
For they have pardons, being asked, as free
As words to little purpose.

105 VOLUMNIA   Prithee now,
Go, and be ruled: although I know thou hadst rather
Follow thine enemy in a fiery gulf
Than flatter him in a bower.

Enter Cominius
Here is Cominius.

110 COMINIUS   I have been i'th'market-place: and, sir, 'tis fit
You make strong party, or defend yourself
By calmness or by absence: all's in anger.

MENENIUS   Only fair speech.

COMINIUS   I think 'twill serve, if he can thereto frame his spirit.

115 VOLUMNIA   He must, and will:
Prithee now, say you will, and go about it.

CORIOLANUS   Must I go show them my unbarbèd sconce?
Must I with my base tongue give to my noble heart
A lie that it must bear? Well, I will do't:
120   Yet were there but this single plot to lose,
This mould of Martius, they to dust should grind it

---

92 **stout** proud   94 **hold** withstand   95 **broils** turmoil, battles   96 **soft** sociable/gentle
97 **fit** as fit   98 **asking** asking for   **frame** adapt, make   99 **forsooth** in truth   100 **person**
personal authority, influential presence   102 **Even . . . speaks** exactly as she describes
103 **free** freely granted   108 **bower** arbor/boudoir   111 **make** gather   **party** faction, side
117 **unbarbèd sconce** unarmed head   120 **plot** piece of earth, i.e. body   121 **mould**
earth/frame

And throw't against the wind. To th'market-place:
You have put me now to such a part which never
I shall discharge to th'life.

125 COMINIUS Come, come, we'll prompt you.

VOLUMNIA I prithee now, sweet son, as thou hast said
My praises made thee first a soldier, so
To have my praise for this, perform a part
Thou hast not done before.

130 CORIOLANUS Well, I must do't:
Away, my disposition, and possess me
Some harlot's spirit: my throat of war be turned,
Which choirèd with my drum, into a pipe
Small as an eunuch, or the virgin voice

135 That babies lull asleep: the smiles of knaves
Tent in my cheeks, and schoolboys' tears take up
The glasses of my sight: a beggar's tongue
Make motion through my lips, and my armed knees,
Who bowed but in my stirrup, bend like his

140 That hath received an alms. I will not do't,
Lest I surcease to honour mine own truth
And by my body's action teach my mind
A most inherent baseness.

VOLUMNIA At thy choice, then:

145 To beg of thee, it is my more dishonour
Than thou of them. Come all to ruin: let
Thy mother rather feel thy pride than fear
Thy dangerous stoutness: for I mock at death
With as big heart as thou. Do as thou list:

150 Thy valiantness was mine, thou sucked'st it from me,
But owe thy pride thyself.

CORIOLANUS Pray, be content:

---

124 discharge to th'life perform convincingly   **132 harlot's** beggar's/whore's   **throat of war**
i.e. soldier's voice   **133 choirèd** sang in harmony   **134 Small** high-pitched   **135 babies lull**
lulls, soothes babies   **136 Tent** encamp   **take up** occupy   **137 The . . . sight** my eyeballs
140 alms charitable gift   **141 surcease** cease   **143 inherent** permanent, abiding   **147 feel**
experience, undergo the effects of   **148 stoutness** obstinacy   **149 heart** i.e. courage   **list**
please   **151 owe** own

Mother, I am going to the market-place:
Chide me no more. I'll mountebank their loves,
155   Cog their hearts from them, and come home beloved
Of all the trades in Rome. Look, I am going:
Commend me to my wife. I'll return consul,
Or never trust to what my tongue can do
I'th'way of flattery further.

160 **VOLUMNIA**   Do your will.   *Exit*

    COMINIUS   Away, the tribunes do attend you: arm yourself
To answer mildly: for they are prepared
With accusations, as I hear, more strong
Than are upon you yet.

165 **CORIOLANUS** The word is 'mildly'. Pray you, let us go:
Let them accuse me by invention: I
Will answer in mine honour.

    MENENIUS   Ay, but mildly.

    CORIOLANUS Well, mildly be it then: mildly.   *Exeunt*

[Act 3 Scene 3]   *running scene 10*

Enter Sicinius and Brutus

    BRUTUS   In this point charge him home, that he affects
Tyrannical power: if he evade us there,
Enforce him with his envy to the people,
And that the spoil got on the Antiates
5   Was ne'er distributed.

Enter an Aedile

                      What, will he come?

    AEDILE   He's coming.

    BRUTUS   How accompanied?

    AEDILE   With old Menenius, and those senators
That always favoured him.

---

154 **mountebank** use trickery to win   155 **Cog** cheat   161 **arm** prepare   165 **word** watchword, password   166 **by invention** with invented charges   **3.3** *Location: Rome (the marketplace)*   1 **charge him home** press home your accusations   **affects** seeks out/is drawn to   3 **Enforce** urge against/attack/constrain   **envy** malice   4 **spoil got on** booty won from

10	SICINIUS	Have you a catalogue
		Of all the voices that we have procured
		Set down by th'poll?
	AEDILE	I have: 'tis ready.
	SICINIUS	Have you collected them by tribes?
15	AEDILE	I have.
	SICINIUS	Assemble presently the people hither:

SICINIUS   Assemble presently the people hither:
And when they hear me say 'It shall be so,
I'th'right and strength o'th'commons', be it either
For death, for fine, or banishment, then let them
20 If I say 'Fine', cry 'Fine!', if 'Death', cry 'Death!',
Insisting on the old prerogative
And power i'th'truth o'th'cause.

AEDILE   I shall inform them.

BRUTUS   And when such time they have begun to cry,
25 Let them not cease, but with a din confused
Enforce the present execution
Of what we chance to sentence.

AEDILE   Very well.

SICINIUS   Make them be strong and ready for this hint
30 When we shall hap to give't them.

BRUTUS   Go about it.   [*Exit Aedile*]
Put him to choler straight: he hath been used
Ever to conquer, and to have his worth
Of contradiction. Being once chafed, he cannot
35 Be reined again to temperance: then he speaks
What's in his heart, and that is there which looks
With us to break his neck.

Enter Coriolanus, Menenius and Cominius, with others [*Senators and Patricians*]

---

10 catalogue list   **12 by th'poll** by head, individually   **14 tribes** divisions of the populace of Rome   **16 presently** immediately   **21 old prerogative** traditional rights (of the people)   **22 i'th'truth o'th'cause** in the justice of the case   **24 cry** cry out, shout   **26 present execution** immediate carrying out   **30 hap** happen   **32 Put . . . straight** rouse him to anger straightaway   **33 worth Of contradiction** full share of answering back, pennyworth of defiance   **34 chafed** roused, angered   **36 looks** looks likely, promises   **37 us** i.e. our assistance

SICINIUS   Well, here he comes.

MENENIUS   Calmly, I do beseech you.   *To Coriolanus*

40 CORIOLANUS   Ay, as an ostler, that for th'poorest piece
Will bear the knave by th'volume. Th'honoured gods
Keep Rome in safety and the chairs of justice
Supplied with worthy men: plant love among's,
Throng our large temples with the shows of peace,
45 And not our streets with war!

FIRST SENATOR   Amen, amen.

MENENIUS   A noble wish.

Enter the Aedile with the Plebians [Citizens]

SICINIUS   Draw near, ye people.

AEDILE   List to your tribunes. Audience: peace, I say.

50 CORIOLANUS   First, hear me speak.

SICINIUS and BRUTUS   Well, say.— Peace, ho!

CORIOLANUS   Shall I be charged no further than this present?
Must all determine here?

SICINIUS   I do demand
55 If you submit you to the people's voices,
Allow their officers, and are content
To suffer lawful censure for such faults
As shall be proved upon you.

CORIOLANUS   I am content.

60 MENENIUS   Lo, citizens, he says he is content.
The warlike service he has done, consider: think
Upon the wounds his body bears, which show
Like graves i'th'holy churchyard.

CORIOLANUS   Scratches with briers, scars to move laughter only.

65 MENENIUS   Consider further
That when he speaks not like a citizen,
You find him like a soldier: do not take

---

40 ostler stable groom   **piece** coin   **41 bear . . . th'volume** put up with being called knave
any number of times/endure any degree of ill treatment from a knave   **Th'honoured** may the
honored   **43 among's** among us   **44 shows** ceremonies   **49 List** listen   **Audience** listen,
pay attention   **52 this present** with this present allegation   **53 determine** be settled
54 demand ask   **56 Allow** acknowledge   **57 censure** judgment

His rougher accents for malicious sounds,
But, as I say, such as become a soldier,
70   Rather than envy you.

COMINIUS   Well, well, no more.

CORIOLANUS   What is the matter
That being passed for consul with full voice,
I am so dishonoured that the very hour
75   You take it off again?

SICINIUS   Answer to us.

CORIOLANUS   Say, then: 'tis true, I ought so.

SICINIUS   We charge you that you have contrived to take
From Rome all seasoned office, and to wind
80   Yourself into a power tyrannical,
For which you are a traitor to the people.

CORIOLANUS   How? Traitor?

MENENIUS   Nay, temperately: your promise.

CORIOLANUS   The fires i'th'lowest hell fold in the people!
85   Call me their traitor, thou injurious tribune?
Within thine eyes sat twenty thousand deaths,
In thy hands clutched as many millions, in
Thy lying tongue both numbers, I would say
'Thou liest' unto thee with a voice as free
90   As I do pray the gods.

SICINIUS   Mark you this, people?

ALL CITIZENS   To th'rock, to th'rock with him!

SICINIUS   Peace!
We need not put new matter to his charge:
95   What you have seen him do and heard him speak,
Beating your officers, cursing yourselves,
Opposing laws with strokes, and here defying
Those whose great power must try him.

---

68 accents ways of speaking/words   **70 envy you** display malice toward you   **74 very** very
same   **76 Answer to us** i.e. you have no right to ask the questions   **77 so** to do so, i.e. answer
to you   **78 contrived** plotted   **79 seasoned** established (or perhaps "qualified, moderate" as
opposed to **tyrannical**)   **wind** insinuate   **82 How?** What?   **84 fold in** enfold, encircle
85 their traitor traitor to them   **injurious** insulting, wrongful   **86 Within** Even if within, i.e.
whatever you might do to me   **89 free** frank/honest/unrestrained   **90 I . . . the** that with
which I pray to the   **94 put** add   **97 strokes** blows, assaults

Even this, so criminal, and in such capital kind,
100 Deserves th'extremest death.

BRUTUS   But since he hath served well for Rome—

CORIOLANUS   What do you prate of service?

BRUTUS   I talk of that, that know it.

CORIOLANUS   You?

105 MENENIUS   Is this the promise that you made your mother?

COMINIUS   Know, I pray you—

CORIOLANUS   I'll know no further:
Let them pronounce the steep Tarpeian death,
Vagabond exile, flaying, pent to linger
110 But with a grain a day, I would not buy
Their mercy at the price of one fair word,
Nor check my courage for what they can give,
To have't with saying 'Good morrow.'

SICINIUS   For that he has,
115 As much as in him lies, from time to time
Envied against the people, seeking means
To pluck away their power, as now at last
Given hostile strokes, and that not in the presence
Of dreaded justice, but on the ministers
120 That doth distribute it. In the name o'th'people,
And in the power of us the tribunes, we,
Even from this instant, banish him our city,
In peril of precipitation
From off the rock Tarpeian, never more
125 To enter our Rome gates. I'th'people's name,
I say it shall be so.

ALL CITIZENS   It shall be so, it shall be so: let him away:
He's banished, and it shall be so.

COMINIUS   Hear me, my masters, and my common friends—

130 SICINIUS   He's sentenced: no more hearing.

---

99 capital i.e. worthy of the death penalty   **102 prate** chatter, babble   **109 pent** imprisoned
linger barely survive, linger on   **112 check** restrain, curb   **113 have't** have it (i.e. the people's
mercy)   **114 For that** because   **115 in him lies** he possibly could   **116 Envied against** shown
malice toward   **117 as** inasmuch as (he has)   **118 not** not only   **123 precipitation** being
thrown

COMINIUS   Let me speak:
I have been consul, and can show for Rome
Her enemies' marks upon me. I do love
My country's good with a respect more tender,
135   More holy and profound, than mine own life,
My dear wife's estimate, her womb's increase,
And treasure of my loins: then if I would
Speak that—
SICINIUS   We know your drift. Speak what?
140   BRUTUS   There's no more to be said, but he is banished,
As enemy to the people and his country.
It shall be so.
ALL CITIZENS   It shall be so, it shall be so.
CORIOLANUS   You common cry of curs, whose breath I hate
145   As reek o'th'rotten fens: whose loves I prize
As the dead carcasses of unburied men
That do corrupt my air: I banish you,
And here remain with your uncertainty.
Let every feeble rumour shake your hearts:
150   Your enemies, with nodding of their plumes,
Fan you into despair: have the power still
To banish your defenders, till at length
Your ignorance, which finds not till it feels,
Making but reservation of yourselves,
155   Still your own foes, deliver you
As most abated captives to some nation
That won you without blows, despising,
For you, the city. Thus I turn my back:
There is a world elsewhere.
Exeunt Coriolanus, Cominius, [Menenius, Senators and Patricians.
The Citizens] all shout, and throw up their caps

---

136 estimate reputation, honor   **womb's . . . loins** i.e. children   **144 cry** pack   **145 reek**
stench/foggy vapor   **148 remain** may you remain   **150 plumes** feathers on a helmet
151 have may you have   **still** always   **153 finds . . . feels** only learns through experience
154 Making . . . yourselves trying only to protect yourselves/having banished everyone except
yourselves   **155 Still . . . foes** always your own worst enemies   **156 abated** humbled, beaten
down   **158 For** because of

160 AEDILE   The people's enemy is gone, is gone!

ALL CITIZENS Our enemy is banished, he is gone. Hoo-oo!

SICINIUS   Go see him out at gates, and follow him
    As he hath followed you, with all despite:
    Give him deserved vexation. Let a guard
165   Attend us through the city.

ALL CITIZENS Come, come, let's see him out at gates: come.
    The gods preserve our noble tribunes! Come.   *Exeunt*

Act 4 [Scene 1]   *running scene 11*

*Enter Coriolanus, Volumnia, Virgilia, Menenius, Cominius, with the
young nobility of Rome*

CORIOLANUS Come, leave your tears: a brief farewell: the beast
    With many heads butts me away. Nay, mother,
    Where is your ancient courage? You were used
    To say extremities was the trier of spirits,
5   That common chances common men could bear:
    That when the sea was calm, all boats alike
    Showed mastership in floating. Fortune's blows,
    When most struck home, being gentle wounded, craves
    A noble cunning. You were used to load me
10   With precepts that would make invincible
    The heart that conned them.

VIRGILIA   O heavens! O heavens!

CORIOLANUS Nay, I prithee, woman—

VOLUMNIA   Now the red pestilence strike all trades in Rome,
15   And occupations perish!

CORIOLANUS What, what, what?
    I shall be loved when I am lacked. Nay, mother,
    Resume that spirit, when you were wont to say,

---

163 despite disdain, contempt   **164 vexation** torment, mortification   **4.1 *Location: Rome
(near the city gates)***   **1 leave** cease   **3 ancient** former   **used** accustomed   **4 extremities**
extreme circumstances, crisis   **5 common chances** ordinary events   **7 Fortune's . . . cunning**
when fortune strikes hardest, it takes noble skill to bear one's wounds like a gentleman
11 conned learned, memorized   **14 red pestilence** red sores were characteristic of the plague
15 occupations trades   **17 lacked** absent/missed   **18 wont** accustomed

If you had been the wife of Hercules,
20   Six of his labours you'd have done, and saved
Your husband so much sweat. Cominius,
Droop not: adieu. Farewell, my wife, my mother:
I'll do well yet. Thou old and true Menenius,
Thy tears are salter than a younger man's,
25   And venomous to thine eyes. My sometime general,
I have seen thee stern, and thou hast oft beheld
Heart-hardening spectacles. Tell these sad women
'Tis fond to wail inevitable strokes,
As 'tis to laugh at 'em. My mother, you wot well
30   My hazards still have been your solace, and
Believe't not lightly: though I go alone,
Like to a lonely dragon, that his fen
Makes feared and talked of more than seen: your son
Will or exceed the common, or be caught
35   With cautelous baits and practice.

VOLUMNIA   My first son,
Whither will thou go? Take good Cominius
With thee awhile: determine on some course
More than a wild exposture to each chance
40   That starts i'th'way before thee.

VIRGILIA   O the gods!

COMINIUS   I'll follow thee a month, devise with thee
Where thou shalt rest, that thou mayst hear of us
And we of thee. So if the time thrust forth
45   A cause for thy repeal, we shall not send
O'er the vast world to seek a single man,
And lose advantage, which doth ever cool
I'th'absence of the needer.

19 **Hercules** legendary Greek hero who achieved twelve seemingly impossible **labours**
22 **Droop** look downcast, despair   25 **venomous** i.e. stinging, causing inflammation
sometime former   28 **fond** foolish   **strokes** blows, afflictions   29 **wot** know   30 **still** always
31 **Believe't not lightly** do not doubt this   32 **fen** swamp   34 **or** either   **exceed the common**
outdo ordinary men, exceed ordinary expectations   35 **cautelous . . . practice** deceitful snares
and plotting   39 **exposture** exposure   40 **starts** leaps up   42 **follow** accompany   45 **repeal**
recall from exile   47 **advantage** the advantageous opportunity

CORIOLANUS Fare ye well:
50   Thou hast years upon thee, and thou art too full
        Of the wars' surfeits to go rove with one
        That's yet unbruised: bring me but out at gate.
        Come, my sweet wife, my dearest mother, and
        My friends of noble touch: when I am forth,
55   Bid me farewell, and smile. I pray you, come:
        While I remain above the ground, you shall
        Hear from me still, and never of me aught
        But what is like me formerly.
MENENIUS   That's worthily
60   As any ear can hear. Come, let's not weep:
        If I could shake off but one seven years
        From these old arms and legs, by the good gods,
        I'd with thee, every foot.
CORIOLANUS Give me thy hand: come.   *Exeunt*

[Act 4 Scene 2]   *running scene 12*

Enter the two Tribunes, Sicinius and Brutus, with the Aedile

SICINIUS   Bid them all home: he's gone, and we'll no further.
        The nobility are vexed, whom we see have sided
        In his behalf.
BRUTUS   Now we have shown our power,
5   Let us seem humbler after it is done
        Than when it was a-doing.
SICINIUS   Bid them home: say their great enemy is gone,
        And they stand in their ancient strength.
BRUTUS   Dismiss them home.   [*Exit Aedile*]
        Enter Volumnia, Virgilia and Menenius
10   Here comes his mother.
SICINIUS   Let's not meet her.

---

51 **wars' surfeits** excesses of military service   52 **bring** accompany   54 **noble touch** noble qualities/proven nobility (as the quality of gold is proved with a touchstone)   61 **one seven** i.e. seven   63 **foot** step of the way   **4.2 *Location: Rome (a street)*   1 home** go home
8 ancient former

BRUTUS	Why?	

SICINIUS   They say she's mad.

BRUTUS   They have ta'en note of us: keep on your way.

15 VOLUMNIA   O, you're well met:
Th'hoarded plague o'th'gods requite your love!

MENENIUS   Peace, peace: be not so loud.

VOLUMNIA   If that I could for weeping, you should hear—
Nay, and you shall hear some. Will you be gone?

20 VIRGILIA   You shall stay too: I would I had the power

To the Tribunes

To say so to my husband.

SICINIUS   Are you mankind?   *To Volumnia*

VOLUMNIA   Ay, fool: is that a shame? Note but this, fool:
Was not a man my father? Hadst thou foxship
25 To banish him that struck more blows for Rome
Than thou hast spoken words?

SICINIUS   O blessèd heavens!

VOLUMNIA   More noble blows than ever thou wise words,
And for Rome's good. I'll tell thee what: yet go:
30 Nay, but thou shalt stay too: I would my son
Were in Arabia, and thy tribe before him,
His good sword in his hand.

SICINIUS   What then?

VIRGILIA   What then? He'd make an end of thy posterity.

35 VOLUMNIA   Bastards and all.
Good man, the wounds that he does bear for Rome!

MENENIUS   Come, come, peace.

SICINIUS   I would he had continued to his country
As he began, and not unknit himself
40 The noble knot he made.

---

13 mad furious/wild, high-spirited/mentally disturbed   **16 Th'hoarded** the stored-up
requite repay   **22 mankind** masculine/furious (Volumnia replies to the sense of "human")
24 foxship sly cunning   **30 would** wish   **31 Arabia** i.e. the desert (a suitably lawless place for
death, and one with nowhere for the enemy to hide)   **tribe** supporters/family   **before** in front
of, facing   **34 posterity** descendants   **39 unknit** untied for   **40 knot** bond between him and
Rome

BRUTUS   I would he had.

VOLUMNIA   'I would he had'? 'Twas you incensed the rabble:
Cats, that can judge as fitly of his worth
As I can of those mysteries which heaven
45   Will not have earth to know.

BRUTUS   Pray, let's go.

VOLUMNIA   Now pray, sir, get you gone.
You have done a brave deed: ere you go, hear this:
As far as doth the Capitol exceed
50   The meanest house in Rome, so far my son —
This lady's husband here, this, do you see? —
Whom you have banished, does exceed you all.

BRUTUS   Well, well, we'll leave you.

SICINIUS   Why stay we to be baited
55   With one that wants her wits?   *Exeunt Tribunes*

VOLUMNIA   Take my prayers with you.
I would the gods had nothing else to do
But to confirm my curses. Could I meet 'em
But once a day, it would unclog my heart
60   Of what lies heavy to't.

MENENIUS   You have told them home,
And, by my troth, you have cause. You'll sup with me?

VOLUMNIA   Anger's my meat: I sup upon myself,
And so shall starve with feeding. Come, let's go:
65   Leave this faint puling and lament as I do,
In anger, Juno-like. Come, come, come.

Exeunt [Volumnia and Virgilia]

MENENIUS   Fie, fie, fie!   *Exit*

---

43 Cats i.e. wretched creatures (contemptuous)   **48 brave** splendid/courageous (sarcastic)
50 meanest poorest, humblest   **54 baited With** harassed by   **58 'em** i.e. the tribunes   **60 to't**
on it   **61 told** chastised   **home** thoroughly   **62 sup** dine   **63 meat** food   **64 starve with
feeding** i.e. consume myself/starve from not eating actual food   **65 faint puling** feeble whining
66 Juno-like like the supreme Roman goddess, Juno; her merciless fury is described in Virgil's
Aeneid

[Act 4 Scene 3]

Enter [Nicanor], a Roman, and [Adrian] a Volsce

NICANOR   I know you well, sir, and you know me: your name, I think, is Adrian.

ADRIAN   It is so, sir: truly, I have forgot you.

NICANOR   I am a Roman, and my services are, as you are,
5   against 'em. Know you me yet?

ADRIAN   Nicanor? No?

NICANOR   The same, sir.

ADRIAN   You had more beard when I last saw you, but your favour is well appeared by your tongue. What's the news in
10   Rome? I have a note from the Volscian state to find you out there. You have well saved me a day's journey.

NICANOR   There hath been in Rome strange insurrections: the people against the senators, patricians and nobles.

ADRIAN   Hath been? Is it ended then? Our state thinks not so:
15   they are in a most warlike preparation, and hope to come upon them in the heat of their division.

NICANOR   The main blaze of it is past, but a small thing would make it flame again. For the nobles receive so to heart the banishment of that worthy Coriolanus, that they are in a
20   ripe aptness to take all power from the people and to pluck from them their tribunes for ever. This lies glowing, I can tell you, and is almost mature for the violent breaking out.

ADRIAN   Coriolanus banished?

NICANOR   Banished, sir.

25   ADRIAN   You will be welcome with this intelligence, Nicanor.

NICANOR   The day serves well for them now. I have heard it said, the fittest time to corrupt a man's wife is when she's fallen out with her husband. Your noble Tullus Aufidius will appear well in these wars, his great opposer Coriolanus being
30   now in no request of his country.

4.3 *Location: on the road, between Rome and Antium*   **5 'em** i.e. the Romans
9 favour . . . tongue identity is confirmed by your voice   **favour** appearance/face   **10 note** i.e.
of instruction   **20 ripe** ready   **21 glowing** smoldering   **22 mature** ready   **26 them** i.e. the
Volscians   **30 of** from

ADRIAN   He cannot choose. I am most fortunate, thus accidentally to encounter you. You have ended my business, and I will merrily accompany you home.

NICANOR   I shall between this and supper tell you most
35   strange things from Rome, all tending to the good of their adversaries. Have you an army ready, say you?

ADRIAN   A most royal one: the centurions and their charges, distinctly billeted already in th'entertainment, and to be on foot at an hour's warning.

40   NICANOR   I am joyful to hear of their readiness, and am the man, I think, that shall set them in present action. So, sir, heartily well met, and most glad of your company.

ADRIAN   You take my part from me, sir: I have the most cause to be glad of yours.

45   NICANOR   Well, let us go together.   *Exeunt*

[Act 4 Scene 4]   *running scene 14*

Enter Coriolanus in mean apparel, disguised and muffled

CORIOLANUS   A goodly city is this Antium. City,
'Tis I that made thy widows: many an heir
Of these fair edifices 'fore my wars
Have I heard groan and drop: then know me not,
5   Lest that thy wives with spits and boys with stones
In puny battle slay me.

Enter a Citizen

Save you, sir.

CITIZEN   And you.

CORIOLANUS   Direct me, if it be your will,
10   Where great Aufidius lies: is he in Antium?

---

31 **choose** do otherwise (than **appear well**)   34 **this** this time, now   37 **centurions** officers, each in charge of one hundred men   **charges** i.e. troops   38 **distinctly billeted** individually enrolled   **in th'entertainment** on the payroll, employed   41 **present** immediate   43 **part** role, words   **4.4** *Location: Antium (outside Aufidius' house)*   *mean* humble, poor   3 **'fore my wars** in the face of my attacks   6 **puny** inexperienced   7 **Save** God save   10 **lies** lives

CITIZEN   He is, and feasts the nobles of the state
At his house this night.

CORIOLANUS   Which is his house, beseech you?

CITIZEN   This here before you.

15   CORIOLANUS   Thank you, sir: farewell.   *Exit Citizen*
O world, thy slippery turns! Friends now fast sworn,
Whose double bosoms seem to wear one heart,
Whose hours, whose bed, whose meal and exercise
Are still together: who twin, as 'twere, in love,
20   Unseparable, shall within this hour,
On a dissension of a doit, break out
To bitterest enmity: so fellest foes,
Whose passions and whose plots have broke their sleep
To take the one the other, by some chance,
25   Some trick not worth an egg, shall grow dear friends
And interjoin their issues. So with me:
My birthplace hate I, and my love's upon
This enemy town. I'll enter: if he slay me,
He does fair justice: if he give me way,
30   I'll do his country service.   *Exit*

[Act 4 Scene 5]   *running scene 15*

Music plays. Enter a Servingman

FIRST SERVINGMAN   Wine, wine, wine! What service is here? I
think our fellows are asleep.   *[Exit]*

Enter another Servingman

SECOND SERVINGMAN   Where's Cotus? My master calls for him.
Cotus!   *Exit*

Enter Coriolanus

---

16 slippery turns fickle, treacherous changes   **fast** firmly   **17 double** two (plays on the sense
of "deceitful")   **19 still** always   **21 dissension . . . doit** dispute over something trivial   **doit**
Dutch coin of small value   **22 fellest** fiercest, most cruel   **23 plots . . . other** plots to capture
one another have kept them awake   **25 trick** trifle   **26 interjoin their issues** unite their
fortunes/join their children in marriage   **29 give me way** allow me to go freely/grant my
request   **4.5 *Location: Antium (inside Aufidius' house)*   2 fellows** fellow servants

5   CORIOLANUS   A goodly house: the feast smells well; but I
         Appear not like a guest.

Enter the First Servingman

FIRST SERVINGMAN   What would you have, friend? Whence are
         you? Here's no place for you: pray, go to the door.   *Exit*

CORIOLANUS   I have deserved no better entertainment,
10   In being Coriolanus.

Enter Second Servingman

SECOND SERVINGMAN   Whence are you, sir? Has the porter his eyes
         in his head, that he gives entrance to such companions?
         Pray, get you out.

CORIOLANUS   Away.

15   SECOND SERVINGMAN   Away? Get you away.

CORIOLANUS   Now thou'rt troublesome.

SECOND SERVINGMAN   Are you so brave? I'll have you talked with
         anon.

Enter Third Servingman: the first meets him

THIRD SERVINGMAN   What fellow's this?

20   FIRST SERVINGMAN   A strange one as ever I looked on: I cannot get
         him out o'th'house: prithee, call my master to him.

THIRD SERVINGMAN   What have you to do here, fellow? Pray you,
         avoid the house.

CORIOLANUS   Let me but stand: I will not hurt your hearth.

25   THIRD SERVINGMAN   What are you?

CORIOLANUS   A gentleman.

THIRD SERVINGMAN   A marvellous poor one.

CORIOLANUS   True, so I am.

THIRD SERVINGMAN   Pray you, poor gentleman, take up some
30   other station: here's no place for you: pray you, avoid: come.

CORIOLANUS   Follow your function: go and batten on cold bits.

                                        Pushes him away from him

---

7 **Whence** from what place   8 **go . . . door** i.e. leave   9 **entertainment** hospitality, reception
12 **companions** rogues   17 **brave** defiant   18 **anon** in a moment   23 **avoid** leave   30 **station**
place to stand   31 **Follow your function** get on with your job   **batten** grow fat   **cold bits** i.e.
leftovers

THIRD SERVINGMAN   What, you will not? Prithee, tell my master
what a strange guest he has here.

SECOND SERVINGMAN   And I shall.   *Exit Second Servingman*

35   **THIRD SERVINGMAN**   Where dwell'st thou?

CORIOLANUS   Under the canopy.

THIRD SERVINGMAN   Under the canopy?

CORIOLANUS   Ay.

THIRD SERVINGMAN   Where's that?

40   **CORIOLANUS**   I'th'city of kites and crows.

THIRD SERVINGMAN   I'th'city of kites and crows? What an ass it is:
then thou dwell'st with daws too?

CORIOLANUS   No, I serve not thy master.

THIRD SERVINGMAN   How, sir! Do you meddle with my master?

45   **CORIOLANUS**   Ay, 'tis an honester service than to meddle with thy
mistress. Thou prat'st, and prat'st: serve with thy trencher,
hence!   *Beats him away*

Enter Aufidius with the [Second] Servingman

AUFIDIUS   Where is this fellow?

SECOND SERVINGMAN   Here, sir: I'd have beaten him like a dog, but

50   for disturbing the lords within.   *Servingmen stand aside*

AUFIDIUS   Whence com'st thou? What wouldst thou? Thy
name?

Why speak'st not? Speak, man: what's thy name?

CORIOLANUS   If, Tullus,   *Unmuffling*

Not yet thou know'st me, and seeing me dost not

55   Think me for the man I am, necessity

Commands me name myself.

AUFIDIUS   What is thy name?

CORIOLANUS   A name unmusical to the Volscians' ears,

And harsh in sound to thine.

---

36 canopy i.e. the sky   **40 kites and crows** birds of prey, scavengers   **42 daws** jackdaws,
proverbially foolish birds   **44 meddle** concern yourself, interfere (Coriolanus then shifts the
sense to "have sex with")   **46 prat'st** speak insolently/to little purpose   **trencher** wooden
serving dish   **49 but** were it not

60   **AUFIDIUS**   Say, what's thy name?
        Thou hast a grim appearance, and thy face
        Bears a command in't: though thy tackle's torn,
        Thou show'st a noble vessel: what's thy name?

    CORIOLANUS   Prepare thy brow to frown: know'st thou me yet?

65   **AUFIDIUS**   I know thee not: thy name?

    CORIOLANUS   My name is Caius Martius, who hath done
        To thee particularly, and to all the Volsces,
        Great hurt and mischief: thereto witness may
        My surname, Coriolanus. The painful service,

70   The extreme dangers, and the drops of blood
        Shed for my thankless country, are requited
        But with that surname: a good memory
        And witness of the malice and displeasure
        Which thou shouldst bear me: only that name remains.

75   The cruelty and envy of the people,
        Permitted by our dastard nobles, who
        Have all forsook me, hath devoured the rest,
        And suffered me by th'voice of slaves to be
        Whooped out of Rome. Now this extremity

80   Hath brought me to thy hearth, not out of hope —
        Mistake me not — to save my life: for if
        I had feared death, of all the men i'th'world
        I would have 'voided thee. But in mere spite
        To be full quit of those my banishers,

85   Stand I before thee here. Then if thou hast
        A heart of wreak in thee, that wilt revenge
        Thine own particular wrongs and stop those maims
        Of shame seen through thy country, speed thee straight,
        And make my misery serve thy turn: so use it

---

61 grim fierce, cruel/forbidding, severe   **62 command** authority   **tackle** gear, equipment—i.e. clothing (plays on sense of "ship's rigging")   **63 show'st** seem to be   **67 particularly** in person, individually   **68 mischief** injury   **thereto . . . Coriolanus** which is attested by my honorary surname, "Coriolanus"   **69 painful** arduous, diligent   **72 memory** memorial/reminder   **76 dastard** cowardly   **77 forsook** rejected, abandoned   **79 Whooped** jeered, hooted   **83 in mere** out of pure   **84 be . . . of** fully pay back   **86 wreak** vengeance   **87 maims Of shame** shameful wounds   **88 through** throughout

90   That my revengeful services may prove
      As benefits to thee, for I will fight
      Against my cankered country with the spleen
      Of all the under-fiends. But if so be
      Thou dar'st not this, and that to prove more fortunes
95   Thou'rt tired, then, in a word, I also am
      Longer to live most weary, and present
      My throat to thee and to thy ancient malice,
      Which not to cut would show thee but a fool,
      Since I have ever followed thee with hate,
100   Drawn tuns of blood out of thy country's breast,
      And cannot live but to thy shame, unless
      It be to do thee service.
AUFIDIUS   O Martius, Martius!
      Each word thou hast spoke hath weeded from my heart
105   A root of ancient envy. If Jupiter
      Should from yond cloud speak divine things,
      And say ''Tis true', I'd not believe them more
      Than thee, all noble Martius. Let me twine
      Mine arms about that body, where against
110   My grainèd ash an hundred times hath broke,
      And scarred the moon with splinters: here I clip   *He embraces*
      The anvil of my sword, and do contest   *Coriolanus*
      As hotly and as nobly with thy love
      As ever in ambitious strength I did
115   Contend against thy valour. Know thou first,
      I loved the maid I married: never man
      Sighed truer breath. But that I see thee here,
      Thou noble thing, more dances my rapt heart
      Than when I first my wedded mistress saw
120   Bestride my threshold. Why, thou Mars, I tell thee,

---

92 **cankered** corrupted, diseased   93 **under-fiends** hell's devils   94 **prove more fortunes** try your fortunes further   97 **ancient** long-standing   100 **tuns** barrels   109 **where against** against which   110 **grainèd ash** strong spear (made of straight-grained ash)   111 **clip** embrace   112 **anvil** i.e. Coriolanus, who has been struck by Aufidius' **sword** as an anvil is hit with a hammer   118 **dances** sets dancing, excites   **rapt** enraptured   120 **Bestride** step across   **Mars** Roman god of war; may pun on "Martius"

We have a power on foot, and I had purpose
Once more to hew thy target from thy brawn,
Or lose mine arm for't: thou hast beat me out
Twelve several times, and I have nightly since
125   Dreamt of encounters 'twixt thyself and me:
We have been down together in my sleep,
Unbuckling helms, fisting each other's throat,
And waked half dead with nothing. Worthy Martius,
Had we no other quarrel else to Rome, but that
130   Thou art thence banished, we would muster all
From twelve to seventy, and pouring war
Into the bowels of ungrateful Rome,
Like a bold flood o'erbear't. O, come, go in,
And take our friendly senators by th'hands
135   Who now are here, taking their leaves of me,
Who am prepared against your territories,
Though not for Rome itself.

CORIOLANUS   You bless me, gods.

AUFIDIUS   Therefore, most absolute sir, if thou wilt have
140   The leading of thine own revenges, take
Th'one half of my commission, and set down —
As best thou art experienced, since thou know'st
Thy country's strength and weakness — thine own ways:
Whether to knock against the gates of Rome,
145   Or rudely visit them in parts remote,
To fright them, ere destroy. But come in:
Let me commend thee first to those that shall
Say yea to thy desires. A thousand welcomes!

---

121 a . . . foot an army mobilized   122 target shield   brawn muscular arm   123 out
outright, fully   124 several separate   126 down together fighting with each other on the
ground; the speech betrays a perhaps unconscious homoeroticism, with many of its terms
having sexual connotations (hotly, encounters, half dead)   127 helms helmets   fisting
clutching, throttling; also slang for "breaking wind," so anal connotations are not impossible
128 waked I have waked   130 muster all recruit all men   133 o'erbear't overwhelm it
(Rome)   136 am prepared have forces drawn up   139 absolute incomparable, perfect
141 commission authority/those in my command   set down determine   145 rudely
violently   146 ere destroy before destroying them   147 commend introduce (favorably)

And more a friend than ere an enemy:

150 Yet, Martius, that was much. Your hand: most welcome!

Exeunt [Coriolanus and Aufidius]

The two Servingmen come forward

FIRST SERVINGMAN Here's a strange alteration!

SECOND SERVINGMAN By my hand, I had thought to have strucken him with a cudgel, and yet my mind gave me his clothes made a false report of him.

155 FIRST SERVINGMAN What an arm he has! He turned me about with his finger and his thumb, as one would set up a top.

SECOND SERVINGMAN Nay, I knew by his face that there was something in him. He had, sir, a kind of face, methought . . . I cannot tell how to term it.

160 FIRST SERVINGMAN He had so, looking, as it were — would I were hanged, but I thought there was more in him than I could think.

SECOND SERVINGMAN So did I, I'll be sworn: he is simply the rarest man i'th'world.

165 FIRST SERVINGMAN I think he is: but a greater soldier than he you wot on.

SECOND SERVINGMAN Who, my master?

FIRST SERVINGMAN Nay, it's no matter for that.

SECOND SERVINGMAN Worth six on him.

170 FIRST SERVINGMAN Nay, not so neither: but I take him to be the greater soldier.

SECOND SERVINGMAN Faith, look you, one cannot tell how to say that: for the defence of a town, our general is excellent.

FIRST SERVINGMAN Ay, and for an assault too.

Enter the Third Servingman

175 THIRD SERVINGMAN O slaves, I can tell you news: news, you rascals!

FIRST *and* SECOND SERVINGMAN What, what, what? Let's partake.

---

153 gave told   156 set up set spinning   163 rarest most exceptional/most splendid
165 he . . . on you know who (i.e. Aufidius)   168 it's . . . for never mind about   169 on of
him like him in the following line, this may refer either to Coriolanus or to Aufidius
175 slaves rogues/servants

THIRD SERVINGMAN   I would not be a Roman of all nations: I had
as lief be a condemned man.

180   FIRST *and* SECOND SERVINGMAN   Wherefore? Wherefore?

THIRD SERVINGMAN   Why, here's he that was wont to thwack our
general, Caius Martius.

FIRST SERVINGMAN   Why do you say 'thwack our general'?

THIRD SERVINGMAN   I do not say 'thwack our general', but he was
185   always good enough for him.

SECOND SERVINGMAN   Come, we are fellows and friends: he was
ever too hard for him: I have heard him say so himself.

FIRST SERVINGMAN   He was too hard for him directly, to say the
truth on't: before Corioles he scotched him and notched him
190   like a carbonado.

SECOND SERVINGMAN   An he had been cannibally given, he might
have boiled and eaten him too.

FIRST SERVINGMAN   But more of thy news!

THIRD SERVINGMAN   Why, he is so made on here within, as if he
195   were son and heir to Mars: set at upper end o'th'table: no
question asked him by any of the senators, but they stand
bald before him. Our general himself makes a mistress of
him: sanctifies himself with's hand and turns up the white
o'th'eye to his discourse. But the bottom of the news is, our
200   general is cut i'th'middle and but one half of what he was
yesterday: for the other has half, by the entreaty and grant of
the whole table. He'll go, he says, and sowl the porter of
Rome gates by th'ears. He will mow all down before him, and
leave his passage polled.

205   SECOND SERVINGMAN   And he's as like to do't as any man I can
imagine.

---

179 as lief rather   180 Wherefore? Why?   181 was wont used   189 on't of it   scotched
slashed   190 carbonado meat scored for cooking   191 An if   given inclined   194 on much
of   195 upper end o'th'table i.e. in the place of honor   196 but . . . bald without them
standing hatless (a mark of respect)   198 sanctifies . . . hand touches Coriolanus' hand as if
it were holy   199 bottom essence, bottom line   202 sowl roughly seize   204 polled stripped
bare (literally, with the branches lopped away)

THIRD SERVINGMAN   Do't? He will do't: for look you, sir, he has as
many friends as enemies: which friends, sir, as it were, durst
not, look you, sir, show themselves, as we term it, his friends
210   whilst he's in directitude.

FIRST SERVINGMAN   Directitude? What's that?

THIRD SERVINGMAN   But when they shall see, sir, his crest up
again, and the man in blood, they will out of their burrows,
like conies after rain, and revel all with him.

215   FIRST SERVINGMAN   But when goes this forward?

THIRD SERVINGMAN   Tomorrow, today, presently: you shall have
the drum struck up this afternoon: 'tis as it were a parcel of
their feast, and to be executed ere they wipe their lips.

SECOND SERVINGMAN   Why, then we shall have a stirring world
220   again. This peace is nothing but to rust iron, increase tailors,
and breed ballad-makers.

FIRST SERVINGMAN   Let me have war, say I: it exceeds peace as far
as day does night: it's sprightly walking, audible, and full of
vent. Peace is a very apoplexy, lethargy, mulled, deaf, sleepy,
225   insensible: a getter of more bastard children than war's a
destroyer of men.

SECOND SERVINGMAN   'Tis so: and as wars in some sort may be said
to be a ravisher, so it cannot be denied but peace is a great
maker of cuckolds.

230   FIRST SERVINGMAN   Ay, and it makes men hate one another.

THIRD SERVINGMAN   Reason: because they then less need one
another. The wars for my money: I hope to see Romans as
cheap as Volscians. They are rising, they are rising.

FIRST and SECOND SERVINGMAN   In, in, in, in.   *Exeunt*

---

210 **directitude** a nonsense word; perhaps the Third Servingman means "discredit"
212 **crest** cockerel's crest/feathers on a helmet   213 **in blood** in good condition, full of life
(hunting term)   **will** will come   214 **conies** rabbits   216 **presently** immediately   217 **parcel**
part   219 **stirring** lively, active   223 **audible** noisy/keen of hearing (like a hunting dog)   **full**
of vent full of shouts and noise/has picked up the scent of a hunted animal   224 **apoplexy**
paralysis   **mulled** numbed, stupefied   225 **getter** begetter, conceiver   228 **ravisher** rapist
229 **cuckolds** men with unfaithful wives   233 **rising** i.e. from the table

[Act 4 Scene 6]   *running scene 16*

Enter the two Tribunes, Sicinius and Brutus

SICINIUS   We hear not of him, neither need we fear him:
His remedies are tame: the present peace
And quietness of the people, which before
Were in wild hurry. Here do we make his friends
5   Blush that the world goes well, who rather had,
Though they themselves did suffer by't, behold
Dissentious numbers pest'ring streets than see
Our tradesmen singing in their shops and going
About their functions friendly.

Enter Menenius

10   BRUTUS   We stood to't in good time. Is this Menenius?

SICINIUS   'Tis he, 'tis he: O, he is grown most kind of late.—
Hail, sir.

MENENIUS   Hail to you both.

SICINIUS   Your Coriolanus is not much missed
15   But with his friends: the commonwealth doth stand,
And so would do, were he more angry at it.

MENENIUS   All's well, and might have been much better if
He could have temporized.

SICINIUS   Where is he, hear you?

20   MENENIUS   Nay, I hear nothing:
His mother and his wife hear nothing from him.

Enter three or four Citizens

ALL CITIZENS The gods preserve you both.   *To the Tribunes*

SICINIUS   Good e'en, our neighbours.

BRUTUS   Good e'en to you all, good e'en to you all.

25   FIRST CITIZEN   Ourselves, our wives and children, on our knees,
Are bound to pray for you both.

SICINIUS   Live and thrive.

4.6 Location: Rome   2 His . . . tame the remedies needed to get rid of Coriolanus (i.e. the
protesting **people**) are quiet   **4 hurry** commotion, urgent activity   **7 pest'ring** obstructing
9 functions tasks, occupations   **10 stood to't** made a stand against it   **15 But** except
16 were even were   **18 temporized** compromised, been moderate   **23 e'en** evening (i.e. any
time after noon)

BRUTUS	Farewell, kind neighbours.

We wished Coriolanus had loved you as we did.

30 ALL CITIZENS Now the gods keep you!

SICINIUS and BRUTUS   Farewell, farewell.   *Exeunt Citizens*

SICINIUS   This is a happier and more comely time

Than when these fellows ran about the streets,

Crying confusion.

35 BRUTUS   Caius Martius was

A worthy officer i'th'war, but insolent,

O'ercome with pride, ambitious past all thinking,

Self-loving—

SICINIUS   And affecting one sole throne, without assistance.

40 MENENIUS   I think not so.

SICINIUS   We should by this, to all our lamentation,

If he had gone forth consul, found it so.

BRUTUS   The gods have well prevented it, and Rome

Sits safe and still without him.

Enter an Aedile

45 AEDILE   Worthy tribunes,

There is a slave, whom we have put in prison,

Reports the Volsces with two several powers

Are entered in the Roman territories,

And with the deepest malice of the war

50 Destroy what lies before 'em.

MENENIUS   'Tis Aufidius,

Who, hearing of our Martius' banishment,

Thrusts forth his horns again into the world

Which were inshelled when Martius stood for Rome,

55 And durst not once peep out.

SICINIUS   Come, what talk you of Martius?

BRUTUS   Go see this rumourer whipped.— It cannot be

To the Aedile

The Volsces dare break with us.

---

32 comely decent, pleasing   **39 affecting** aiming for/desiring   **assistance** partners   **41 this** this time, now   **47 several powers** separate armies   **53 horns** i.e. like those of a snail   **54 inshelled** within his (snail's) shell, withdrawn   **stood** fought   **56 what** why   **58 break with us** i.e. break the terms of our treaty

MENENIUS   Cannot be?
60   We have record that very well it can,
            And three examples of the like hath been
            Within my age. But reason with the fellow,
            Before you punish him, where he heard this,
            Lest you shall chance to whip your information
65   And beat the messenger who bids beware
            Of what is to be dreaded.

SICINIUS   Tell not me: I know this cannot be.

BRUTUS   Not possible.

Enter a Messenger

MESSENGER   The nobles in great earnestness are going
70   All to the senate house: some news is come
            That turns their countenances.

SICINIUS   'Tis this slave:—
            Go whip him, fore the people's eyes.— His raising,   *To the Aedile*
            Nothing but his report.

75 MESSENGER   Yes, worthy sir,
            The slave's report is seconded and more,
            More fearful, is delivered.

SICINIUS   What more fearful?

MESSENGER   It is spoke freely out of many mouths —
80   How probable I do not know — that Martius,
            Joined with Aufidius, leads a power gainst Rome,
            And vows revenge as spacious as between
            The young'st and oldest thing.

SICINIUS   This is most likely!

85 BRUTUS   Raised only, that the weaker sort may wish
            Good Martius home again.

SICINIUS   The very trick on't.

MENENIUS   This is unlikely:

---

62 age lifetime   **reason with** converse with, question   **64 information** source of information
71 turns transforms   **73 His raising** this is his rumormongering   **76 seconded** corroborated
82 as . . . between wide enough to include   **85 Raised** stirred up, rumored   **87 trick on't**
nature, aim of it

He and Aufidius can no more atone
90   Than violent'st contrariety.

Enter [another] Messenger

SECOND MESSENGER   You are sent for to the senate:
A fearful army, led by Caius Martius,
Associated with Aufidius, rages
Upon our territories, and have already
95   O'erborne their way, consumed with fire, and took
What lay before them.

Enter Cominius

COMINIUS   O, you have made good work!

MENENIUS   What news? What news?

COMINIUS   You have holp to ravish your own daughters and
100   To melt the city leads upon your pates,
To see your wives dishonoured to your noses.

MENENIUS   What's the news? What's the news?

COMINIUS   Your temples burnèd in their cement, and
Your franchises, whereon you stood, confined
105   Into an auger's bore.

MENENIUS   Pray now, your news?
You have made fair work, I fear me.—   *To the Tribunes*
                         Pray, your news.— *To Cominius*
If Martius should be joined with Volscians.

COMINIUS   If? He is their god: he leads them like a thing
110   Made by some other deity than nature,
That shapes man better, and they follow him
Against us brats, with no less confidence
Than boys pursuing summer butterflies,
Or butchers killing flies.

115 MENENIUS   You have made good work,   *To the Tribunes*
You and your apron-men: you that stood so much

---

89 atone be reconciled   **90 violent'st contrariety** most extreme opposites   **95 O'erborne**
overcome (everything in)   **took** captured   **99 holp** helped   **ravish** rape   **100 leads** lead roofs
pates heads   **101 to your noses** in front of you, in your faces   **103 in their cement** i.e. to
their foundations   **104 franchises** rights, freedom   **105 auger's bore** small hole made with a
carpenter's tool (**auger**)   **112 brats** children   **116 apron-men** tradesmen

Upon the voice of occupation and
The breath of garlic-eaters!

COMINIUS   He'll shake your Rome about your ears.   *To the Tribunes*

120   MENENIUS   As Hercules did shake down mellow fruit.
You have made fair work.

BRUTUS   But is this true, sir?

COMINIUS   Ay, and you'll look pale
Before you find it other. All the regions

125   Do smilingly revolt, and who resists
Are mocked for valiant ignorance,
And perish constant fools. Who is't can blame him?
Your enemies and his find something in him.

MENENIUS   We are all undone, unless

130   The noble man have mercy.

COMINIUS   Who shall ask it?
The tribunes cannot do't for shame: the people
Deserve such pity of him as the wolf
Does of the shepherds: for his best friends, if they

135   Should say 'Be good to Rome', they charged him even
As those should do that had deserved his hate,
And therein showed like enemies.

MENENIUS   'Tis true: if he were putting to my house the brand
That should consume it, I have not the face

140   To say 'Beseech you, cease.'— You have made fair
   hands,   *To the Tribunes*
You and your crafts: you have crafted fair!

COMINIUS   You have brought
A trembling upon Rome, such as was never

145   S'incapable of help.

SICINIUS and BRUTUS   Say not we brought it.

---

117 voice of occupation working men's votes   **118 garlic-eaters** i.e. the lower classes
120 Hercules . . . fruit the eleventh labor of Hercules was to pluck the golden apples of the
Hesperides (the three sisters who guarded them)   **124 other** otherwise   **125 smilingly**
willingly   **who** whoever   **127 constant** steadfast, loyal   **128 something** some admirable
quality   **129 undone** ruined   **134 for** as for   **135 charged** would be entreating   **137 showed**
would appear   **138 brand** flaming torch   **141 hands** i.e. work (sarcastic)   **142 crafts** skills/
craftsmen/guiles   **crafted** worked skillfully/been cunning   **145 S'incapable of help** so
incapable of being helped

MENENIUS   How? Was't we? We loved him,
But, like beasts and cowardly nobles,
Gave way unto your clusters, who did hoot
150   Him out o'th'city.

COMINIUS   But I fear
They'll roar him in again. Tullus Aufidius,
The second name of men, obeys his points
As if he were his officer: desperation
155   Is all the policy, strength and defence
That Rome can make against them.

Enter a troop of Citizens

MENENIUS   Here come the clusters.
And is Aufidius with him? You are they
That made the air unwholesome when you cast
160   Your stinking greasy caps in hooting at
Coriolanus' exile. Now he's coming,
And not a hair upon a soldier's head
Which will not prove a whip: as many coxcombs
As you threw caps up will he tumble down,
165   And pay you for your voices. 'Tis no matter:
If he could burn us all into one coal,
We have deserved it.

ALL CITIZENS   Faith, we hear fearful news.

FIRST CITIZEN   For mine own part,
170   When I said 'Banish him' I said 'twas pity.

SECOND CITIZEN   And so did I.

THIRD CITIZEN   And so did I: and to say the truth, so did very many
of us: that we did, we did for the best, and though we willingly
consented to his banishment, yet it was against our will.

175   COMINIUS   You're goodly things, you voices.

MENENIUS   You have made good work,
You and your cry. Shall's to the Capitol?

---

149 clusters crowd, mobs   **152 roar** i.e. with fear   **153 name** greatest (after Coriolanus)   **his points** Coriolanus' instructions   **163 coxcombs** i.e. fool's heads (literally, headgear with a crest like a cock's comb)   **166 coal** smoldering piece of charcoal   **177 cry** pack (of dogs)/shouting, noise   **Shall's** shall we go

COMINIUS	O, ay, what else? *Exeunt [Cominius and Menenius]*
SICINIUS	Go, masters, get you home: be not dismayed:

180   These are a side that would be glad to have
            This true which they so seem to fear. Go home,
            And show no sign of fear.

FIRST CITIZEN   The gods be good to us! Come, masters, let's home.
            I ever said we were i'th'wrong when we banished him.

185   SECOND CITIZEN   So did we all. But, come, let's home.

Exeunt Citizens

BRUTUS   I do not like this news.

SICINIUS   Nor I.

BRUTUS   Let's to the Capitol. Would half my wealth
             Would buy this for a lie.

190   SICINIUS   Pray, let's go.   *Exeunt Tribunes*

[Act 4 Scene 7]   *running scene 17*

Enter Aufidius with his Lieutenant

AUFIDIUS   Do they still fly to th'Roman?

LIEUTENANT   I do not know what witchcraft's in him, but
             Your soldiers use him as the grace fore meat,
             Their talk at table, and their thanks at end;

5   And you are darkened in this action, sir,
             Even by your own.

AUFIDIUS   I cannot help it now,
             Unless by using means I lame the foot
             Of our design. He bears himself more proudlier,

10   Even to my person, than I thought he would
             When first I did embrace him. Yet his nature
             In that's no changeling, and I must excuse
             What cannot be amended.

LIEUTENANT   Yet I wish, sir —

---

180 side faction   **188 Would . . . lie** i.e. I would give half my wealth to have this be untrue
4.7 *Location: the Volscian camp, near Rome*   5 darkened obscured, eclipsed   **6 own** own
men, followers   **8 using means** taking action   **lame . . . design** cripple our plans (for Rome)
12 changeling fickle thing

15   I mean for your particular — you had not
            Joined in commission with him, but either
            Have borne the action of yourself, or else
            To him had left it solely.
      AUFIDIUS   I understand thee well, and be thou sure,
20   When he shall come to his account, he knows not
            What I can urge against him. Although it seems,
            And so he thinks, and is no less apparent
            To th'vulgar eye, that he bears all things fairly,
            And shows good husbandry for the Volscian state,
25   Fights dragon-like, and does achieve as soon
            As draw his sword: yet he hath left undone
            That which shall break his neck or hazard mine,
            Whene'er we come to our account.
      LIEUTENANT   Sir, I beseech you, think you he'll carry Rome?
30   AUFIDIUS   All places yields to him ere he sits down,
            And the nobility of Rome are his:
            The senators and patricians love him too:
            The tribunes are no soldiers, and their people
            Will be as rash in the repeal, as hasty
35   To expel him thence. I think he'll be to Rome
            As is the osprey to the fish, who takes it
            By sovereignty of nature. First he was
            A noble servant to them, but he could not
            Carry his honours even: whether 'twas pride,
40   Which out of daily fortune ever taints
            The happy man: whether defect of judgement,
            To fail in the disposing of those chances
            Which he was lord of: or whether nature,
            Not to be other than one thing, not moving

---

15 for your particular as far as you personally are concerned   **16 Joined in commission**
decided to share power   **17 Have . . . yourself** had orchestrated the campaign by yourself
20 account reckoning, judgment   **21 urge** bring forward   **23 th'vulgar** the common   **bears**
manages   **24 husbandry for** management on behalf of   **25 achieve** succeed in his aims
29 carry overcome, capture   **30 sits down** begins a siege   **34 repeal** recall from exile
36 osprey fish-hawk, thought to be so kingly that fish turned belly-up in surrender to it
39 even steadily, evenly   **40 out . . . fortune** due to repeated success   **41 happy** fortunate
42 disposing management   **43 nature** his character

45   From th'casque to th'cushion, but commanding peace
          Even with the same austerity and garb
          As he controlled the war. But one of these —
          As he hath spices of them all — not all,
          For I dare so far free him — made him feared,
50   So hated, and so banished: but he has a merit,
          To choke it in the utt'rance. So our virtues
          Lie in th'interpretation of the time,
          And power, unto itself most commendable,
          Hath not a tomb so evident as a chair
55   T'extol what it hath done.
          One fire drives out one fire: one nail, one nail:
          Rights by rights foulder, strengths by strengths do fail.
          Come, let's away. When, Caius, Rome is thine,
          Thou art poor'st of all: then shortly art thou mine.   *Exeunt*

Act 5 [Scene 1]
                                 running scene 18

Enter Menenius, Cominius, Sicinius, Brutus, the two Tribunes, with
others

MENENIUS   No, I'll not go: you hear what he hath said
          Which was sometime his general: who loved him
          In a most dear particular. He called me 'father':
          But what o'that?— Go, you that banished him: *To the Tribunes*
5   A mile before his tent fall down, and knee
          The way into his mercy: nay, if he coyed
          To hear Cominius speak, I'll keep at home.

---

45 casque helmet   **cushion** i.e. senator's seat/comfort of peacetime   **46 austerity and garb** severe manner   **48 spices** traces, a flavor   **49 free** absolve   **50 So** therefore **he . . . utt'rance** his merit stifles itself even as it is being praised/his merit is sufficient to stifle any talk of whatever fault was responsible   **52 time** current age, contemporary opinion **53 power . . . done** while power may be inherently worthy of praise it never entombs itself more surely than when it is publicly proclaimed   **54 chair** public rostrum   **55 T'extol** to raise up with praise   **57 Rights . . . fail** i.e. other, more dominant rights or strengths overcome the original ones; **foulder**, which could mean either "fire out" or "crumble," is the most satisfactory emendation of Folio's senseless "fouler," though some editors prefer "falter" **5.1 *Location: Rome***   **1 he** i.e. Cominius   **2 Which** who   **sometime** formerly   **3 In . . . particular** with heartfelt personal affection   **He** i.e. Coriolanus   **5 knee** crawl   **6 coyed** was reluctant

COMINIUS   He would not seem to know me.

MENENIUS   Do you hear?

10 COMINIUS   Yet one time he did call me by my name:
I urged our old acquaintance, and the drops
That we have bled together. 'Coriolanus'
He would not answer to: forbad all names:
He was a kind of nothing, titleless,
15 Till he had forged himself a name o'th'fire
Of burning Rome.

MENENIUS   Why, so! You have made good work: *To the Tribunes*
A pair of tribunes that have wracked for Rome,
To make coals cheap: a noble memory!

20 COMINIUS   I minded him how royal 'twas to pardon
When it was less expected. He replied
It was a bare petition of a state
To one whom they had punished.

MENENIUS   Very well: could he say less?

25 COMINIUS   I offered to awaken his regard
For's private friends. His answer to me was
He could not stay to pick them in a pile
Of noisome musty chaff. He said 'twas folly
For one poor grain or two to leave unburnt,
30 And still to nose th'offence.

MENENIUS   For one poor grain or two?
I am one of those: his mother, wife, his child,
And this brave fellow too: we are the grains.
You are the musty chaff, and you are smelt
35 Above the moon. We must be burnt for you.

SICINIUS   Nay, pray, be patient: if you refuse your aid
In this so never-needed help, yet do not

---

8 would . . . to acted as if he did not   18 wracked ruined (puns on "racked," i.e. strained,
worked)   19 coals charcoal (because Rome will be burned down)   memory memorial
20 minded reminded   22 bare worthless/threadbare   25 offered attempted   26 private
personal   27 stay delay, make time   in from   28 noisome foul-smelling   30 nose th'offence
smell the offensive matter (the **musty chaff**)   33 brave fine   37 so never-needed help matter
in which help is needed more than ever before

Upbraid's with our distress. But sure, if you
Would be your country's pleader, your good tongue,
40   More than the instant army we can make,
Might stop our countryman.

MENENIUS   No, I'll not meddle.

SICINIUS   Pray you, go to him.

MENENIUS   What should I do?

45 BRUTUS   Only make trial what your love can do
For Rome, towards Martius.

MENENIUS   Well, and say that Martius return me,
As Cominius is returned, unheard: what then?
But as a discontented friend, grief-shot
50   With his unkindness? Say't be so?

SICINIUS   Yet your good will
Must have that thanks from Rome, after the measure
As you intended well.

MENENIUS   I'll undertake't:
55   I think he'll hear me. Yet to bite his lip
And hum at good Cominius much unhearts me.
He was not taken well, he had not dined:
The veins unfilled, our blood is cold, and then
We pout upon the morning, are unapt
60   To give or to forgive: but when we have stuffed
These pipes and these conveyances of our blood
With wine and feeding, we have suppler souls
Than in our priest-like fasts: therefore I'll watch him
Till he be dieted to my request,
65   And then I'll set upon him.

BRUTUS   You know the very road into his kindness,
And cannot lose your way.

MENENIUS   Good faith, I'll prove him,

---

38 distress hardship, affliction   **40 instant** quickly mobilized   **49 grief-shot** grief-stricken
52 after . . . well in proportion to your good intentions   **55 bite . . . hum** signs of anger
56 unhearts discourages   **57 taken well** tackled at the right moment   **59 pout upon** look
moodily on   **61 conveyances** channels (i.e. veins)   **62 suppler** more yielding, receptive
64 dieted to sufficiently well-fed to hear   **68 prove** test

Speed how it will. I shall ere long have knowledge

70   Of my success.   *Exit*

COMINIUS   He'll never hear him.

SICINIUS   Not?

COMINIUS   I tell you, he does sit in gold, his eye
Red as 'twould burn Rome, and his injury

75   The jailer to his pity. I kneeled before him:
'Twas very faintly he said 'Rise': dismissed me
Thus with his speechless hand. What he would do
He sent in writing after me: what he would not,
Bound with an oath to yield to his conditions:

80   So that all hope is vain, unless his noble mother
And his wife, who, as I hear, mean to solicit him
For mercy to his country. Therefore, let's hence,
And with our fair entreaties haste them on.   *Exeunt*

[Act 5 Scene 2]   *running scene 19*

Enter Menenius to the Watch or Guard

FIRST WATCHMAN   Stay: whence are you?

SECOND WATCHMAN   Stand, and go back.

MENENIUS   You guard like men: 'tis well.
But, by your leave, I am an officer

5   Of state, and come to speak with Coriolanus.

FIRST WATCHMAN   From whence?

MENENIUS   From Rome.

FIRST WATCHMAN   You may not pass, you must return: our
general will no more hear from thence.

10   SECOND WATCHMAN   You'll see your Rome embraced with fire
before you'll speak with Coriolanus.

---

69 Speed prosper, fare   **70 success** outcome   **73 gold** i.e. splendor, a chair of state
74 injury sense of having been wronged   **76 faintly** indifferently, disinterestedly
77 What . . . conditions i.e. he listed the concessions that he would and would not make,
provided that the Romans swore to comply with his conditions/he stated exactly what he
would and would not do to Rome, swearing that he would abide by his intentions/he stated his
wishes, and swore to stick to them   **5.2 Location: the Volscian camp**

MENENIUS Good my friends,
　　　If you have heard your general talk of Rome,
　　　And of his friends there, it is lots to blanks,
15　　My name hath touched your ears: it is Menenius.
FIRST WATCHMAN Be it so: go back: the virtue of your name is not
　　　here passable.
MENENIUS I tell thee, fellow,
　　　The general is my lover: I have been
20　　The book of his good acts, whence men have read
　　　His fame unparalleled, happily amplified:
　　　For I have ever verified my friends,
　　　Of whom he's chief, with all the size that verity
　　　Would without lapsing suffer: nay, sometimes,
25　　Like to a bowl upon a subtle ground,
　　　I have tumbled past the throw: and in his praise
　　　Have almost stamped the leasing. Therefore, fellow,
　　　I must have leave to pass.
FIRST WATCHMAN Faith, sir, if you had told as many lies in his
30　　behalf as you have uttered words in your own, you should
　　　not pass here: no, though it were as virtuous to lie as to live
　　　chastely. Therefore, go back.
MENENIUS Prithee, fellow, remember my name is Menenius,
　　　always factionary on the party of your general.
35　SECOND WATCHMAN Howsoever you have been his liar, as you say
　　　you have, I am one that, telling true under him, must say you
　　　cannot pass. Therefore, go back.
MENENIUS Has he dined, canst thou tell? For I would not speak
　　　with him till after dinner.
40　FIRST WATCHMAN You are a Roman, are you?

---

14 lots to blanks a certainty (literally, prize-winning tickets in a lottery compared to worthless ones) **16 virtue** power/worth **17 passable** valid **19 lover** good friend **20 book** record **21 happily** favorably **22 verified** supported, guaranteed the worth of **23 size** magnitude **verity** truth **24 without lapsing suffer** permit without collapsing **25 bowl** bowling ball **subtle** deceptive **26 tumbled . . . throw** overshot the mark **27 stamped the leasing** given the stamp of truth to falsehood **32 chastely** honestly (**lie . . . chastely** plays on the sense of "have sex as to be sexually chaste") **34 factionary** active as a partisan **36 under** while serving under

MENENIUS   I am as thy general is.

FIRST WATCHMAN   Then you should hate Rome, as he does. Can
you, when you have pushed out your gates the very defender
of them, and in a violent popular ignorance, given your
45 enemy your shield, think to front his revenges with the easy
groans of old women, the virginal palms of your daughters,
or with the palsied intercession of such a decayed dotant as
you seem to be? Can you think to blow out the intended fire
your city is ready to flame in, with such weak breath as this?
50 No, you are deceived: therefore back to Rome, and prepare
for your execution: you are condemned, our general has
sworn you out of reprieve and pardon.

MENENIUS   Sirrah, if thy captain knew I were here, he would
use me with estimation.

55 **FIRST WATCHMAN**   Come, my captain knows you not.

MENENIUS   I mean, thy general.

FIRST WATCHMAN   My general cares not for you. Back, I say, go:
lest I let forth your half-pint of blood. Back: that's the utmost
of your having: back.

60 **MENENIUS**   Nay, but fellow, fellow—

Enter Coriolanus with Aufidius

CORIOLANUS   What's the matter?

MENENIUS   Now, you companion, I'll say an errand for   *To First*
you: you shall know now that I am in estimation: *Watchman*
you shall perceive that a jack guardant cannot office me
65 from my son Coriolanus: guess but my entertainment with
him: if thou stand'st not i'th'state of hanging, or of
some death more long in spectatorship, and crueller in
suffering, behold now presently, and swoon for what's to

---

44 **violent popular ignorance** surge of ignorant public violence   45 **shield** i.e. Coriolanus
front confront, meet   **easy** ready   46 **palms** outstretched hands   47 **palsied** trembling
dotant dotard, i.e. imbecile/in senile decay   52 **out of** beyond   53 **Sirrah** sir (used to address
an inferior)   54 **use** treat   **estimation** respect   58 **utmost . . . having** all you're going to
get/the furthest you're going to go   62 **companion** fellow, rogue   **say . . . for** deliver the
report for you   64 **jack guardant** knavish guardsman   **office** officiously keep
65 **entertainment** (favorable) reception   66 **stand'st . . . of** are not already condemned to
67 **spectatorship** watching

come upon thee.— The glorious gods sit in hourly　*To Coriolanus*
70　synod about thy particular prosperity, and love thee no
worse than thy old father Menenius does! O my son, my
son! Thou art preparing fire for us: look thee, here's　*He weeps*
water to quench it. I was hardly moved to come to thee, but
being assured none but myself could move thee, I have been
75　blown out of our gates with sighs, and conjure thee to
pardon Rome, and thy petitionary countrymen. The good
gods assuage thy wrath, and turn the dregs of it upon this
varlet here: this, who like a block hath denied my access
to thee.

80　CORIOLANUS　Away!

MENENIUS　How? Away?

CORIOLANUS　Wife, mother, child, I know not. My affairs
Are servanted to others: though I owe
My revenge properly, my remission lies
85　In Volscian breasts. That we have been familiar,
Ingrate forgetfulness shall poison, rather
Than pity note how much. Therefore, be gone.
Mine ears against your suits are stronger than
Your gates against my force. Yet, for I loved thee,
90　Take this along: I writ it for thy sake,　*He gives him a letter*
And would have sent it. Another word, Menenius,
I will not hear thee speak. This man, Aufidius,
Was my beloved in Rome: yet thou behold'st.

AUFIDIUS　You keep a constant temper.

Exeunt [Coriolanus and Aufidius]

The Guard and Menenius [remain]

95　FIRST WATCHMAN　Now, sir, is your name Menenius?

SECOND WATCHMAN　'Tis a spell, you see, of much power: you
know the way home again.

---

70 synod council, assembly　**73 hardly moved** persuaded with great difficulty　**75 conjure**
solemnly ask　**76 petitionary** entreating　**78 varlet** knave　**block** idiot/impediment
83 servanted in service　**owe** own　**84 properly** personally, as my own　**remission**
inclination to forgive　**85 That . . . much** our friendship shall be poisoned by Rome's
ungrateful forgetfulness rather than recalled through compassion　**89 for** because
94 constant temper steadfast state of mind

FIRST WATCHMAN Do you hear how we are shent for keeping your
greatness back?

100 SECOND WATCHMAN What cause, do you think, I have to swoon?

MENENIUS I neither care for th'world nor your general: for such
things as you, I can scarce think there's any, you're so slight.
He that hath a will to die by himself fears it not from another:
let your general do his worst. For you, be that you are long,
105 and your misery increase with your age. I say to you, as I was
said to, 'Away!'   *Exit*

FIRST WATCHMAN A noble fellow, I warrant him.

SECOND WATCHMAN The worthy fellow is our general. He's the
rock, the oak not to be wind-shaken.   *Exeunt*

[Act 5 Scene 3]

running scene 19 continues

Enter Coriolanus and Aufidius

CORIOLANUS We will before the walls of Rome tomorrow
Set down our host. My partner in this action,
You must report to th'Volscian lords, how plainly
I have borne this business.

5 AUFIDIUS Only their ends you have respected,
Stopped your ears against the general suit of Rome:
Never admitted a private whisper, no, not with such friends
That thought them sure of you.

CORIOLANUS This last old man,
10 Whom with a cracked heart I have sent to Rome,
Loved me above the measure of a father,
Nay, godded me, indeed. Their latest refuge
Was to send him, for whose old love I have,
Though I showed sourly to him, once more offered
15 The first conditions, which they did refuse
And cannot now accept, to grace him only

98 **shent** rebuked/blamed   101 **for** as for   102 **slight** worthless   103 **die by himself** kill
himself   104 **be . . . long** may you live a long life   **5.3**   2 **Set down** encamp   **host** army
3 **plainly** openly, straightforwardly   5 **their ends** Volscian aims   12 **godded me** treated me
like a god   **latest refuge** last resort   14 **showed** appeared   16 **grace** do honor to

That thought he could do more. A very little
I have yielded to. Fresh embassies and suits,
Nor from the state nor private friends, hereafter
20   Will I lend ear to.— Ha? What shout is this?   *Shout within*
Shall I be tempted to infringe my vow
In the same time 'tis made? I will not.

Enter Virgilia, Volumnia, Valeria, young Martius, with Attendants

My wife comes foremost, then the honoured mould
Wherein this trunk was framed, and in her hand
25   The grandchild to her blood. But out, affection!
All bond and privilege of nature break:
Let it be virtuous to be obstinate.   *Virgilia curtsies*
What is that curtsy worth? Or those dove's eyes,
Which can make gods forsworn? I melt, and am not
30   Of stronger earth than others. My mother bows,   *Volumnia bows*
As if Olympus to a molehill should
In supplication nod: and my young boy
Hath an aspect of intercession, which
Great nature cries 'Deny not'. Let the Volsces
35   Plough Rome and harrow Italy: I'll never
Be such a gosling to obey instinct, but stand,
As if a man were author of himself
And knew no other kin.

VIRGILIA   My lord and husband.

40   CORIOLANUS These eyes are not the same I wore in Rome.

VIRGILIA   The sorrow that delivers us thus changed
Makes you think so.

CORIOLANUS Like a dull actor now,
I have forgot my part, and I am out,
45   Even to a full disgrace. Best of my flesh,

---

19 Nor neither   **23 mould** i.e. form of his mother, Volumnia   **24 this trunk** my body   **framed**
formed, created   **25 affection** emotion/love   **27 obstinate** unyielding, hard-hearted
28 dove's eyes i.e. (Virgilia's) beautiful eyes; the dove symbolized peace and fidelity in love
29 forsworn perjured, oath-breakers   **31 Olympus** the mountain home of the Greek gods
33 aspect look   **36 gosling** young goose, i.e. fool   **to** as to   **stand** resist   **37 author** creator,
originator   **41 delivers** presents   **43 dull** stupid/inactive   **44 am out** have forgotten my lines
45 Best . . . flesh i.e. Virgilia (refers to the idea that husband and wife are one flesh)

Forgive my tyranny, but do not say
For that 'Forgive our Romans'. O, a kiss   *Virgilia kisses him*
Long as my exile, sweet as my revenge!
Now, by the jealous queen of heaven, that kiss
50 I carried from thee, dear, and my true lip
Hath virgined it e'er since. You gods, I prate,
And the most noble mother of the world
Leave unsaluted: sink, my knee, i'th'earth: *Kneels*
Of thy deep duty more impression show
55 Than that of common sons.
VOLUMNIA   O, stand up blest!   *Coriolanus rises*
Whilst, with no softer cushion than the flint,
I kneel before thee, and unproperly
Show duty as mistaken all this while
60 Between the child and parent.   *She kneels*
CORIOLANUS What's this? Your knees to me?
To your corrected son?
Then let the pebbles on the hungry beach   *He raises her*
Fillip the stars: then let the mutinous winds
65 Strike the proud cedars gainst the fiery sun,
Murd'ring impossibility, to make
What cannot be, slight work.
VOLUMNIA   Thou art my warrior: I holp to frame thee.
Do you know this lady?
70 **CORIOLANUS** The noble sister of Publicola,
The moon of Rome, chaste as the icicle
That's curdied by the frost from purest snow
And hangs on Dian's temple: dear Valeria!

---

46 tyranny cruelty   **49 jealous . . . heaven** i.e. Juno, Roman goddess of marriage   **51 virgined it** kept it chaste   **prate** talk idly   **54 more impression** a deeper indentation   **58 unproperly** unfittingly, against propriety   **59 Show . . . parent** show that all this time duty has been wrongly supposed to be owed by a child to its parent   **62 corrected** reprimanded   **63 hungry** sterile, barren   **64 Fillip** strike smartly   **66 Murd'ring impossibility** destroying the laws by which some things are impossible   **67 slight** easy   **68 holp** helped   **70 Publicola** one of Rome's first consuls   **71 moon** i.e. chaste one   **72 curdied** congealed   **73 Dian** Diana, Roman goddess of the moon and chastity

VOLUMNIA This is a poor epitome of yours, *Indicating Young Martius*
75 Which by th'interpretation of full time
May show like all yourself.

CORIOLANUS The god of soldiers, *To Young Martius*
With the consent of supreme Jove, inform
Thy thoughts with nobleness, that thou mayst prove
80 To shame unvulnerable, and stick i'th'wars
Like a great sea-mark standing every flaw,
And saving those that eye thee!

VOLUMNIA Your knee, sirrah. *To Young Martius, who then kneels*

CORIOLANUS That's my brave boy.

85 VOLUMNIA Even he, your wife, this lady, and myself,
Are suitors to you.

CORIOLANUS I beseech you, peace:
Or if you'd ask, remember this before:
The thing I have forsworn to grant may never
90 Be held by you denials. Do not bid me
Dismiss my soldiers, or capitulate
Again with Rome's mechanics. Tell me not
Wherein I seem unnatural: desire not t'allay
My rages and revenges with your colder reasons.

95 VOLUMNIA O, no more, no more!
You have said you will not grant us anything:
For we have nothing else to ask, but that
Which you deny already: yet we will ask
That, if you fail in our request, the blame
100 May hang upon your hardness: therefore hear us.

CORIOLANUS Aufidius, and you Volsces, mark: for we'll
Hear nought from Rome in private. Your request? *He sits*

---

74 epitome miniature, summary   **75 th'interpretation** the expounding, unfolding   **76 show like all** resemble in full   **77 The . . . soldiers** i.e. Mars   **78 inform** infuse, invest   **80 shame** being shamed/shameful deeds   **stick** stand out   **81 sea-mark** sailor's guide, either a beacon or landmark   **standing** withstanding   **flaw** gust of wind   **82 eye** see, i.e. follow   **89 The . . . denials** i.e. I have already sworn not to and therefore can never grant certain requests; therefore you must not consider me to be denying you personally   **91 capitulate** negotiate, come to terms   **92 mechanics** laborers   **93 t'allay** to lessen/temper/dilute   **94 colder** calmer, less impassioned

VOLUMNIA   Should we be silent and not speak, our raiment
         And state of bodies would bewray what life
105   We have led since thy exile. Think with thyself
         How more unfortunate than all living women
         Are we come hither: since that thy sight, which should
         Make our eyes flow with joy, hearts dance with comforts,
         Constrains them weep and shake with fear and sorrow,
110   Making the mother, wife and child to see
         The son, the husband and the father tearing
         His country's bowels out: and to poor we
         Thine enmity's most capital: thou barr'st us
         Our prayers to the gods, which is a comfort
115   That all but we enjoy. For how can we,
         Alas, how can we for our country pray?
         Whereto we are bound, together with thy victory,
         Whereto we are bound? Alack, or we must lose
         The country, our dear nurse, or else thy person,
120   Our comfort in the country. We must find
         An evident calamity, though we had
         Our wish, which side should win. For either thou
         Must as a foreign recreant be led
         With manacles through our streets, or else
125   Triumphantly tread on thy country's ruin,
         And bear the palm for having bravely shed
         Thy wife and children's blood. For myself, son,
         I purpose not to wait on fortune till
         These wars determine: if I cannot persuade thee
130   Rather to show a noble grace to both parts
         Than seek the end of one, thou shalt no sooner
         March to assault thy country than to tread —
         Trust to't, thou shalt not — on thy mother's womb
         That brought thee to this world.

---

103 Should we were we to   **raiment** clothing   **104 bewray** betray, reveal   **105 Think with thyself** reflect   **109 Constrains them** compels them to   **113 capital** fatal   **118 or** either **121 evident** certain, unavoidable   **122 which** whichever   **123 foreign recreant** deserter to a foreign power   **126 palm** palm leaf, symbol of victory   **128 purpose** intend   **129 determine** decide the matter   **130 grace** favor/mercy   **parts** sides

135 VIRGILIA   Ay, and mine, that brought you forth this boy,
        To keep your name living to time.

    YOUNG MARTIUS   A shall not tread on me:
        I'll run away till I am bigger, but then I'll fight.

    CORIOLANUS   Not of a woman's tenderness to be,
140   Requires nor child nor woman's face to see:
        I have sat too long.   *He rises and turns to leave*

    VOLUMNIA   Nay, go not from us thus:
        If it were so that our request did tend
        To save the Romans, thereby to destroy
145   The Volsces whom you serve, you might condemn us
        As poisonous of your honour. No, our suit
        Is that you reconcile them: while the Volsces
        May say 'This mercy we have showed', the Romans,
        'This we received', and each in either side
150   Give the all-hail to thee, and cry 'Be blest
        For making up this peace!' Thou know'st, great son,
        The end of war's uncertain: but this certain,
        That if thou conquer Rome, the benefit
        Which thou shalt thereby reap is such a name
155   Whose repetition will be dogged with curses:
        Whose chronicle thus writ: 'The man was noble,
        But with his last attempt he wiped it out,
        Destroyed his country, and his name remains
        To th'ensuing age abhorred.' Speak to me, son:
160   Thou hast affected the fine strains of honour,
        To imitate the graces of the gods,
        To tear with thunder the wide cheeks o'th'air,
        And yet to charge thy sulphur with a bolt
        That should but rive an oak. Why dost not speak?

---

137 A he   **139 Not . . . see** to avoid womanly tenderness one must not look at the faces of
women or children   **141 sat** i.e. stayed   **143 tend** aim   **147 while** so that while   **150 Give
the all-hail** i.e. welcome, praise   **152 but this** only this is   **157 it** i.e. his nobility   **160 affected**
been drawn to/sought   **161 gods** specifically Jupiter/Jove, whose weapon was the thunderbolt
163 charge load   **sulphur** lightning   **bolt** thunderbolt   **164 but . . . oak** i.e. do no harm to
mankind   **rive** split

165 Think'st thou it honourable for a noble man
Still to remember wrongs? Daughter, speak you:
He cares not for your weeping. Speak thou, boy:
Perhaps thy childishness will move him more
Than can our reasons. There's no man in the world
170 More bound to's mother, yet here he lets me prate
Like one i'th'stocks. Thou hast never in thy life
Showed thy dear mother any courtesy,
When she, poor hen, fond of no second brood,
Has clucked thee to the wars and safely home,
175 Loaden with honour. Say my request's unjust,
And spurn me back: but if it be not so,
Thou art not honest, and the gods will plague thee
That thou restrain'st from me the duty which
To a mother's part belongs. He turns away:
180 Down, ladies: let us shame him with our knees.
To his surname 'Coriolanus' 'longs more pride
Than pity to our prayers. Down: an end:
This is the last. So we will home to Rome,   *The Ladies and Young*
And die among our neighbours. Nay, behold's: *Martius kneel*
185 This boy, that cannot tell what he would have,
But kneels and holds up hands for fellowship,
Does reason our petition with more strength
Than thou hast to deny't. Come, let us go:
This fellow had a Volscian to his mother:
190 His wife is in Corioles, and his child
Like him by chance. Yet give us our dispatch:
I am hushed until our city be afire,
And then I'll speak a little.
        [*Coriolanus*] *holds her by the hand, silent*

---

166 Still constantly   **171 i'th'stocks** the stocks were a public instrument of punishment in
which the arms and/or legs were confined   **173 fond . . . brood** i.e. with no other children
fond of doting on/desirous of   **177 honest** honorable/truthful   **178 restrain'st** withhold
181 'longs belongs   **185 cannot . . . have** does not know what he asks   **187 reason** argue for
189 to for   **191 dispatch** dismissal

CORIOLANUS O mother, mother!
195 What have you done? Behold, the heavens do ope,
The gods look down, and this unnatural scene
They laugh at. O my mother, mother, O!
You have won a happy victory to Rome.
But for your son, believe it, O believe it,
200 Most dangerously you have with him prevailed,
If not most mortal to him. But let it come. *The Ladies and Young*
Aufidius, though I cannot make true wars, *Martius rise*
I'll frame convenient peace. Now, good Aufidius,
Were you in my stead, would you have heard
205 A mother less? Or granted less, Aufidius?
AUFIDIUS   I was moved withal.
CORIOLANUS I dare be sworn you were:
And, sir, it is no little thing to make
Mine eyes to sweat compassion. But, good sir,
210 What peace you'll make, advise me. For my part,
I'll not to Rome: I'll back with you, and pray you
Stand to me in this cause.— O mother! Wife!
AUFIDIUS   I am glad thou hast set thy mercy and thy
honour *Aside*
At difference in thee: out of that I'll work
215 Myself a former fortune.
CORIOLANUS Ay, by and by: *To the Ladies*
But we will drink together, and you shall bear
A better witness back than words, which we,
On like conditions, will have counter-sealed.
220 Come, enter with us. Ladies, you deserve
To have a temple built you: all the swords
In Italy, and her confederate arms,
Could not have made this peace. *Exeunt*

---

201 **mortal** fatally   202 **true** i.e. true to my word   203 **convenient** appropriate, suitable
206 **withal** by it   209 **sweat** i.e. weep   211 **back** go back   212 **Stand to** support
215 **former fortune** fortune like my former one   218 **A better witness** i.e. an official treaty
219 **On . . . counter-sealed** having agreed to the same terms, will have countersigned
222 **her confederate arms** the weapons of her allies

[Act 5 Scene 4]

Enter Menenius and Sicinius

MENENIUS   See you yond coign o'th'Capitol, yond corner-stone?

SICINIUS   Why, what of that?

MENENIUS   If it be possible for you to displace it with your little
finger, there is some hope the ladies of Rome, especially his
5   mother, may prevail with him. But I say there is no hope in't:
our throats are sentenced and stay upon execution.

SICINIUS   Is't possible that so short a time can alter the
condition of a man?

MENENIUS   There is difference between a grub and a butterfly,
10   yet your butterfly was a grub. This Martius is grown from
man to dragon: he has wings: he's more than a creeping
thing.

SICINIUS   He loved his mother dearly.

MENENIUS   So did he me, and he no more remembers his
15   mother now than an eight-year-old horse. The tartness of
his face sours ripe grapes. When he walks, he moves like
an engine, and the ground shrinks before his treading. He is
able to pierce a corslet with his eye, talks like a knell, and his
hum is a battery. He sits in his state, as a thing made for
20   Alexander. What he bids be done is finished with his bidding.
He wants nothing of a god but eternity and a heaven to
throne in.

SICINIUS   Yes, mercy, if you report him truly.

MENENIUS   I paint him in the character. Mark what mercy his
25   mother shall bring from him. There is no more mercy in him
than there is milk in a male tiger: that shall our poor city
find: and all this is long of you.

SICINIUS   The gods be good unto us!

5.4 *Location: Rome*   **1 coign** corner (of a building)   **6 stay upon** await   **8 condition**
disposition   **9 difference** difference   **17 engine** instrument of war   **18 corslet** armor
protecting the torso   **knell** the tolling of a funeral bell   **19 hum** sound of displeasure or
impatience   **battery** assault   **state** chair of state   **as . . . Alexander** like a statue of
Alexander the Great   **20 with his bidding** as soon as he asks   **21 wants** lacks   **22 throne** be
enthroned   **24 in the character** to the life, accurately   **27 long of** on account of

MENENIUS   No, in such a case the gods will not be good unto us.
30   When we banished him, we respected not them, and, he
     returning to break our necks, they respect not us.

Enter a Messenger

MESSENGER   Sir, if you'd save your life, fly to your house: *To Sicinius*
     The plebeians have got your fellow tribune
     And hale him up and down, all swearing if
35   The Roman ladies bring not comfort home,
     They'll give him death by inches.

Enter another Messenger

SICINIUS   What's the news?

SECOND MESSENGER   Good news, good news: the ladies have
          prevailed,
     The Volscians are dislodged, and Martius gone:
40   A merrier day did never yet greet Rome,
     No, not th'expulsion of the Tarquins.

SICINIUS   Friend, art thou certain this is true?
     Is't most certain?

SECOND MESSENGER   As certain as I know the sun is fire:
45   Where have you lurked that you make doubt of it?
     Ne'er through an arch so hurried the blown tide
     As the recomforted through th'gates.

Trumpets, hautboys, drums beat all together

                                        Why, hark you:
     The trumpets, sackbuts, psalteries and fifes,
     Tabors and cymbals and the shouting Romans
50   Make the sun dance.   *A shout within*
                    Hark you!

MENENIUS   This is good news:
     I will go meet the ladies. This Volumnia
     Is worth of consuls, senators, patricians,

---

34 hale haul, drag   **36 death by inches** i.e. a slow death   **39 are dislodged** i.e. have
withdrawn   **41 Tarquins** last kings of Rome (before it became a republic)   **46 blown**
swollen/roused by the wind   **47 recomforted** relieved/refreshed   *hautboys* oboe-like
instruments   **48 sackbuts** trumpet-like instruments   **psalteries** ancient or medieval stringed
instruments   **fifes** flute-like instruments, often used for military music   **49 Tabors** small
drums

55   A city full of tribunes, such as you,
       A sea and land full. You have prayed well today:
       This morning for ten thousand of your throats
       I'd not have given a doit. Hark, how they joy!
       [*Music*] *sound still with the shouts*
       SICINIUS   First, the gods bless you for your tidings: next,   *To the*
60   Accept my thankfulness.   *Messenger*
       SECOND MESSENGER   Sir, we have all great cause to give great
           thanks.
       SICINIUS   They are near the city?
       SECOND MESSENGER   Almost at point to enter.
       SICINIUS   We'll meet them, and help the joy.   *Exeunt*

[Act 5 Scene 5]   *running scene 20 continues*

Enter two Senators with Ladies [*Volumnia, Virgilia and Valeria*]
passing over the stage, with other Lords

A SENATOR   Behold our patroness, the life of Rome!
       Call all your tribes together, praise the gods,
       And make triumphant fires: strew flowers before them:
       Unshout the noise that banished Martius:
5   Repeal him with the welcome of his mother:
       Cry 'Welcome, ladies, welcome!'
       ALL   Welcome, ladies, welcome!
       A flourish with Drums and Trumpets   [*Exeunt*]

[Act 5 Scene 6]   *running scene 21*

Enter Tullus Aufidius with Attendants

AUFIDIUS   Go tell the lords o'th'city I am here:
       Deliver them this paper: having read it,
       Bid them repair to th'market-place, where I,
       Even in theirs and in the commons' ears,

---

58 doit small Dutch coin, worth half an English farthing   **63 at point** about   **5.6 *Location:***
Corioli   **3 repair** go

5   Will vouch the truth of it. Him I accuse
     The city ports by this hath entered, and
     Intends t'appear before the people, hoping
     To purge himself with words. Dispatch.   [*Exeunt Attendants*]
Enter three or four Conspirators of Aufidius' faction
     Most welcome.

10   FIRST CONSPIRATOR   How is it with our general?

     AUFIDIUS   Even so as with a man by his own
     Alms impoisoned, and with his charity slain.

     SECOND CONSPIRATOR   Most noble sir, if you do hold the same
          intent
     Wherein you wished us parties, we'll deliver you
15   Of your great danger.

     AUFIDIUS   Sir, I cannot tell:
     We must proceed as we do find the people.

     THIRD CONSPIRATOR   The people will remain uncertain whilst
     'Twixt you there's difference: but the fall of either
20   Makes the survivor heir of all.

     AUFIDIUS   I know it,
     And my pretext to strike at him admits
     A good construction. I raised him, and I pawned
     Mine honour for his truth: who being so heightened,
25   He watered his new plants with dews of flattery,
     Seducing so my friends: and to this end
     He bowed his nature, never known before
     But to be rough, unswayable, and free.

     THIRD CONSPIRATOR   Sir, his stoutness
30   When he did stand for consul, which he lost
     By lack of stooping—

     AUFIDIUS   That I would have spoke of:
     Being banished for't, he came unto my hearth,
     Presented to my knife his throat: I took him,

---

5 Him he whom   **6 ports** gates   **this** this time, now   **12 his** his own   **14 parties** supporters
15 Of from   **19 difference** disagreement, opposition   **22 admits** allows   **23 construction**
interpretation   **pawned** pledged   **24 truth** allegiance   **heightened** raised to a position of
importance   **25 plants** i.e. followers   **28 free** frank, honorable   **29 stoutness** stubbornness,
firmness   **32 That . . . of** I was about to mention that

35	Made him joint-servant with me, gave him way
	In all his own desires, nay, let him choose
	Out of my files, his projects to accomplish,
	My best and freshest men: served his designments
	In mine own person: holp to reap the fame
40	Which he did end all his, and took some pride
	To do myself this wrong: till at the last
	I seemed his follower, not partner, and
	He waged me with his countenance, as if
	I had been mercenary.
45	**FIRST CONSPIRATOR** So he did, my lord:
	The army marvelled at it, and in the last,
	When he had carried Rome and that we looked
	For no less spoil than glory—
	AUFIDIUS There was it,
50	For which my sinews shall be stretched upon him.
	At a few drops of women's rheum, which are
	As cheap as lies, he sold the blood and labour
	Of our great action: therefore shall he die,
	And I'll renew me in his fall.

Drums and Trumpets sound, with great shouts of the people
                                    But hark.

55	**FIRST CONSPIRATOR** Your native town you entered like a post,
	And had no welcomes home: but he returns
	Splitting the air with noise.
	SECOND CONSPIRATOR And patient fools,
	Whose children he hath slain, their base throats tear
60	With giving him glory.
	THIRD CONSPIRATOR Therefore, at your vantage,

---

35 joint-servant i.e. equal partner   **gave him way** let him have his way/gave him opportunity
37 files troops   **38 designments** enterprises   **39 holp** helped   **40 end** gather in as
(harvesting term)   **43 waged** paid, rewarded   **countenance** patronage, approval
44 mercenary a hired soldier   **46 in** at   **47 had carried** was about to overcome   **49 There
was it** i.e. that was the thing   **50 sinews . . . stretched** strength will be exerted to the utmost
against   **51 rheum** i.e. tears   **55 post** messenger (sent in advance of the main arrival);
Aufidius' native town is Antium, where this scene is set in Plutarch, but for the dramatic effect
of Coriolanus' downfall, Shakespeare locates it in Corioli   **61 your vantage** this opportune
moment for you

Ere he express himself, or move the people
With what he would say, let him feel your sword,
Which we will second. When he lies along,

65   After your way his tale pronounced shall bury
His reasons with his body.

Enter the Lords of the city

AUFIDIUS   Say no more: here come the lords.

ALL THE LORDS   You are most welcome home.

AUFIDIUS   I have not deserved it.

70   But, worthy lords, have you with heed perused
What I have written to you?

ALL THE LORDS   We have.

FIRST LORD   And grieve to hear't.
What faults he made before the last, I think

75   Might have found easy fines: but there to end
Where he was to begin, and give away
The benefit of our levies, answering us
With our own charge, making a treaty where
There was a yielding — this admits no excuse.

80   AUFIDIUS   He approaches: you shall hear him.

Enter Coriolanus marching with Drum and Colours, the Commoners being with him

CORIOLANUS   Hail, lords! I am returned your soldier,
No more infected with my country's love
Than when I parted hence, but still subsisting
Under your great command. You are to know

85   That prosperously I have attempted and
With bloody passage led your wars even to
The gates of Rome. Our spoils we have brought home
Doth more than counterpoise a full third part
The charges of the action. We have made peace

---

64 along stretched out   65 After . . . pronounced his story told in your words   66 reasons explanations, justifications   70 heed care   75 easy fines lenient penalties   77 levies expenses incurred in raising troops   answering rewarding   78 charge expenses   79 yielding surrender   85 prosperously . . . attempted my endeavors have been prosperous   88 more . . . part outweigh by a full third   89 charges costs

90   With no less honour to the Antiates
          Than shame to th'Romans. And we here deliver,
          Subscribed by th'consuls and patricians,
          Together with the seal o'th'senate, what
          We have compounded on.   *He gives the Lords a paper*
95   AUFIDIUS   Read it not, noble lords,
          But tell the traitor in the highest degree
          He hath abused your powers.
     CORIOLANUS Traitor? How now?
     AUFIDIUS   Ay, traitor, Martius.
100 CORIOLANUS Martius?
     AUFIDIUS   Ay, Martius, Caius Martius: dost thou think
          I'll grace thee with that robbery, thy stol'n name,
          'Coriolanus' in Corioles?
          You lords and heads o'th'state, perfidiously
105   He has betrayed your business, and given up,
          For certain drops of salt, your city Rome:
          I say 'your city' to his wife and mother,
          Breaking his oath and resolution like
          A twist of rotten silk, never admitting
110   Counsel o'th'war: but at his nurse's tears
          He whined and roared away your victory,
          That pages blushed at him and men of heart
          Looked wond'ring each at others.
     CORIOLANUS Hear'st thou, Mars?
115 AUFIDIUS   Name not the god, thou boy of tears.
     CORIOLANUS Ha?
     AUFIDIUS   No more.
     CORIOLANUS Measureless liar, thou hast made my heart
          Too great for what contains it. Boy? O slave!—
120   Pardon me, lords, 'tis the first time that ever
          I was forced to scold. Your judgements, my grave lords,

---

90 Antiates citizens of Antium   **92 Subscribed** signed   **94 compounded** agreed
104 perfidiously treacherously   **106 drops of salt** i.e. tears   **109 twist** twined thread
admitting Counsel o'th'war taking advice from fellow soldiers   **112 heart** courage   **121 scold**
speak violently

Must give this cur the lie: and his own notion —
Who wears my stripes impressed upon him, that
Must bear my beating to his grave — shall join
125   To thrust the lie unto him.

FIRST LORD   Peace, both, and hear me speak.

CORIOLANUS   Cut me to pieces, Volsces: men and lads,
Stain all your edges on me. 'Boy'! False hound,
If you have writ your annals true, 'tis there,
130   That, like an eagle in a dovecote, I
Fluttered your Volscians in Corioles.
Alone I did it. 'Boy'!

AUFIDIUS   Why, noble lords,
Will you be put in mind of his blind fortune,
135   Which was your shame, by this unholy braggart,
'Fore your own eyes and ears?

ALL CONSPIRATORS   Let him die for't.

ALL [THE] PEOPLE   Tear him to pieces! Do it presently!   *Shouting*
He killed my son! My daughter! He killed my cousin   *individually*
140   Marcus! He killed my father!

SECOND LORD   Peace, ho! No outrage: peace!
The man is noble, and his fame folds in
This orb o'th'earth. His last offences to us
Shall have judicious hearing. Stand, Aufidius,
145   And trouble not the peace.

CORIOLANUS   O that I had him, with six Aufidiuses,   *Drawing his sword*
Or more, his tribe, to use my lawful sword!

AUFIDIUS   Insolent villain!   *Drawing his sword*

ALL CONSPIRATORS   Kill, kill, kill, kill, kill him!

*Draw both the Conspirators, and kill Martius, who falls: Aufidius
stands on him*

150   LORDS   Hold, hold, hold, hold!

AUFIDIUS   My noble masters, hear me speak.

---

122 **give . . . lie** accuse this dog of lying   **notion** understanding   123 **stripes** lashes
128 **edges** swords' edges   131 **Fluttered** threw into agitation, caused to flutter in panic
134 **blind fortune** random good luck (fortune was traditionally depicted as a blind woman)
138 **presently** immediately   141 **outrage** violence   142 **folds in** enfolds   144 **judicious
hearing** i.e. lawful trial   **Stand** stop

FIRST LORD   O Tullus!

SECOND LORD   Thou hast done a deed whereat   *To Aufidius*
    Valour will weep.

155 THIRD LORD   Tread not upon him, masters: *To Aufidius and the*
    All be quiet: put up your swords.   *Conspirators*

AUFIDIUS   My lords,
    When you shall know — as in this rage,
    Provoked by him, you cannot — the great danger
160   Which this man's life did owe you, you'll rejoice
    That he is thus cut off. Please it your honours
    To call me to your senate, I'll deliver
    Myself your loyal servant, or endure
    Your heaviest censure.

165 FIRST LORD   Bear from hence his body,
    And mourn you for him. Let him be regarded
    As the most noble corpse that ever herald
    Did follow to his urn.

SECOND LORD   His own impatience
170   Takes from Aufidius a great part of blame.
    Let's make the best of it.

AUFIDIUS   My rage is gone,
    And I am struck with sorrow. Take him up:
    Help three o'th'chiefest soldiers: I'll be one.
175   Beat thou the drum, that it speak mournfully:
    Trail your steel pikes. Though in this city he
    Hath widowed and unchilded many a one,
    Which to this hour bewail the injury,
    Yet he shall have a noble memory. Assist.

Exeunt bearing the body of Martius. A dead march sounded

---

153 whereat at which   **160 owe** have in store for   **161 Please it** if it please   **162 deliver** prove, demonstrate   **164 censure** criticism/judgment   **174 one** i.e. the fourth bearer of the body   **176 Trail** i.e. turn the pikes upside down and carry them so that the metal heads trail along the ground; a customary practice at military funerals   **179 memory** memorial/ posthumous reputation   ***dead march*** solemn piece of music accompanying a funeral; probably played with a muffled drum

TEXTUAL NOTES

F = First Folio text of 1623, the only authority for the play
F2 = a correction introduced in the Second Folio text of 1632
F3 = a correction introduced in the Third Folio text of 1663–64
F4 = a correction introduced in the Fourth Folio text of 1685
Ed = a correction introduced by a later editor
SD = stage direction
SH = speech heading (i.e. speaker's name)

List of parts = Ed

1.1.13 on = Ed. F = one **56 you. For** = Ed. F = you for **81 stale't** = Ed. F = scale't **98 tauntingly** = Ed. F = taintingly **166 geese: you are** = Ed. F = Geese you are: **195 pick** = F. Ed = pitch **210 Shouting** = Ed. F = Shooting **215 unroofed** = Ed. F = vnroo'st **225 SD** *Junius* = F4 *(Iunius)*. F = *Annius* **242 Lartius** = Ed. F = *Lucius* **255 your** = F4. F = you **259 SD** *remain* = Ed. F = *Manet* **280 of** = F. Ed = on
1.2.5 on = Ed. F = one **17 Whither** = Ed. F = Whether
1.3.33 that's = F2. F = that **40 sword, contemning.** = Ed. F = sword. *Contenning,* **79 yarn** = Ed. F = yearne **Ithaca** = Ed. F = *Athica*
1.4.36 boils = Ed. F = Byles **47 followed** = F2. F = followes. Ed = Follow/ Follow me **50 SD** *gates* = F2. F = *Gati* **52 SD** *is shut in* this direction is *transferred from the end of the stage direction five lines previously. It has been repositioned because Martius has lines to speak after this direction in* F; *furthermore, the gates do not shut until the soldier remarks upon it* **63 left** = F. Ed = lost **66 Cato's** = Ed. F = *Calues*
1.5.4 honours = Ed. F = hours **7 them,** = F3. F = them. **9 him.** = F3. F = him
1.6.6 The = F. Ed = Ye **63 Antiates** = Ed. F = Antients. F *could make sense as "ancients" is a common spelling of "ensigns"; however, seven lines later reference is made to the "Antiats," suggesting an earlier error* **83 Lesser** = F3. F = Lessen **97 I** = Ed. F = foure
1.9.0 SD *Flourish moved from before "Alarum" since it should herald the entry of the Romans* **45 beheld** = F. Ed = upheld **51 An overture** = F. Ed = a coverture/an ovator. *If the* coverture *reading is preferred, it would mean a "covering," possibly signifying a special garment.* Ovator *means "one who receives a public ovation"* **54 shout** = Ed. F = shoot **70, 71 Martius** = Ed. F = *Marcus* **72 SH CORIOLANUS** = Ed. F = *Martius* (F speech

heading changes to Cor., Corio., Coriol. with effect from return to Rome in Act 2)

1.10.23 Embarquements = F. Ed = Embargements

2.1.13 SH SICINIUS *and* BRUTUS = Ed. F = *Both. This emendation, for the purposes of clarification, also occurs at lines 22 and 25*   **16 with all** = F3. F = withall   **22 How are** = F2. F = ho ware   **52 can** = F. Ed = cannot. *The Folio reading can be defended if one agrees that Menenius is being sarcastic*   **56 tell you** = F. Ed = tell you, you   **58 bisson** = Ed. F = beesome   **64 faucet** = Ed. F = Forset   **77 are. When . . . purpose, it** = F4. F = are, when . . . purpose. It   **84 Good e'en** = Ed. F = Godden   **97 SH VIRGILIA *and* VALERIA** = Ed. F = 2.*Ladies.*   **144 SD *A . . . flourish** moved from F's original positioning after "Hark, the trumpets"*   **153 'Coriolanus'** = Ed. F = *Martius Caius Coriolanus*   **169 wear** = F2. F = were   **172 SH CORIOLANUS** = Ed. F = *Com.*   **213 gauded** = F *(gawded)*. Ed = guarded   **247 authorities . . . end.** = F *(Authorities, . . . end.)*. Ed = authorities. For an end,   **259 teach** = F. Ed = touch

2.2.65 SH FIRST SENATOR = Ed. F = *Senat.*   **83 one on's** = Ed. F = on ones   **93 chin** = F *(Shinne)*   **110 took: . . . foot** = Ed. F = tooke . . . foot: Ed = took. . . . foot   **155 thus':** = F3 *(thus,)*. F = thus   **163 SH SENATORS** = Ed. F = *Senat.*

2.3.25 wedged = F *(wadg'd)*   **34 it. I say,** = Ed. F = it, I say.   **37 all together** = F *(altogether)*   **61 SD *three** = F. Ed = two. The speech headings were also altered by Rowe, in keeping with the emendation*   **66 but not** = Ed. F = but   **84 SH FOURTH CITIZEN** = Ed. F = I. *This is to distinguish between these two other citizens and the three who have just exited*   **99 SH FIFTH CITIZEN** = Ed. F = 2.   **108 starve** = Ed. F = sterue   **109 hire** = F2 *(hier)*. F = higher   **110 tongue** = F. Ed = toge   **127 SH SIXTH CITIZEN** = Ed. F = I.*Cit.*   **129 SH SEVENTH CITIZEN** = Ed. F = 2.*Cit.*   **246 And . . . surnamed** = Ed. *Delius suggests inserting a line derived from North's* Plutarch, *possibly missed by the compositor's eyeskip from* And *to* And.

3.1.5 road = F *(roade)*. Ed = raid   **38 SH FIRST SENATOR** = Ed. F = *Senat. (throughout scene)*   **54 suppliants** = F4. F = Suppliants: **60 SH CORIOLANUS** = Ed. F = *Com.*   **72 on.** = Ed. F = on,   **111 good** = Ed. F = God!   **117 he** = F. Ed = they   **118 ignorance** = F. Ed = impotence   **153 native** = F. Ed = motive   **155 bosom multiplied** = F. Ed = bisson multitude   **169 Where one** = Ed. F = Whereon   **188, 189 He's** = F *(Ha's)*   **194 bench?** = Ed. F = Bench,   **208 SH ALL PATRICIANS** = Ed. F = *All.*   **216 SH ALL CITIZENS** = Ed. F = *All. (throughout scene)*   **238 SH CORIOLANUS** = Ed. F = *Com.*   **260 poisonous** = F. Ed = poisons   **271 your** = Ed. F = our   **274 SH CORIOLANUS** = Ed. F = *Com.*   **281 SH COMINIUS** = F2. F = *Corio.*   **282 SH CORIOLANUS** = Ed. F = *Mene.*   **285 SH MENENIUS** = Ed. *The speech heading has been moved from three lines above*

302 SH A PATRICIAN = F *(Patri.)* **343 our** = Ed. F = one **385 him** = Ed. F = bring him in peace *(thought to be an error by the compositor, anticipating two lines later)* **402 SH FIRST SENATOR** = F *(Sena.)*

3.2.7 SH A PATRICIAN = Ed. F = *Noble.* **31 SH FIRST SENATOR** = F *(Sen.)* **39 herd** = Ed. F = heart **65 you on** = F. Ed = on you **92 With** = Ed. F = Which **119 bear? Well,** = Ed. F = beare well? **120 plot to lose** = Ed. F = Plot, to loose

3.3.12 poll = F *(Pole)* **40 for th'** = F2 *(forth).* F = fourth **44 Throng** = Ed. F = Through **51 SH SICINIUS** *and* **BRUTUS** = F *(Both Tri.)* **68 accents** = Ed. F = Actions **84 hell fold** = Ed. F = hell.Fould **87 clutched** = Ed. F = clutcht: **92 SH ALL CITIZENS** = Ed. F = *All. (throughout scene)* **132 for** = Ed. F = from **159 SD** *Menenius . . . Patricians* = Ed. F = *with Cumalijs. It seems that the compositor misunderstood a direction for Coriolanus and Cominius to exit "with the others" and set it as a proper name*

4.1.5 chances = F2. F = chances. **26 thee** = F *(the)* **37 will thou** = F. F2 = will you. Ed = wilt thou **41 SH VIRGILIA** = Ed. F = *Corio.*

4.2.28 words, = Ed. F = words.

4.3.1 SH NICANOR = Ed. F = *Rom. The speech heading "Roman" has been altered to the character's proper name throughout the scene* **3 SH ADRIAN** = Ed. F = *Volsce. The speech heading "Volsce" has been altered to the character's proper name throughout the scene* **9 appeared** = F. Ed = approved **33 will** = F2. F = well

4.4.17 seem = F4 *(seeme).* F = seemes **27 hate** = Ed. F = haue. Ed = leave

4.5.10 SD *Servingman* = Ed. F = *Seruant.* **79 Whooped** = Ed. F = Hoop'd **129 no other** = F. F3 = no **133 o'erbear't** = Ed. F = o're-beate. Ed = o'erbear **150 SD** *The . . . forward* = Ed. F = *Enter two of the Seruingmen. The Servingmen have clearly overheard the dialogue between Aufidius and Coriolanus, so it is necessary for them to remain onstage, rather than exit and reenter* **169 on** = F *(one)* **177 SH FIRST** *and* **SECOND SERVINGMAN** = Ed. F = *Both. (throughout scene)* **179 lief** = F *(liue)* **192 boiled** = F *(boyld).* Ed = broiled **223 sprightly walking** = F. Ed = sprightly, walking **224 sleepy** = F3 *(sleepie).* F = sleepe

4.6.22 SH ALL CITIZENS = F *(All.) (throughout scene)* **70 come** = Ed. F = comming **91 SH SECOND MESSENGER** = Ed. F = *Mes.* **146 SH SICINIUS** *and* **BRUTUS** = F *(Tri.)* **168 SH ALL CITIZENS** = Ed. F = *Omnes.*

4.7.39 'twas = F3. F = 'was **41 defect** = F2. F = detect **51 virtues** = F2. F = Vertue **57 foulder** = Ed. F = fouler.

5.1.18 for = F. Ed = fair **79 yield to his** = F. Ed = hold to his/yield no new/ yield to no

5.2.62 errand = Ed. F = arrant **68 swoon** = Ed. F = swoond **75 our** = F4. F = your **87 pity** = Ed. F = pitty: **100 swoon** = Ed. F = swoond

5.3.51 prate = Ed. F = pray **68 holp** = Ed. F = hope **72 curdied** = F. Ed =

candied **89 thing** = F. Ed = things **124 through** = F. Ed = thorough
137 SH YOUNG MARTIUS = Ed. F = *Boy.* **160 fine** = Ed. F = fiue
163 charge = Ed. F = change **165 noble man** = F2. F = Nobleman
174 clucked = Ed. F = clock'd **180 him with** = F2. F = him with him
with **190 his** = F. Ed = this
5.5.4 Unshout = F *(Vnshoot)*
5.6.37 projects to accomplish, = F3. F = projects, to accomplish **64–65**
second. . . . way = Ed. F = second, . . . way. **131 Fluttered** = F3. F =
Flatter'd **149 SD** *kill* = F4. F = *kils*

SCENE-BY-SCENE ANALYSIS

ACT 1 SCENE 1

Lines 1–157: Roman citizens are preparing to mutiny over recent food shortages, believing that the patricians are hoarding corn and charging high prices for it. One citizen urges them all "rather to die than to famish," and the crowd agrees. He tells them that Caius Martius (later Coriolanus) is "chief enemy to the people," and again the crowd agrees. Another citizen says they must acknowledge Martius' reputation as a war hero, but the First Citizen argues that Martius "pays himself with being proud." Shouts are heard and they realize that the "other side o'th'city is risen." As they set off for the Capitol, they meet Menenius and tell him the senate has known of the people's discontent for a fortnight and that they now intend to exchange "strong breaths" for "strong arms." Menenius argues that the patricians have the "most charitable care" for them and tells them "a pretty tale": an allegory about "a time when all the body's members / Rebelled against the belly," believing that it was hoarding all the food for itself, while they did all the work. The "belly" replied that it was "the storehouse and the shop / Of the whole body," responsible for distributing the nutrition that enabled all the parts to work. They are interrupted by Martius.

Lines 158–259: Martius shows his contempt for the citizens, calling them "dissentious rogues" and "scabs." He accuses them of being fickle, liking "nor peace nor war" and "call[ing] him noble that was now your hate." Menenius explains that the citizens believe the "city is well stored" with grain, and Martius scornfully exclaims that the citizens know nothing: their beliefs are all stories told "by th'fire." He reports that the other uprising has been quelled, and that the senate have allowed the citizens to choose "Five tribunes to defend their vulgar wisdoms," including Sicinius and Brutus. He expresses disapproval and tells the "fragments" of the crowd to go home. A messenger brings news that the Volsces are prepared for war, and Martius callously suggests that this will help rid Rome of the "musty superfluity" of citizens. Members of the senate arrive to confirm that war is imminent, and Martius mentions the leader of the Volsces, Tullus Aufidius, calling him a "lion." A senator reminds Martius of his promise to serve as second to Cominius, and Martius says that he will be "constant" to this. The senators ask Cominius to lead them to the Capitol and the citizens disperse.

Lines 260–294: Sicinius and Brutus discuss Martius' pride. Sicinius wonders that Martius' "insolence can brook to be commanded / Under Cominius," but Brutus points out that if they fail, Cominius will be blamed, but if it goes well, the credit will go to Martius.

ACT 1 SCENE 2

In Corioles, Aufidius and the Volscian senators discuss the forthcoming conflict. Aufidius is angry that the Romans appear to be informed about Volscian military plans, although, ironically, he has a letter informing him of movements in Rome. The senators send Aufidius into battle, confident that Rome will not be prepared, although he is certain it will be and telling them that he and his "old enemy" Caius Martius have sworn to fight to the death.

ACT 1 SCENE 3

In Rome, the focus shifts from the public/political sphere to a private, domestic setting as Martius' mother and wife sit sewing, although their conversation concerns Martius and the forthcoming conflict. Volumnia tells Virgilia that she should "rejoice" in her husband's absence, as the "honour" that he wins at war is better than "the embracements of his bed." She describes how, even though he was "the only son of [her] womb," and still "tender-bodied," she encouraged Martius to go to war when he was younger. Virgilia asks how she would have felt if Martius had died, but Volumnia argues that she would have been proud that her son had died "nobly" for Rome. The arrival of Valeria is announced, and Virgilia begs to be allowed to retire. Volumnia refuses her request, telling her that she expects news of Martius, and imagining his valiant but bloody deeds in battle. She describes how Martius will "beat Aufidius' head below his knee / And tread upon his neck." Virgilia is horrified, but her mother-in-law calls her a "fool." Valeria enters and comments on the ladies' sewing, a strange counterpoint to the talk of violence, before asking after Martius and Virgilia's son. Volumnia boasts of her grandson's bloodthirsty nature, describing how he caught a "gilded butterfly" and then "set his teeth to tear it." Valeria invites the ladies to go visiting with her, but Virgilia refuses, insisting that she will not leave her home until Martius returns from the wars. The others try to persuade her but she is unmoved.

ACT 1 SCENE 4

Martius and Lartius wait outside Corioles, betting their horses on whether Cominius and Aufidius have met. A messenger brings the news that the generals have not spoken, and Martius calls for a parley. The Volscian senators appear and Martius asks for Aufidius, but he is already doing battle with Cominius, confirmed by the sounds of a distant drum and alarum. Lartius calls for ladders to scale the walls of Corioles, but the Volscian army advances. Martius' call to arms, to "fight / With hearts more proof than shields," demonstrates his courage. The Volsces beat the Romans back to their trenches and Martius is furious. He curses his soldiers, a "herd" of men who have the "souls of geese," wishing "boils and plagues" upon them. As the gates open, Martius pursues the enemy inside, but the Roman soldiers do not follow, regarding his actions as "Foolhardiness." The gates close behind Martius and Lartius assumes that he has been killed. As he delivers a eulogy on Martius' bravery, Martius himself reemerges, bleeding, but still fighting. Inspired, his men follow him into Corioles.

ACT 1 SCENE 5

Martius and Lartius find soldiers dividing their "spoils," while the fighting continues elsewhere. Martius is disgusted by the "base slaves" who value worthless goods, such as "a cracked drachma" and "leaden spoons," and leave before the fighting's finished. He hears the sounds of the battle, and imagines Aufidius "Piercing" the Roman troops. He sends Lartius to secure Corioles while he goes to help Cominius. Lartius argues that Martius is heavily wounded, but Martius insists he will fight.

ACT 1 SCENE 6

Cominius and his soldiers retreat. He praises his men, in contrast to Martius' contempt for the common soldiers. A messenger reports that he saw Lartius and Martius' troops driven back to their trenches outside Corioles. They are interrupted, however, by the arrival of a bleeding Martius. Martius and Cominius embrace, and Cominius calls him a "Flower of warriors." Martius reveals that they have taken Corioles and demands to know why Cominius is not fighting. Cominius tells him of their retreat, and Martius asks Cominius to "Set [him] against Aufidius." He urges him to fill "the air with swords advanced and darts." Martius rallies the soldiers, calling for anyone who believes "brave death outweighs bad life." The men all take up arms and prepare to fight, urged on by Cominius who promises a share of any booty, revealing another contrast in the attitudes of the two leaders: Martius fights for honor, Cominius for financial reward.

ACT 1 SCENE 7

Lartius leaves a guard on the gates of Corioles and goes to find Cominius and Martius.

ACT 1 SCENE 8

Martius and Aufidius fight. Their enmity is apparent as Martius announces that he "hates" Aufidius "Worse than a promise-breaker." They agree to fight to the death, but Aufidius breaks his word and retreats, assisted by Volscian soldiers.

ACT 1 SCENE 9

Cominius praises Martius, saying the tribunes and the "fusty ple-beians" will "thank the gods" that "Rome hath such a soldier." They are joined by Lartius, who joins in with Cominius' fulsome praise, to Martius' discomfort. Cominius insists that "Rome must know the value of her own" and offers Martius "a tenth" of the spoils, but Mar-tius refuses any "bribe to pay [his] sword." The soldiers cheer and Lartius and Cominius bare their heads in respect but Martius repeats that he does not want their praise. Cominius says he is "Too modest" and insists on giving Martius his own horse. He adds that, "from this time," Martius shall be known as "Martius Caius Coriolanus" in recognition of "what he did before Corioles." The soldiers call out his new name, and "Coriolanus" thanks Cominius before inquiring after a Volscian prisoner, "a poor man" who allowed him to rest at his house. He requests the man's freedom (the first and only time he shows concern for a commoner) but cannot remember his name, and the moment passes.

ACT 1 SCENE 10

Defeated, Aufidius is furious and swears his revenge on Martius/Coriolanus. He acknowledges that Martius has beaten him five times, and probably would do so "should we encounter / As often as we eat." He swears that if he cannot beat him "True sword to sword" then he will do so by some other means, emphasizing the contrast between his own character and Martius' inflexible honesty. He sends a soldier to Corioles to discover who are "hostages to Rome," and goes to make his plans.

ACT 2 SCENE 1

Lines 1–87: Menenius says that the augurer has predicted that it will be good news from the wars, although the people will not think so "for they love not Martius." Brutus and Sicinius discuss Martius' faults, particularly his pride, and Menenius retorts that they are themselves "censured" by the honorable and noble men of the city for being "unmeriting, proud, violent, testy magistrates, alias fools." He enlarges on the faults of the people's tribunes, "the herdsmen of the beastly plebeians," and tells them that Martius is "worth all [their] predecessors." He prepares to leave, saying that their conversation might "infect" his brain. He meets Volumnia, Virgilia, and Valeria.

Lines 88–200: Volumnia tells Menenius that Martius is on his way, showing him letters to this effect, and adding that there is a letter for him too. Menenius is overjoyed and asks if Martius is wounded. Despite Virgilia's protests, Volumnia insists that he will be, and both she and Menenius are pleased at this sign of his military prowess. They discuss his defeat of Aufidius and how the senate has had a full report of Martius' bravery. Volumnia proudly boasts that Martius has been given "the whole name of the war," and Menenius tells Brutus and Sicinius that Martius now has even "more cause to be proud." As Menenius and Volumnia discuss the wounds that Martius has received over the years, they hear a shout and a flourish. The procession arrives, the victorious Martius crowned with "an oaken garland." A herald announces that he is to be known henceforth as "Coriolanus." The Romans cheer and Coriolanus silences them before greeting his mother. He kneels before her, but she tells him to stand and greet his wife. Coriolanus turns to Virgilia, who is weeping, and tells her that her behavior is more like that of a widow, although his tone is gentle. He takes her hand, and his mother's, and says that they must go to the Capitol before they go home. Volumnia claims that now there is only "one thing wanting" in her dreams for her son, but he insists that he would rather serve Rome as a soldier than have political power.

Lines 201–277: Alone, Brutus and Sicinius discuss Coriolanus' recent triumph and popularity. Brutus predicts that Coriolanus will be offered the consulship, which Sicinius foresees will lessen their own powers. They take comfort from the fact that he will not be able to sustain his popularity because of his pride. They decide to remind the people of Coriolanus' previous "hatred" for them. A messenger arrives to call the tribunes to the Capitol, where Coriolanus is celebrated by "nobles" and "commons" alike.

ACT 2 SCENE 2

Two officers prepare the Capitol for the election of the consulship. One comments that "Coriolanus will carry it," but the other says that despite his bravery, Coriolanus is "vengeance proud, and loves not the common people." A sennet is heard, and the official procession of patricians and tribunes arrives. Menenius announces that the main purpose of the meeting is to report on the "worthy work performed / By Martius Caius Coriolanus." Cominius is invited to speak, and Brutus and Sicinius are asked to listen and then report what they hear "toward the common body." Coriolanus leaves, insisting that he does not want to hear his deeds recounted. Menenius makes a point of commenting on Coriolanus' modesty, and Cominius begins his speech in praise of Coriolanus' bravery in war, from the start of his career to Corioles. He describes how Coriolanus "waxèd like a sea" and "struck / Corioles like a planet," adding that he refused the spoils he was offered, believing he "rewards / His deeds with doing them." Coriolanus is sent for, and Menenius tells him he will be made consul, but he must now "speak to the people." Coriolanus replies that he cannot "entreat" the people for their vote by displaying his wounds and asks to "o'erleap that custom," but Sicinius insists that "the people must have their voices." Coriolanus argues that he will "blush in acting" such a part and does not wish it to be thought his valor in battle was merely to win the good opinion of the people. Menenius urges him to speak to them and they all leave except Brutus and Sicinius, who again condemn Coriolanus' arrogance.

ACT 2 SCENE 3

Lines 1–61: The citizens await Coriolanus, discussing how they must show "noble acceptance" of his noble deeds, although aware of his dislike. Coriolanus enters, dressed in a gown of humility, to ask for their votes. Menenius encourages Coriolanus, but he is reluctant and cannot see why he should show his battle scars to win approval. Menenius urges him to speak "In wholesome manner," otherwise he will "mar all." Menenius leaves, and three citizens come before Coriolanus.

Lines 62–132: Coriolanus is brusque and awkward as he asks the citizens the "price o'th'consulship," adding that he has "wounds to show" if they wish. They give him their vote. The next two citizens enter, and again Coriolanus asks for their vote, but one of the citizens challenges him, accusing him of being both a friend and enemy of the people: he has proved "a scourge" to the enemies of Rome, but also "a rod" to her friends, as he does not love "the common people." Coriolanus cynically promises to "flatter" the citizens, and to "practise the insinuating nod," and the citizens give him their vote. When they have left, Coriolanus' soliloquy reveals his contempt for the process and the citizens: "Better it is to die, better to starve / Than crave the hire which first we do deserve." More citizens enter and he reminds them of the battles he has fought before they give him their votes.

Lines 133–270: Menenius returns with Brutus and Sicinius. Menenius tells him that he has "the people's voice" and can now meet the senate. Coriolanus wishes to change out of his robes of humility. Coriolanus and Menenius leave, and Brutus observes how "With a proud heart he wore his humble weeds." The citizens return and report that Coriolanus has their vote, although most of them feel he "mocked" them, saying they did not see his wounds, the "marks of merit" that won their votes. Sicinius questions why, therefore, they gave their votes and both he and Brutus tell the citizens what they should have said, using the opportunity to remind them of Coriolanus' faults, arguing that "his contempt" will be "bruising" to them once he has "power to crush." The citizens are swayed, as, encouraged by Brutus and Sicinius, they prepare to march to the senate and "revoke" their "ignorant election" of Coriolanus.

ACT 3 SCENE 1

Lines 1–212: Coriolanus questions Lartius about Aufidius, who has raised a new army. Coriolanus believes they will soon be at war again but Lartius says that this is unlikely. He reports that Aufidius has retired to Antium, where he curses the Volsces for yielding Corioles. Aufidius hates Coriolanus most "of all things upon the earth," and wants to become his "vanquisher." As Coriolanus is expressing his desire to meet Aufidius again, Brutus and Sicinius stop the procession. Coriolanus tells Lartius how much he despises the two tribunes, "The tongues o'th'common mouth." Brutus and Sicinius say that it would be dangerous to process any further: the people are "incensed against" Coriolanus. Coriolanus asks why the tribunes cannot control their "herd" and accuses them of inciting the citizens against him.

Despite Menenius' and Cominius' repeated appeals for calm, an argument begins as Brutus and Sicinius say that Coriolanus "mocked" the people and remind him of his past attitude toward them. In turn, Coriolanus accuses them of a "plot" against him. He cannot contain his true feelings about the commoners, "the mutable, rank-scented meinie," arguing that in "soothing" them, and "mingling" with them, the senate has "nourished" the masses and given "power" to "beggars." He denies all of Menenius' attempts to excuse his words and continues to criticize the senate for their tolerance toward the people. Sicinius accuses Coriolanus of treachery and calls for him to be arrested. The patricians back Coriolanus, but the Aediles arrive with the rabble of plebeians to arrest him.

Lines 213–300: Menenius calls for "respect" from all sides, but Brutus and Sicinius incite the crowd, telling them that Coriolanus would take their power and urging the Aediles to "seize him." A disturbance breaks out and Menenius urges Sicinius to call the crowd to order. As Menenius observes, however, Sicinius' words serve more to "kindle" rather than "quench" as he tells the crowd that "Martius" would have them "lose [their] liberties." Coriolanus argues that giving the people their own tribunes "is the way to lay the city flat." Brutus and Sicinius claim "Martius is worthy / Of present death" and urge the masses to seize him and throw him from "th'rock Tarpeian." Coriolanus draws his sword and declares he will die fighting. Again, Menenius urges calm and Cominius calls on the nobility to help Coriolanus. The mutiny begins and the tribunes, officers, and people are beaten offstage. Despite Coriolanus' desire to stay and fight, the senators urge him to leave. Cominius leads him away, while Menenius stays to try and "patch" matters.

Lines 301–402: Menenius explains that Coriolanus is "too noble" to flatter and that "his tongue must vent" what is in his heart. The "rabble" returns led by Brutus and Sicinius who have complete control over them. Menenius tries to describe their new consul's "worthiness," but they deny that Coriolanus is consul. Sicinius argues that they are keen to "dispatch" him, describing Coriolanus as a "disease that must be cut away." Menenius asks what he has "done to Rome that's worthy death," reminding them of his bravery in battle and the blood that he has shed "for his country." He asks the people to allow him to bring Coriolanus to answer them in a fair trial and, urged by the senators, they agree. Menenius and the senators go to fetch Coriolanus, and Brutus and Sicinius lead the people to wait in the marketplace.

ACT 3 SCENE 2

The defiant Coriolanus is surprised that his mother urges him to be "milder." He asks if she wants him to be "false" to his own nature when he would rather "play" the part of himself. Volumnia answers that she would rather that he had been secure in his new power before he "had worn it out." Menenius arrives and explains to Coriolanus that, for the sake of "the whole state," he must "Repent." Coriolanus is reluctant, but Volumnia encourages him to think of it as tactical, "as in war," "to seem / The same you are not." She tells him to go with his head uncovered and kneel before the people, as "Action is eloquence," and to tell them that as a soldier he does not have "the soft way" with words. Cominius comes to fetch Coriolanus to the marketplace. He revolts at the idea that he must turn his "throat of war" into "a pipe / Small as an eunuch." Volumnia continues to urge him, and he agrees that he will go and behave "mildly."

ACT 3 SCENE 3

Lines 1–47: An Aedile tells Sicinius and Brutus that Coriolanus is coming, accompanied by Menenius and several senators. Sicinius tells him to "assemble the people." He adds instructions that, whatever he pronounces against Coriolanus, whether it be "For death, for finė, or banishment," the crowd are to repeat his declaration, showing the power he has over the citizens. The Aedile leaves and Brutus advises Sicinius to provoke Coriolanus "to choler," as he will speak "his heart," thus giving them the opportunity to "break his neck." Coriolanus arrives, accompanied by various noble figures. Menenius begs him to behave calmly, and Coriolanus vows that he will keep the peace.

Lines 48–167: The Aedile brings in the citizens and Coriolanus asks to speak. Sicinius says that he must accept the "lawful censure" of the people once his faults are "proved upon" him. Menenius tells the crowd they must allow for Coriolanus' "rougher accents" because he is a soldier. Coriolanus asks to know why the citizens changed their minds about the consulship, and Sicinius accuses him of desiring "a power tyrannical," which would make him "a traitor to the people." Coriolanus is unable to control his proud temper and declares he will not "buy" the citizens' "mercy" and would rather take his punishment. Sicinius seizes the opportunity to banish him. Cominius' attempts to intervene are ineffectual and Coriolanus proclaims his hatred of the common "curs," claiming that their ignorance leads them to "banish [their] defenders." He leaves, accompanied by the noblemen, and the citizens celebrate that "the people's enemy is gone," before heading to the gates to see Coriolanus cast out of Rome.

ACT 4 SCENE 1

The short scenes that distinguish this act create both a sense of pace and of the inevitable progression toward the tragic conclusion.

This scene is personal, contrasting with the heated and violent politics throughout the previous act, as Coriolanus says "a brief farewell" to his family and friends. Volumnia and Virgilia weep and Coriolanus asks where his mother's "ancient courage" is. Volumnia asks him to take Cominius, who offers to go with him for a month, but Coriolanus refuses, showing concern for Cominius' age and health, and says he must go alone.

ACT 4 SCENE 2

Brutus and Sicinius give orders that the crowds are to be dispersed. They decide they should "seem humbler" for a while, to placate Coriolanus' noble supporters. Volumnia, Virgilia, and Menenius arrive and both women angrily attack the tribunes. Volumnia reminds them of the "noble blows" Coriolanus has struck "for Rome," and accuses them of having "incensed the rabble." The tribunes leave quickly.

ACT 4 SCENE 3

Nicanor and Adrian meet between Rome and Antium and exchange military secrets. Nicanor recounts the unrest in Rome and the banishment of Coriolanus, and we learn that the Volscians have an army ready to attack.

ACT 4 SCENE 4

Coriolanus arrives in Antium in disguise and asks for Aufidius' house. His soliloquy reflects on how friends can suddenly turn in "bitterest enmity," and how he hopes that Aufidius, once his enemy, will "interjoin" with him against Rome.

ACT 4 SCENE 5

Lines 1–150: In Aufidius' house, the servants are in attendance at a feast. Coriolanus enters and the servingmen try to make him leave. When they cannot, one goes to fetch Aufidius while the others trade insults with Coriolanus. Aufidius questions him, seeing that although he has a "grim appearance," Coriolanus "show'st a noble vessel." The tension builds until Coriolanus reveals his identity. He explains his circumstances to Aufidius and reveals that "in mere spite" to his "banishers" he has come to fight with him against the "cankered" Rome. He acknowledges that Aufidius may cut his throat and accepts his fate if so. In another of the play's swift reversals, Aufidius claims that "each word" Coriolanus has spoken has "weeded" out the "root of ancient envy" from his heart. He expresses his delight before inviting him to meet the senators he is entertaining as they prepare their attack on Rome's territories. He goes on to invite Coriolanus to take "one half of [his] commission," and advise them how best to defeat Rome.

Lines 151–234: The two servingmen discuss what has just occurred. As they argue over who is the better soldier, Aufidius or Coriolanus, a third man arrives to report that Coriolanus has been well received by the senators, "as if he were son and heir to Mars." He comments that, in accepting Coriolanus' offer and giving him power, Aufidius has made himself "but one half of what he was yesterday," a dangerous position. They agree, however, that "peace is nothing but to rust iron" and that they had rather be at war, an opinion that suits the martial tone of the play.

ACT 4 SCENE 6

Lines 1–96: Sicinius and Brutus gloat that there has been no news of Coriolanus, and that there has been peace in Rome since his departure. Menenius arrives and they observe that "Coriolanus is not much missed." He is forced to admit that "All's well," but wishes that Coriolanus had been more moderate. He has heard nothing from his friend, and neither has Volumnia nor Virgilia. Several citizens exchange pleasantries with the tribunes, who again take the opportunity to gloat over the "happier time" and criticize Coriolanus for helping to create civil unrest with his pride and ambition, insisting that he was aiming for "one sole throne." An Aedile brings the news that a slave claims that "the Volsces with two several powers / Are entered in the Roman territories." Menenius says that it is Aufidius taking advantage of Coriolanus' absence, but the tribunes refuse to believe it until a messenger brings confirmation. He adds that Coriolanus has "joined with Aufidius" and "vows revenge" on Rome. It is Menenius' turn to deny the report, but a second messenger arrives to announce that Coriolanus, "Associated with Aufidius, rages / Upon [their] territories."

Lines 97–190: Cominius arrives and says that the Volscians view Coriolanus as "their god." He and Menenius accuse the tribunes of bringing this upon their country through their treatment of Coriolanus. Menenius says that unless "noble" Coriolanus has "mercy" they are "all undone." Sicinius and Brutus feebly deny responsibility. Several citizens arrive and Menenius points out to them that they cast up their "stinking greasy caps" in joy when Coriolanus was exiled, and now they have no one to fight for them. The citizens also deny responsibility, but Menenius is scornful. He and Cominius leave for the Capitol and Sicinius and Brutus follow, hoping the rumors are untrue.

ACT 4 SCENE 7

Aufidius listens as his lieutenant describes Coriolanus' influence over the Volscian troops, which, he says, eclipses Aufidius' own power. Aufidius acknowledges this but says he "cannot help it now" without ruining their plans to take Rome. He adds that Coriolanus "bears himself more proudlier" than he anticipated. The lieutenant wishes that Aufidius had not joined with Coriolanus, but he reassures him that he will defeat Coriolanus eventually, and in the meantime Coriolanus is fighting "dragon-like" for the Volsces. Coriolanus is necessary for them to "carry Rome": he will take it easily, but his pride and inflexible nature will be his downfall. Aufidius swears that when Coriolanus has defeated Rome, he will defeat Coriolanus.

ACT 5 SCENE 1

Menenius will not ask Coriolanus for mercy, arguing that it should be those who banished him that do so. Cominius tried but Coriolanus refused to acknowledge him, or to answer to any name, considering himself "titleless, / Till he had forged himself a name o'th'fire / Of burning Rome." He refused to consider mercy for his "private friends" or even his family, telling Cominius that he could not separate "one poor grain or two" from "a pile / Of noisome musty chaff," an image that evokes the opening of the play and the role of the tribunes and citizens in recent events. Menenius points out that

Sicinius and Brutus are responsible. They appeal to his patriotism, asking him to speak with Coriolanus, and he relents. After he has left, Cominius tells the tribunes that Coriolanus "will never hear" Menenius, as his sense of betrayal by Rome is too great. He adds that Volumnia and Virgilia may perhaps solicit him "For mercy to his country" and they go to urge the women to try.

ACT 5 SCENE 2

At the Volscian camp, Menenius asks to speak to Coriolanus. The watchmen tell him that their new general will not talk with anyone from Rome, despite Menenius' assurances that he is a good friend of Coriolanus. They tell him that Rome has "pushed out" its "very defender" through "violent popular ignorance" and now cannot hope that a "decayed dotant" such as Menenius will prevent his revenge. As Menenius begs to be allowed in, Coriolanus and Aufidius arrive. Menenius tells the watchman that his "son Coriolanus" will punish him for trying to stop their meeting, then turns to Coriolanus, weeping, to beg for his mercy, reiterating the paternal role he has played in his life. Coriolanus tells him to go away, adding that he "know[s] not" "Wife, mother, child." He gives Menenius a letter but will not hear him speak, and the generals leave again. The watchmen mock Menenius.

ACT 5 SCENE 3

Lines 1–141: Coriolanus and Aufidius discuss their attack on Rome and Coriolanus asks Aufidius to tell the Volscian senators how he has conducted himself. Aufidius confirms that Coriolanus has worked only to Volscian ends and has not admitted any "private whisper" from his former friends. Coriolanus says that he will not yield, even to Menenius who, he acknowledges, loved him "above the measure of a father." They are interrupted by the arrival of Volumnia, Virgilia, and his son, young Martius. Clearly moved, Coriolanus wills himself to "out affection" and refuses to "obey instinct." He is cold toward them but softens as his wife kisses him and his mother and son kneel before him. He begs them not to ask what he cannot grant but his mother pleads with him to hear them. His resolve hardens and he says she must speak before Aufidius and the Volsces as he will "Hear nought from Rome in private." Volumnia makes an emotional speech, saying that in order to attack Rome Coriolanus must march over his mother's body. Virgilia threatens the same but young Martius says that he will not be trodden on, but will run away and return to fight his father when he is "bigger." Coriolanus replies he has "sat too long" and starts to leave.

Lines 142–223: Volumnia tries again, arguing that he could be known for showing noble mercy toward Rome, rather than for destroying it. She urges Coriolanus to "speak" to her, and Virgilia and young Martius to "speak" to him, placing words above action for the first time. Again they kneel before him and Coriolanus silently takes his mother's hand before agreeing to "frame convenient peace" between Volsces and Rome. He asks Aufidius if he could have refused such a request and Aufidius says that he was moved, but adds in an aside that he is glad Coriolanus has acted in this way as it gives him an excuse to destroy him.

ACT 5 SCENE 4

In Rome, Menenius is pessimistic about the possibility that Coriolanus' family can sway him, saying that "There is no more mercy in him than there is milk in a male tiger." A messenger arrives, telling Sicinius to flee to the safety of his home: the plebeians have Brutus and are threatening to kill him if Volumnia and Virgilia cannot move Coriolanus. A second messenger brings the news that "the ladies have prevailed, / The Volscians are dislodged, and Martius gone." Celebrations are heard and Menenius hurries to meet the women, saying that Volumnia is "worth" a "city full of tribunes."

ACT 5 SCENE 5

Volumnia and Virgilia are welcomed into Rome in triumph.

ACT 5 SCENE 6

Aufidius sends attendants with written accusations against Coriolanus to the lords of Corioles. He asks them to come to the marketplace where he will "vouch the truth" of his written statement to the commoners. His conspirators arrive and offer to kill Coriolanus but he says they must follow public opinion. The conspirators advise him that public opinion is divided between him and Coriolanus but that, if one falls, the other will become "heir of all." Aufidius is aware of this and outlines his case against Coriolanus: he will argue that he "pawned" his own honor for him only to find that Coriolanus "sold the blood and labour" of the Volscian army for women's tears. Again, the conspirators urge Coriolanus' death, and the lords arrive, angry with Coriolanus for making the treaty with Rome. Coriolanus enters, claiming he is a Volscian soldier, no longer "infected" with the love of Rome, and presents them with the peace treaty. Aufidius calls Coriolanus a "traitor" and reverts to calling him "Martius" rather than giving him a "stol'n name." They argue, and Aufidius provokes Coriolanus' pride and temper. The conspirators call for his death with the crowd who are swayed by the moment. Despite a lord calling for peace, the crowd are bloodthirsty and Coriolanus and Aufidius draw their swords. The conspirators draw also and kill Coriolanus. Aufidius, who has brought about his enemy's death without acting himself, stands on the body. The lords reprove him but Aufidius says he will answer to the senate. The lords order that Coriolanus be mourned as a "noble corpse" and Aufidius agrees, helping to bear the body away.

CORIOLANUS IN PERFORMANCE: THE RSC AND BEYOND

The best way to understand a Shakespeare play is to see it or ideally to participate in it. By examining a range of productions, we may gain a sense of the extraordinary variety of approaches and interpretations that are possible—a variety that gives Shakespeare his unique capacity to be reinvented and made "our contemporary" four centuries after his death.

We begin with a brief overview of the play's theatrical and cinematic life, offering historical perspectives on how it has been performed. We then analyze in more detail a series of productions staged over the last half century by the Royal Shakespeare Company. The sense of dialogue between productions that can only occur when a company is dedicated to the revival and investigation of the Shakespeare canon over a long period, together with the uniquely comprehensive archival resource of promptbooks, program notes, reviews, and interviews held on behalf of the RSC at the Shakespeare Birthplace Trust in Stratford-upon-Avon, allows an "RSC stage history" to become a crucible in which the chemistry of the play can be explored.

Finally, we go to the horse's mouth. Modern theater is dominated by the figure of the director, who must hold together the whole play, whereas the actor must concentrate on his or her part. The director's viewpoint is therefore especially valuable. Shakespeare's plasticity is wonderfully revealed when we hear directors of highly successful productions answering the same questions in very different ways.

FOUR CENTURIES OF *CORIOLANUS:* AN OVERVIEW

One must admit that it will never achieve popularity purely as a stage production. For a stage production must always make strong calls upon the emotionalism of the audience, whereas here the appeal is almost entirely to the intellect.[30]

These words of one reviewer epitomize long-held feelings toward *Coriolanus*, an infrequently revived play more respected than loved in performance. Yet theater-makers bold enough to tackle it have found *Coriolanus* a striking and powerful political tool, and the play has particularly thrived in adaptation and translation.

No performance is recorded until 1681 when Nahum Tate's *The Ingratitude of a Commonwealth* was performed at Drury Lane's Theatre Royal. Tate's adaptation was explicitly political:

> What offence to any good Subject in Stygmatizing on the Stage, those Troublers of the State, that out of private Interest or Mallice, Seduce the Multitude to Ingratitude, against Persons that are not only plac't in Rightful Power above them; but also the Heroes and Defenders of their Country . . . The moral therefore of these Scenes being to Recommend Submission and Adherence to Establisht Lawful Power.[31]

The new character of Nigridius, a former officer of Coriolanus who defects to Aufidius, increases the element of "ingratitude" in Coriolanus' murder. Aufidius is killed by Coriolanus and dies taunting him. Coriolanus watches his wife and son die, and in his bathetic dying lines he embraces his dead family and hopes for a peaceful afterlife. Tate's adaptation met with little success, his attempts to inject sentiment into a play normally considered intellectual falling flat.

John Dennis's *The Invader of his Country, or the Fatal Resentment* premiered at Drury Lane in 1719. Again, Aufidius dies first, but here pleads for forgiveness from Coriolanus, who is then beset by vengeful Volscian tribunes. Virgilia and Volumnia watch in horror as Coriolanus dies and Cominius delivers a very different moral from Tate's, warning that traitors inevitably get their deserts.

From 1749, *Coriolanus* held the stage in a version by James Thomson based on Livy rather than Shakespeare, reworking the story as neoclassical tragedy. This was hugely influential on subsequent performances of Shakespeare's play. A conflation of Shakespeare and Thomson was staged by Thomas Sheridan at Dublin's Smock Alley Theatre in 1752 and London in 1754. The advertisement explains:

> Shakespear's [sic] play was purely historical, and had little or no plot. Thomson's plot was regular, but too much of the epic kind, and wanted business. [The adaptor] thought, by blending these, a piece might be produced, which, tho' not perfect, might furnish great entertainment to, and keep up the attention of an audience.[32]

The centerpiece of this version was a spectacular Roman ovation featuring 118 supernumeraries. Aufidius was finally allowed to survive until the end to speak Coriolanus' epitaph. Volumnia is here the name of Coriolanus' wife while his mother is renamed Veturia—symptomatic, perhaps, of a critical tradition that thought of Volumnia and Virgilia as two types of "wife" to Coriolanus.

John Philip Kemble's *Coriolanus; or, the Roman Matron* at Drury Lane was the actor's crowning achievement. It drew heavily on Sheridan, incorporating lines from Thomson and the spectacular ovation. Kemble's team drew on advances in archaeology and art criticism to create a spectacular, historically authentic Roman world. The text acted as a vehicle for Kemble's austere Coriolanus and Sarah Siddons's Volumnia, who drew a dagger on herself in the melodramatic climax to the supplication scene. It was in this role that Kemble bade farewell to the stage in 1817, and his performance was mimicked for decades to come, notably by Charles Macready. It was Kemble's text, too, that formed the basis of the first professional American production in Philadelphia in 1796.

In 1820, Robert Elliston directed Edmund Kean in a production that attempted to break from Kemble's influence by opting to

> stage the play as a celebration of bourgeois individualism . . . Elliston and Kean begged sympathy for a Romantic noble savage, a creature of primordial integrity victimized by corruption at both ends of the social scale.[33]

Cutting all of Thomson, the production claimed to recapture Shakespeare's spirit, but still acted primarily as a study of the lead role, in which Kean was unfavorably compared with Kemble. The production nevertheless reasserted the case for Shakespeare's text, and Kean went some way toward humanizing the character. However, John Vandenhoff, Kean's successor at Drury Lane, was another Coriolanus in the Kemble mold, perpetuating the classically austere tradition through the provinces and American tours over the next thirty years.

Samuel Phelps took over at Drury Lane from 1848. His efforts to create realistic scenery extended to distinguishing between Roman and Volscian cultures, and while the spectacular elements once again dominated attention, "Phelps took pains not only to establish Martius as loving husband and dutiful son, but made him an affectionate and demonstrative father as well,"[34] succeeding in the domestic as well as the heroic.

A succession of productions following Kemble's text dominated the North American stage during the nineteenth century, including those of Thomas Abthorpe Cooper (1799) and Edwin Forrest from 1838 to 1864, who reinvented the play as heroic melodrama. The Italian actor Tommaso Salvini toured his acclaimed and fiery *Coriolanus* around the country in 1885–86, but the play remained even less popular in the United States than in Britain.

Coriolanus made its Stratford-upon-Avon debut in August 1893. Lawrence Alma-Tadema's historically accurate designs were universally praised, a grand ovation with spoils of war provided spectacle, and Frank Benson's redefining performance "displayed a good deal of noble thought and subtle spirit, and it grew in strength and form as it proceeded to its tragic ending."[35] Alice Chapin's Volumnia, an "Amazonian scold," was felt to be "wanting both in force and feeling," while Mrs. Benson's Virgilia was played for sympathetic pathos.

Benson continued in the role until 1919. Chapin was replaced by Genevieve Ward, "a remarkable actress of the old tradition,"[36] and the final performance of this production was presented as excerpts focusing on mother and son. The *Telegraph* commented, "It is easy to understand the attraction of 'Coriolanus' for Sir Frank Benson at this moment. Patriotism rings through it, and civic virtue."[37] Benson's production had long outlasted Henry Irving's competing Lyceum production, in which both he and Ellen Terry were badly miscast.

Coriolanus was next performed in Stratford in 1926 in a tempo-

1. Frank Benson as Coriolanus, 1893–1919, was full of "noble thought and subtle spirit."

rary theater only a month after the Shakespeare Memorial Theatre burned down. Ethel Carrington's "fierce and determined" Volumnia was praised, while George Skillan's Coriolanus "humanised the part from its aloofness, and gave it force."[38] Politically, it was "as fine a picture of a Tory as has ever been committed to paper," and while reviewers assumed that Shakespeare's sympathies were "obviously and strongly on the side of Coriolanus," the production suggested this was "not ambiguously so."[39] Producer W. Bridges-Adams utilized his large crowd to maximum effect:

> [He] realises that Coriolanus and the people—the "voices" as the hero scornfully calls them—are the true and only protagonists. He concentrates all his energy on vitalising the conflict between the individual and the crowd, and the result, all things considered, is a triumph.[40]

In 1931, William Poel confused critics with a radically adapted production at the Chelsea Palace Theatre. This production cut over half the play, reducing the role of the mob and Aufidius in favor of the relationship between Coriolanus and Volumnia. Coriolanus' death occurred offstage; rather than following his mother into Rome after the supplication scene, he turned and strode through the opposite gates of Corioli. This was followed "by a dissonant mixture of sounds: singing and dancing on one side of the platform stage, and the sounds of Coriolanus's death on the other."[41]

René-Louis Piachaud's adaptation caused riots in Paris in 1934, with the play evoking extreme reactions from a crowd sensitive to loaded political statements. *Coriolanus* flourished in Germany under the Third Reich, with Coriolanus mandated to be a powerful, self-willed leader betrayed by unthinking masses. Under these conditions, all Erich Engel could do in his 1937 production was "keep the memory of the play alive in a production that avoided equally the vilifying of the people and the undue heroicizing of Coriolanus,"[42] yet critics responded favorably to the impression of unvarnished truth. The play's Nazi associations caused it to fall out of favor in postwar Germany until Bertolt Brecht's intervention.

The relevance of Ben Iden Payne's Stratford 1939 production was strongly remarked:

> At this time it is especially apt for production, since it deals with the clash of States, the making and breaking of treaties and alliances, the bitter, indissoluble antipathies of the autocrat and the demagogue, the reactions of the common people to various methods of incitement and appeasement, and the unending struggle of private affection against public hate.[43]

Alec Clunes captured the "tyrannical splendour"[44] of Coriolanus, while Sicinius Velutus had transformed from stock villain to something more interesting, "a gaunt, forbidding figure with frightening fingers and a positively terrifying reserve of private and professional hatred against the despot." The large battle scenes, however, were "conducted with a complete failure to recognise the offside rule and a tendency on each side to wear the other's colours."[45] In 1952, the play returned to Stratford. In Glen Byam Shaw's production, "the frightening rabble is the real star."[46] Again, the conflict between man and mob was central: the "general's patriotism and his relapse into defiant dictatorship provide eternal arguments for and against democracy, all as fiercely topical as ever."[47]

Two productions in 1954 continued to explore the play's power. While Michael Benthall's Old Vic production was most noted for his casting of Richard Burton and Fay Compton, the play's final image of Coriolanus' butchered body was powerful, at the sight of which the conspirators, "seized with terror of their old conqueror, slink and run and flee into the darkness, tripping over each other in panic fear."[48] Meanwhile, at New York's Phoenix Theater, John Houseman innovatively avoided taking sides, allowing a "high-profile crowd and sympathetic tribunes [to be] counterbalanced by a Herculean Martius."[49]

The next Stratford production set the tone for all subsequent productions. Laurence Olivier had played the role at the Old Vic in 1938, imagining Coriolanus as a victim of "arrested development" with his "reliance on and subservience to his mother, his almost schoolboy hatred of Aufidius, and the special fury at the taunt of 'boy of tears.'"[50] Twenty-one years later at Stratford, Olivier's proud, majestic, and disdainful Coriolanus had a sardonic smile playing constantly around his lips and was memorably physical, including a "death leap" that saw him stabbed mid-leap and fall dangerously from a high platform.

2. Peter Hall production, 1959. Laurence Olivier as Coriolanus was "memorably physical, including a 'death leap' that saw him stabbed mid-leap and fall dangerously from a high platform."

Laurence Olivier turns Coriolanus into something new. He is a man interested only in war, unhappy when he is not fighting, and taking pleasure only in the sight of blood, even if it is his own . . . Bully and hero by turn, his voice rough and clipped . . . he and his director, Peter Hall, drag us inevitably to their conclusion—that although we need such men in war, this is an argument against war, not for such men.[51]

Brecht's work on the play, which began in 1951, took the play's political implications even further. Although he died before it reached production, Manfred Wekwerth and Joachim Tenschert staged a version of his text in 1964. Brecht depicted the masses

taking an active role in bringing about and defending the Roman Republic and thereby provides role models with which the East German "masses" could identify and from which they could learn . . . Through the collective action of the masses, Roman society develops to a point where it no longer needs military heroes, and Coriolanus falls because he cannot comprehend that military specialists have now become redundant and even dangerous for the state.[52]

Brecht's text had a long afterlife: a 1970 production by the Seville-based Tabanque company was "the first 'Shakespearean' drama to make any impact during the Franco years" in Andalusia.[53] The next major German production was produced by Hans Hollman at Munich's Residenztheater in 1970, and offered a "grim plea for pacifism,"[54] reflecting changing political concerns with a more even-handed approach that allowed for moral ambiguity in all figures. Wekwerth and Tenschert directed a further production of the play in London in 1971.

Michael Langham's 1961 production at Stratford, Ontario, was a box-office disaster despite Paul Scofield's performance in the title role, but was influential in using an unusually full text and Elizabethan-style acting space. Coriolanus was read through a Freudian lens; dominated by Eleanor Stuart's overbearing Volumnia, he found a surrogate parent figure in Aufidius. This latter relationship was gaining increasing prominence: Tyrone Guthrie's 1963 Nottingham production focused on the jealousy of Ian McKellen's Aufidius that directly occasioned his betrayal, emphasized by his stamping on the corpse's crotch and flinging himself over the body. McKellen returned to the play as Coriolanus for Peter Hall's 1984 National Theatre production. Again, the homoerotic relationship between Coriolanus and Greg Hicks's Aufidius was key, with moments such as their embrace of unification made prominent. As Aufidius welcomed Coriolanus to Antium:

> He gazes in exultation at Coriolanus' body, allowing the image to sink in and the dynamic to build before advancing with open arms . . . Aufidius delivers a large portion of his speech while still in Coriolanus's arms, suiting the action to the word as they now contend as hotly for love as ever they did in hate.[55]

Deborah Warner produced an intimate production for London's Almeida in 1986, and in 1993 was invited to direct the play for the Salzburg summer festival. Warner's conception of *Coriolanus* as "a play of overwhelming humanity and touching the heart,"[56] however, did not meet the expectations of German-speaking critics more familiar with Brecht's didactic, antimilitaristic version. British productions were increasingly displaying a general disillusion with war and the very concept of "heroes." The 1990–91 English Shakespeare Company production opened

> with a bang—several bangs—and the flare of searchlights. A Solidarity-style banner is unfurled, sirens wail, police loud-hailers order the crowd to disperse. Before long the riot-shields are out, and tear gas is billowing across the stage.[57]

The grim setting saw the slogan-chanting mob already wielding considerable power. Michael Pennington's Coriolanus "epitomizes the scarred, battle-hardened military machine, mouthing with contempt the popular slogan 'The people are the city.'"[58] Taking a similar political stance, Stephen Berkoff directed the play in Munich in 1991, then again in 1995–96 in the UK. Setting the production to military drums, the production parodied warfare and Berkoff played Coriolanus in the manner of "a cheerfully sinister nightclub bouncer who likes people to think that he had once been a big-time boxer."[59]

Jonathan Kent's epic 2000 production in the hangar-like space of London's Gainsboro Studios starred Ralph Fiennes as Coriolanus. Most praise was reserved for Barbara Jefford's Volumnia who "presents a truly definitive performance. In her fierce, sensual embrace, Coriolanus becomes a little boy again; her domination of him being not merely emotional, but all-consuming."[60] The scale of this production contrasted with Andrew Hilton's intimate 2001 version at Bristol's Tobacco Factory, in which "Gyuri Sarossy's young hero is like an impatient public-school prefect forced to seem friendly to oiks from the local comprehensive."[61] Evoking the French Revolution, Hilton's reading showed an aristocracy being challenged by "the first clamours for democracy."

Following the World Trade Center attacks, Georges Lauvadant's modern-dress staging of the play in 2001 at Spain's Teatre Nacional de Catalunya addressed contemporary paranoia surrounding "the threat to the 'metropolis' from an unspecified 'other,' "[62] and expressed a palpable disillusion with politics itself. Toneelgroep Amsterdam in 2009 had a similar agenda in choosing the play to open its six-hour *Roman Tragedies*. *Coriolanus* introduced a world of self-promotion and bureaucratic wrangling in which Fedja van Huet's Coriolanus, chafing in a suit, was forced to participate in a television debate with the tribunes. The war hero, out of his element in the political arena, eventually rose to the tribunes' insults in the only way he knew how, overturning the tables in an outburst of violence. Increasingly, in the twenty-first century, *Coriolanus* is providing bleak commentary on the hypocrisy and self-serving interests of the political classes.

The play has rarely been filmed. Elijah Moshinsky's television adaptation was one of the more abstract of the BBC Shakespeare series, setting much of the action in narrow streets and enclosed spaces. The homoerotic element between Coriolanus and Aufidius was given particular emphasis, with Coriolanus stripping down for their battle, and Moshinsky took full advantage of the television medium to present Coriolanus' death as a private moment in which

Coriolanus whispered "kill" to Aufidius, willing his own death. In 2011, Ralph Fiennes's movie finally brought the play up to date on the big screen. Set in Belgrade, this visceral version was set in the contemporary theater of war and made a strong case for the play's ongoing relevance in a world where, more than ever, our leaders are held up to intensive public scrutiny.

AT THE RSC

"What Is the City but the People?" (3.1.232)

John Barton's 1967 production in the Royal Shakespeare Theatre was the first at Stratford after Peter Hall's acclaimed production of 1959 with Laurence Olivier as Coriolanus, regarded by many as the "greatest Coriolanus of modern times."[63] Theater historian John Ripley describes designer John Bury's Rome as

> a primitive wooden compound where totems towered above the palisade. Against a permanent black backcloth, figures in black leather armor and black furs bore black shields in black-gloved hands . . . Sharp-edged metal was a pervasive presence: branched iron and copper standards, forests of spears, and gigantic, spiked, oblong shields announced a violent, even sadistic, society, dominated by a ruthless warrior class. The citizens, in straw hats and dark woollens, betrayed, by way of contrast, a visual vulnerability, if no less ferocity and cupidity than their betters.[64]

Critic Milton Shulman saw the production as politically "fence-sitting,"[65] agreeing with Ripley's view that Barton downplayed the politics by presenting corrupt, ineffective Tribunes and few, non-individualized, citizens who, in Ripley's view, "failed to discharge their function in his societal critique."[66] Peter Lewis, however, argued

> There is the smell of a very small-town Rome in the dirty-faced crowds, fussed over by their tribunes (excellently played by

3. Trevor Nunn production, 1972. "Spectacle was of the essence . . . Huge crowds . . . filled the heaving stage . . . the great bronze she-wolf was held aloft on poles . . . a ragged plebeian lay dead." Act 2 Scene 1, Coriolanus (Ian Hogg) returns in triumph and kneels to his mother, Volumnia (Margaret Tyzack).

Nicholas Selby and Clive Swift like a couple of shop stewards with a grudge against management).[67]

In 1972 *Coriolanus* was the first in Trevor Nunn's chronological cycle of Shakespeare's Roman plays. The RST stage had been extended, jutting into the auditorium beyond the proscenium arch.

It was a spectacular production whose urge to impress with special effects provoked Frank Marcus to rechristen Nunn "Cecil B. de Nunn."[68] The opening was particularly impressive:

Spectacle was of the essence . . . Huge crowds, both Roman and Volscian, filled the heaving stage. In an introductory tableau, the great bronze she-wolf was borne aloft on poles by bronze-masked automata while Romulus and Remus were held up to the vulpine teats. This image of a Rome implacably in pursuit of a national destiny, a commitment to which individual ambition must bow or be broken, set the tone for the cycle. In the wake of the procession, a ragged plebeian lay dead—a negligible sacrifice to nationalistic ambition.[69]

In contrast to 1967, Rome was represented as a brightly lit white box. Nunn (with Buzz Goodbody) paid more attention to the plebeians who were individualized and represented as skilled craftsmen at work. The cultural distinctions between Romans and Volsces was emphasized:

> Christopher Morley . . . has provided a beautiful white box: and some singularly efficient stage machinery spirits up moving steps and marble seats for the Senate. For the plebs the stage is hung with black skins, and reverberates with forges and carpenters' shops. The Volsci are beautiful, fighting Incas.[70]

Peter Thomson, however, thought there was "something altogether haywire about the Volsces" and that "the polarity for which the production strove is not present in the text." In contrast he saw the representation of conflict between patricians and plebeians as more successful:

> The Roman opposition of plebeians and patricians was both more effective and more consistent. The finest moments of political confrontation were attended always by the admirably-played tribunes. By letting their voices simply say the words, and by seeming always to be confiding in each other, Raymond Westwell and Gerald James found secret corners all over the stage. They were not content to create so much as to indicate revolutionary processes, like Marxist opportunists exploiting social confrontations without themselves resorting to terrorism: "Let's to the Capitol, / And carry with us ears and eyes for th'time, / But hearts for the event." (2.1.274–76)[71]

Terry Hands's 1977 production with Alan Howard in the title role was widely praised and admired. Many were impressed by its power, energy, and control. Jean Vaché saw it as an example of Artaud's theater of cruelty: "the whole performance is one long, obsessive death-march and no over-simple identifications are possible, either with the enemies of Coriolanus (portrayed as sly demagogues), or with Coriolanus, a none-too-pitiable misfit, more than half in love with himself and self-annihilation."[72] Hands explained how "In this production I am anxious to keep away from extremes . . . I don't think that *Coriolanus* is about politics."[73] Irving Wardle argues that Hands's 1977 production offered a complete contrast to Nunn's:

> There could be no greater contrast with the republican treatment of the play in the RSC's "Romans" season than this new version by Terry Hands. In place of an historically detailed setting, the action is taken out of time and reduced to theatrical essentials. Farrah's set consists simply of two huge doorways at the back wall and mid-stage positions, and instead of crowds, the competing forces are represented by small compact groups who make their statements in formalized riot and slow-motion battle, casting superhuman shadows, and then freeze or vanish into the darkness. The whole show is lit directionally so that individuals get heightened prominence at the expense of democratic spectacle.
>
> A non-political production of *Coriolanus* sounds a contradiction in terms, but Mr Hands has gone as far as it is possible to achieving one. It appears to be rooted in the current dread of collectivism . . . the performance escapes politics by concentrating on the conflict between those who bend to circumstances and the one character who cannot do such violence to his own nature. The two Tribunes (Tim Wylton and Oliver Ford-Davies) are not treated as buffoons; they simply act together, looking to each other for support and often speaking in unison. The same could be said of the patrician faction. All this has the effect of subduing individual character, but in the circumstances the sacrifice is worthwhile.[74]

Not all critics were persuaded by his nonpolitical approach, but Carol Chillington argued that Hands lets the play swing, as if on a heavy pendulum, between its questions and counter-questions, claims and counter-claims . . . The play itself is stark—not even a subplot spaces out the relentless narrative—and nothing in this production's design violates that rigorous austerity. The raked stage is black. Black wedges stripped in metal press in on the sides. Huge vertical blocks stand at the back, swinging open heavily as the gates of Corioli or Rome. Soldier, patrician and apronman alike wear black. The women's gowns are grey. The effect is at once rich— and starved. Virgilia's flowing red hair stuns, like an icon, and banished Coriolanus appals when he stalks the length of the stage, armored now completely in red, deaf to Menenius.[75]

A decade later Hands revisited the play in a less successful production with Charles Dance as Coriolanus. Dance lacked the compelling stage presence exhibited by Howard but perhaps the changing cultural context required a different focus. Opening in December 1989, a month after the fall of the Berlin Wall, military greatcoats seemed to glance toward events in Eastern Europe, but the production did not pick up on such resonances and only Peter Holland referred to them in his review:

Watching *Coriolanus* in December 1989 was a strange experience. Though Terry Hands's production (with unspecified help from John Barton) did nothing whatsoever to conjure up the analogy, exercising admirable restraint, the events in Eastern Europe inevitably became a point of comparison. As the citizens of Rome flexed their political muscles in search of food and freedom from oppression, images from the countries of the dissolving Warsaw Pact whirled through my mind. The patrician world is, of course, nothing like a Soviet-supported regime but the exhilaration of the discovery of the power of mass protest and of the possibility of exerting a previously unsuspected control over government was powerfully present.

It was, though, present *only* in my mind as a reaction to the text; little on stage supported such a weighty comparison. For the production neither managed to explore the social context

for the plebeian revolt nor established a coherent and significant relationship of antagonism between Coriolanus and the
people. But when Sicinius asked "What is the city but the people?" there was a sudden moment of arrest in the impetus of
the scene, a realization, shocked and excited, of the potential
revolutionary power of the crowd, that could have been fed
effectively into the rest of the production.[76]

The Tribunes, as Holland notes, were played by comic actors Joe
Melia and Geoffrey Freshwater and were made ridiculous at every
opportunity. Ripley suggests, however, that the production "demands
attention for its postmodern deference to feminist politics. Women,
who had almost invisibly swelled stage crowds for centuries, were
not only present, but militantly active."[77] He goes on, quoting again
from Holland's perceptive review, that it was the women plebeians in
Act 3 Scene 2

> who provided the switch of mood against Coriolanus with the
> Third Citizen's speech divided between a group of women. In
> 5.1 there was a strong emphasis on the men arming for the
> threat of war and, by the end of the scene, a powerful image of
> the women left behind, the city unmanned . . . Even more
> emphatically the voices of the Volscian people in 5.6 shouting
> against Coriolanus were all women, a female recognition of
> the costs of Coriolanus' actions by the people who are "wid-
> owed and unchilded" . . . The Volscian women urged their
> men to attack Coriolanus who was knifed by Aufidius and then
> mobbed and beaten to death by the crowd.[78]

David Thacker's 1994 production at the Swan Theatre with Toby
Stephens as Coriolanus was set and costumed as a historical period
combining French Revolution and Empire. The Swan setting, as Russell Jackson explained, served the play well:

> The debate scenes benefited from the intimacy of the thrust
> stage and galleried auditorium, while the space was sufficient
> to accommodate the battle in the first act or to emphasize the

isolation of Caius Martius as he stood in his gown of humility waiting for "voices." In this theatre the audience could be appealed to as though they were the Roman public, and the director capitalized on this by placing the plebeians around the auditorium, making us complicit in the decisions taken, as it were, on our behalf.[79]

The gallery was hung with bloody banners proclaiming the revolutionary slogan "Liberty, Equality, Fraternity" and an "exploded back wall"[80] at the back of the set which revealed a sketch of Delacroix's *Liberty Leading the People.* In some ways this was an incompletely satisfactory image since "Delacroix's image was a response to the failed revolution of 1830, not the 1790s." Its potency "lay not only in the symbolism of the revolution in arms" but in the symbolic power it accords a woman: "Delacroix's Liberty became, as it were, the iconic expression of the control over the political world that Volumnia would have wished to have."[81]

Jackson describes how Thacker managed to set up political parallels without attempting to elaborate them too minutely:

The Napoleonic figure of Caius Martius (Toby Stephens) was first glimpsed at the back of the stage, scowling as grain poured from above into a pit centerstage. The store was covered before the starving common people could get their hands on it. With this Thacker provided a neat motivation for the plebeians' discontent while offering a vivid image for the play's opening scene, but he wisely avoided further elaboration on the play's sketchy political economy.[82]

The representation of the plebeians was careful and considered:

Thacker made the citizens consistent in their opinions: it was the same "voices" who objected to Coriolanus's banishment that, when told in 4.6 of his march against Rome, said they were reluctant to make him go. The arguments with which the play opened were serious and seemed to come from genuine

4. David Thacker production, 1994. "The Napoleonic figure of Caius Martius (Toby Stephens) was first glimpsed at the back of the stage, scowling as grain poured from above into a pit centerstage" against a sketch of Delacroix's *Liberty Leading the People.*

hardship, and the disgruntled plebeians listened to Menenius with respect but no real sign of conviction. Caius Martius's arrival cut the debate short in any case. At the end of the first scene, the citizens showed no enthusiasm for the impending campaign against the Volsces but (following the Folio direction) chose instead to "steal away."[83]

David Farr's 2003 production, also in the Swan, took its inspiration from the traditions of samurai warriors and Japanese Noh theater. Russell Jackson saw it as offering "an articulate, sardonic view of heroism, which rose on occasion to great power" and described the striking opening scene:

The stage was lacquered a rich, smooth red, and colored banners hung from the gallery at the back of the platform. With the opening clash of percussion, three figures were revealed at the rear, seated on stools with their backs to the audience.

The citizens, roused by a vehement female worker wielding an ax, were stationed around the auditorium during the first exchanges and then moved onto the platform.[84]

Greg Hicks's Coriolanus was universally admired, but some critics had reservations about the Japanese themed setting:

> As the programme and the costumes emphasise, this Coriolanus is a samurai, and good samurai don't cry. The trouble is that, as a result, Rome has become a half-modern, half-antique Japan. On display are rather a lot of cheap kimonos, obis and such like as well as cigarettes, coffee cups, tennis rackets and, for the secretaries taking notes at Coriolanus's trial, 1920s typewriters. And the scene in which our exiled hero comes disguised as a beggar to Aufidius's house, has become a none-too-funny blend of commedia, kabuki and Bruce Lee.[85]

Russell Jackson, however, saw this as a deliberate process of undercutting of the "oriental" formality of the earlier part of the play:

> The first sign of this was one of the servants in the Capitol lighting his cigarette from the flame that had been placed centerstage. Modern props and costuming indicated the process. The typists in the scene in which Coriolanus is accused of treason marked a further falling-off from the antique codes of honor, as did the café table and coffee cups, the citizen's shorts and the tennis rackets in the "Rome at peace" sequence, and the worker's cloth cap adopted by Menenius in what seemed now to be the People's Socialist Republic of Rome. The tribunes wore natty new costumes that conveyed the sense of their now being successful bureaucrats. The representation of the Volsces was less successful: they seemed to inhabit a colder, windier territory, and the Volscian senators' costumes suggested a society less civilized than that of Rome.[86]

Coriolanus was by chance the final play to be presented at the Royal Shakespeare Theatre in 2007 before its closure for major refurbishment. Gregory Doran and designer Richard Hudson extended the stage with steps leading down into the auditorium, and they deployed this more flexible space to good effect:

> The play opens with a bang as peasants burst down the aisles onto a stage filled with lavish terracotta-coloured stone walls, which open like doors and have shutters which snap up and down. The scenery is offset by costumes in orange, red and grey . . . And actors continue to make their entrances and exits through the audience throughout, sweeping them into the action.[87]

The set was impressive, like blood or rust-streaked red and gray marble. The Romans and Volsces wore indistinguishable schematic Roman costumes: Romans in red, Volsces in gray. The plebeians were strongly played and carefully chosen to represent different constituencies: men, women, black and white. Two of the Roman soldiers joined the plebeian revolt against Coriolanus. The tribunes (Fred Ridgeway and Darren Tunstall) were played with an ambiguous combination of humor, knowingness, and sincerity but the focus of the production was on Coriolanus and his relationship with Aufidius, even more than his relationship with his mother.

Sons and Others

Historical productions of the play, notably John Philip Kemble's eighteenth-century productions with himself in the title role and his sister, Sarah Siddons, as Volumnia, romanticized Coriolanus as a noble hero. Twentieth-century sensibilities proved more skeptical, holding the role and character up to greater scrutiny, especially in light of post-Freudian theories. John Ripley argues that Barton's (1967), Trevor Nunn's (1972), and Terry Hands's (1977) productions all deliberately eschewed the play's politics, focusing on the central role not in order to romanticize it, but as part of contemporary society's drive to demythologize "its collective persona," thus making the "anti-hero . . . the new protagonist."[88] Part of this process involved "a narcissistic quest for individual liberation and relationship as an antidote to the spiritual desolation of modern life."

Within this move, "Martius was a prime candidate for exploitation."[89]

Ripley goes on to argue that

> All three ignore the play's political resonance in favor of a revisionist critique of Roman history and the exploitation of the phenomenon of alienation. All place Martius at the center of the action, but unlike romantic interpretations, invite not identification but estrangement: audiences at Barton's and Nunn's productions were repelled by an antihero; at Hands's, awed by an alien superhero.[90]

Barton's 1967 revival revealed a stylistic rather than ideological debt to Brecht:

> The repellent features of the play, and of Martius in particular, long glossed over in British and American productions ... were now ruthlessly exploited by Barton as a revisionist gesture. From a Rome just emerging from prehistory, Barton culled the bleak aperçu that humankind's triumph over nature freed it only for the pursuit of power.[91]

Barton's own program notes, however, tell a different story:

> If we see the other protagonists clearly the way is open to seeing how far Coriolanus himself is their victim and wherein he is nobler, and at bottom, more human. It's often said the play is dry and inflexible because he does not change or mature. Surely he is the one character who basically *does* change? The others are gradually revealed for what they are. He, though he resists change or self-knowledge (and his temperament is unalterable), is forced by circumstance and his own nature to know himself, and to begin to grow. In that sense he is like Lear. Surely the centre of the play is to be found in Coriolanus's lines:
> > "I melt, and am not
> > Of stronger earth than others."

> His fate is ultimately tragic: victim of the waste, self-deception and muddle of politics, and the domination of his mother.[92]

Repellent as he may appear, Barton suggests, we should see Coriolanus as victim of a brutal and brutalizing social order, finally acknowledging his humanity but at the inevitable cost of his life. The mother's role in reproduction both physiological and ideological is crucial. Mothers such as Volumnia must sacrifice their humanity in order to sacrifice their sons. The degree to which they come to understand this will affect interpretations of the role and development of character. Postwar productions have not shied away from the play's violence, often indeed sensationalizing it; they have swung between poles of representation of the Volsces, traditionally seen as Rome's less civilized neighbor. They are just as often seen as Rome's mirror image rather than its savage "Other." Productions have played with their appearance and the homoerotic potential of the relationship between Coriolanus and Aufidius.

Ian Richardson (Coriolanus) and Edward Cicciarelli (Aufidius) looked like blond-haired, blue-eyed, deeply tanned twins in Barton's production. Critic Alan Brien saw Richardson's Coriolanus as

> a glacial prefect, dedicated to an impossible code of honour, dominated by his mother, unconsciously suppressing a strong crush on a rival schoolfellow, fated to break down when the antagonism between his unacknowledged passions and his boasted ideals becomes too strong to support.
>
> Ian Richardson made up as the blond twin of Aufidius, gives a remarkable impersonation of a man who seems positively varnished under a veneer of upper-class correctness which applies only to social equals and does not forbid the kicking, insulting, even killing on the spot, of inferiors who do not understand or respect his standards. He speaks that peculiar Coriolanian verse, arid, grinding, abrasive language with sudden fluid of oiled movement, with immense intelligence in a careful, metallic voice which never sacrifices sense to sound.[93]

5. Ian Richardson (Coriolanus) and Edward Cicciarelli (Aufidius) looked like blond-haired, blue-eyed, deeply tanned twins in John Barton's 1967 RSC production.

One critic thought his "most impressive moment"

> when he cracks, like an obstinate Brazil nut, in the jaws of his
> mother . . . All the pride and valour and contempt are shaken
> out of him in appalling sobs. The she-dragon mother herself
> is played by Catherine Lacey like an ancient mistress of fox-
> hounds, glorying in her son's wounds, like a huntress blooding
> her young.[94]

Irving Wardle regarded it as "an interpretation that earns sympathy
for the least likeable of all Shakespeare's tragic heroes."[95]

John Barber was one of a number of critics unimpressed by Ian
Hogg's performance in Trevor Nunn's production:

> It is a criticism of Ian Hogg's small, wiry Coriolanus that it does
> not dominate the restless effects. Callous, impatient, ineffably
> proud, his high, flat voice expresses all the man's quirkiness.
> But not for a second, any of his greatness. Once when he was
> referred to as noble, the audience, understandably, laughed.
>
> Without question, the performance of the night was the
> Volumnia of Margaret Tyzack, notably in the great scene at
> the end when she pleads for her son to spare Rome from his
> anger. "I was moved withal," said Aufidius afterwards. Indeed,
> so was I.[96]

John Mortimer, however, was won over:

> When Mr Ian Hogg first appeared I thought he lacked magne-
> tism, and his voice the operatic qualities for the role. But later I
> became convinced by this mother's boy-wonder, to whom wars
> and politics are fun and excitement until he is dragged into fury
> and disaster by the treacherous undertow of his own personal-
> ity. His final surrender to Volumnia's persuasions became par-
> ticularly moving when you realised that part of the self he
> claimed was finally the need to do what his mother asked.[97]

Peter Thomson also saw him as a different sort of Coriolanus, a "temperamental sporting star, a George Best sulkily crossing Manchester

to help the welcoming City defeat a shaken United."[98] When the production transferred to the Aldwych, Hogg was replaced by Nicol Williamson whose charismatic presence produced a more evenly balanced production.

Alan Howard gave a widely acclaimed performance in 1977. This is Irving Wardle's assessment:

> We are used to seeing actors searching out Coriolanus's weak spots. One point about Mr Howard's hero is that he is a strong man full stop. There is nothing reductive in the portrait. That obviously goes for the battle scenes which he dispatches with

6. Terry Hands production, 1977. "The production concluded ominously with the young Martius, now dressed like a young warrior, holding Volumnia's hand, the promise of the future," with Maxine Audley (Volumnia) and Fleur Chandler (Virgilia).

that trumpet voice which is the most thrilling sound at present to be heard on the English stage.

It applies even more to his behaviour in Rome. Whereas everyone else is enacting a social role, Mr Howard strictly observes his character's claim: "I am the man I play" . . . He is incapable of doing otherwise. Trying briefly to follow his mother's instructions and adopt a mask of humility, he turns into an infant barely able to walk. Finally he is not a mother's boy. There is no great emotional crack-up to Volumnia's supplications . . . He simply chooses to spare Rome and is never more thoroughly in command of the situation than when he embraces his family under the baleful eye of Julian Glover's Aufidius. He knows it means death, and it is he who cheerfully impales himself on Aufidius's sword at the end.

With its hand-holding duels and arrays of studded black leather, this is an uninhibitedly romantic treatment of the play; it is also the most exciting I have ever seen.[99]

Carol Chillington also found the production and Howard's performance impressive but unsympathetic:

There is no repository of sympathy in this production. Martius is bound to his mother not by heartstrings, but by the rod of steel that runs up both their backbones . . . No one is honest about his motives or actions in this play, so we don't know who to trust. And the production doesn't tell us. Instead, brilliantly, it brings to our attention all the acting imagery embedded in the play and shows it to us as a metaphoric extension of the characters' wanton self-deception. No one is honest except Coriolanus. Only he disdains compromise and makes us think pride a malicious word for integrity. In this consists his magnificence *and* his tragedy, his utter isolation.[100]

The production concluded ominously with the young Martius, now dressed like a young warrior, holding Volumnia's hand, the promise of the future.

Charles Dance played Coriolanus in Hands's 1989 production. His performance was generally felt to lack conviction:

> Again and again Hands used stagey devices to increase the menace and authority of Dance's performance . . . But such devices only served to emphasize all the more strongly that Dance needed such support to cover his own deficiencies of technique and imagination. At his best as the child of Barbara Jefford's superbly overpowering mother, a performance from her of tigerish authority and control, Dance found it easy to underline the potential comedy of, say, the struggle between them in 3.2; "Look, I am going" [156] sounded like nothing so much as "look I really am off to tidy my room," instantly made serious by the force of Volumnia's implied threat of giving up on him in "Do your will" [160].[101]

After his capitulation to Volumnia, Aufidius insults Coriolanus in terms designed to wound his pride and dignity: "thou boy of tears" (5.6.115). Coriolanus is stung, repeating "Boy" three times in his attempted rebuttal of Aufidius' charge. To most directors this, together with his successful military career, has suggested a Coriolanus of relatively mature years, a seasoned warrior around forty. David Thacker, however, decided to take it literally and cast the twenty-eight-year-old Toby Stephens in the role. In a production centrally concerned with class, Stephens played the part with an unforgettable sneer on his face and curl of his upper-class lip. Russell Jackson summed his performance up as "superbrat":

> Toby Stephens was a strident, energetically disdainful, and very young Coriolanus, exuding the naïve self-assurance of a school captain who excels effortlessly on the playing field and looks forward to a life of hero worship. He was also remarkably good-looking. With a Martius this young, the impressive military record became miraculous, and we lost the possibility of a Coriolanus whose long career of both taints and honors was now coming spectacularly to a head. What we got instead was a superbrat, but this had its own advantages. The hero's

callowness counted as a sort of political innocence, nearly enough to excuse his brashness. This was a Coriolanus whom one could not easily dismiss as a functionary of a militaristic state or a crazed fighter driven by his own testosterone. With the admiring smooth-tongued Menenius around to excuse each new feat of haughtiness, he might have gotten away with a great deal. He was a credible political threat.[102]

Having played Aufidius with distinction in Peter Hall's (1984) National Theatre production, Greg Hicks proved a compelling Coriolanus in 2002:

This is a tremendous performance. Hicks combines the heroic simple-mindedness and intemperate rage of a proud, illiterate zombie with the turbulent feelings of an emotionally underdeveloped boy-man and the awesome physical control and intelligence of a great actor.

He speaks the play's craggy, sinewy language with a clarity, an emotional commitment and an intellectual vigour that I have never seen equalled.[103]

Benedict Nightingale had misgivings about the sheer quantity of gore used, "He appears to have swum three lengths in the stuff,"[104] while Paul Taylor thought Alison Fiske "a more sensitive than normal Volumnia" who "seems to understand the terrible cost of the climb-down she has exacted," concluding:

the production has bags of energy and bite and ends with a deeply moving depiction of the hero's obdurate integrity. In the climactic sword fight with Aufidius, he's felled by a cheating bullet from behind. Twice he drags himself to his feet to continue the contest and twice more he's shot. This haunting sequence symbolising the superannuation of the hero's values leaves you feeling that the world will not be an unequivocally better place without him.[105]

William Houston's boyish looks in Doran's 2007 production belied his thirty-eight years. Robert Hanks argues that "crowd scenes and cameos are invested with a sense of irony, as if the characters, including the plebeians, are perfectly aware that in the drama of politics they too have their parts to play," and he goes on to argue:

> Something of the same spirit infects Houston's Coriolanus. In one sense, the point of the play is that Coriolanus takes himself too seriously: obsessed with making war and his own image of himself, he won't stoop to the petty business of making politics—though all he has to do is tell the truth about his glorious deeds . . . Houston hardly looks the conventional warrior—with his wide, thin-lipped mouth, bulging eyes and sinewy physique, he conjures up Zippy from *Rainbow* as drawn by William Blake. But as the play goes on, his aggression and penchant for bloodshed are persuasive, to a degree that leaves you sympathising with the people of Rome—sure, he wins battles, but would you want this psycho in charge? He never quite throws off an air of amusement; he knows how excessive he is, and finds the spectacle entertaining.[106]

Michael Billington felt that the focus on the central role undercut the play's politics, but, despite that,

> the production notches up several good points. There is no escaping the way Trevor White's Aufidius and Houston's hero are engaged in a permanent homoerotic combat. [Janet] Suzman quietly humanises Volumnia, and Timothy West plays Menenius as a singularly testy patrician.[107]

Referring to the imminent closure of Elizabeth Scott's 1932 New Shakespeare Memorial Theatre, Billington adds, "This closes a chapter of Stratford history with dignity and style."

THE DIRECTOR'S CUT: INTERVIEWS WITH GREGORY DORAN AND DAVID FARR

Gregory Doran, born in 1958, studied at Bristol University and the Bristol Old Vic Theatre School. He began his career as an actor, before becoming associate director at the Nottingham Playhouse. He played some minor roles in the RSC ensemble before directing for the company, first as a freelance, then as associate and subsequently chief associate director. His productions, several of which have starred his partner Antony Sher, are characterized by extreme intelligence and lucidity. He has made a particular mark with several of Shakespeare's lesser-known plays and the revival of works by his Elizabethan and Jacobean contemporaries. His 2007 *Coriolanus* for the RSC featured William Houston as Coriolanus, Trevor White as Aufidius, Timothy West as Menenius, and Janet Suzman as Volumnia.

David Farr is a writer and director, and has had an extraordinarily prolific career for such a young talent. He was artistic director of the Gate Theatre, London, from 1995 to 1998, moving on to the position of joint artistic director of Bristol Old Vic from 2002 to 2005. He became artistic director of the Lyric Theatre Hammersmith in 2005, where his productions included *Water*, *The Resistible Rise of Arturo Ui*, *The Birthday Party*, *The Magic Carpet*, *Ramayana*, *The Odyssey*, and a new version of Kafka's *Metamorphosis*. As a playwright, his work includes *The Nativity*, *Elton John's Glasses*, and *Crime and Punishment in Dalston*. David joined the RSC as an associate director in 2009, since which time he has directed Greg Hicks as Leontes in *The Winter's Tale* (2009) and as the title role in *King Lear* (2010), though his first work with the company came in between his tenures at the Gate and the Old Vic, writing *Night of the Soul* for the company, which was produced at the Pit Theatre in 2001. He returned to direct an award-winning production of *Coriolanus* (also starring Greg Hicks) in 2002 which he discusses here.

Did you and your designer opt for a very Roman setting and look?

Farr: No, but I was looking for a world that had a strong social and political hierarchy. I wasn't interested in updating the play to a time where the modernity of the world somehow forced the lead character into becoming unacceptable, because for me the fascination of the play was the fact that I was morally very attracted to him and at the same time repelled by him. I was deeply attracted to his moral rigor and his refusal to bow to what he sees as easy populist choices. In order not to make that seem horrific or fascist—as he is so often portrayed—you have to find a world in which what he is standing for has depth, history, and meaning. I made quite a bold choice to set it in Samurai Japan. It then became very specific, setting it in nine-teenth-century Japan, toward the end of the Samurai era, which socially is the equivalent of the end of the feudal era in Europe, although the detail of that specific setting was nothing that the audi-ence necessarily needed to know. The visual language in the play therefore showed a development from a totally purist Samurai lan-guage to something with increasing creeping modernity, symbolized by different weaponry and, most crucially, by two typewriters that I think became the visual centerpieces showing that development.

Doran: Rome is a metaphor. Shakespeare chooses a subject with a Roman setting, but clearly engages profoundly with the political issues of his own time. The play works in a startlingly contemporary way because we can still reapply that metaphor to our own times if we choose to do so. However, setting the play in a different time period, or updating it to a specific historical period and trying to appropriate a particular political system, can run the risk of inviting unhelpful comparisons; the parallels you hope to draw can confuse more than they illuminate. On the other hand, if you invent a period or put it in its own historical setting, you may run the danger of exoticizing the play and concealing the intensely political and satiri-cal portrait of a society that Shakespeare has created.

My designer Richard Hudson and I decided to use the basic metaphor of Ancient Rome, filtered to some extent through the Jacobean period (so togas were worn over doublets). We didn't want Hollywood Rome; this is not the Augustan city after all, but a more primitive, volatile, warmongering state. So we created a series of receding walls punctuated with doors. The walls were metallic, stri-ated with a sort of rusty red, echoing the bloody conflicts which Rome had undergone, scarred like Coriolanus' own body with the glorious wounds of battle. These walls also created a sense of the bustling streets, which could be populated and filled, but which could also close down the space.

And was there a significant design difference between the scenes in Rome and the world elsewhere?

Farr: No, not at all. There was a bare red stage, a blood-red stage of wood. There were almost no scene changes of any significance whatsoever. It was largely sculpted by light, as I think is often best, particularly in the Swan, with simple use of furniture and development of the language of the world. There was some small use of vertical banners to create that sense of ritual, particularly in the procession when he returns home in triumph, moving into that more modern language of typewriters—what we called governmental furniture—where suddenly Coriolanus is becoming accountable to the people. It helped to show the journey on which Sicinius and Junius Brutus lead the people, discovering that a new accountability is possible and that an aristocratic system is not necessarily inevitable.

Doran: For Corioli we had a similar metallic look but two huge iron doors to represent the gates of Corioli, and we used them again for Antium in the second half. For Act 5, for the plain before the walls of Rome where the Volsci set up their encampment, we flew everything out and had the vast empty stage of the old RST (seen for the last time in its history in this production). It somehow echoed the barrenness of the relationships between Rome and the Volscians.

Did your production find itself taking sides in the disputes between patricians and plebeians, Coriolanus and the crowd?

Farr: I suppose my production was noted for being much more supportive, or at least sympathetic, toward him. I was determined to make him fully rounded, intelligent, and in a strange way a heroic character. He is heroic to me because, like a lot of Shakespeare's tragic heroes, he stands in defiance against certain easy moral choices. His flaw is that he stands with such pride and obstinacy that it destroys him. I don't feel that I sided with him but I feel that I saw the play through his eyes. I see it as the tragedy of a man who passionately believes in a system which has existed for years and years. I think Shakespeare would be far more sympathetic toward that than people may realize. Shakespeare has his deep conservative impulse as well as an extraordinary social liberal impulse and he doesn't know where he stands. He plays between these two impulses. I think that may come from his being from a family with a strong Catholic past, which is now buried and hidden, and he is moving into a much more modern Protestant world, which is in some sense more democratic. But he has these great longings back to that old world. It is pretty clear to me that Shakespeare doesn't love Junius Brutus or Sicinius. He didn't write them lovably; he writes them absolutely accurately and the points they make are entirely apposite and correct, but they're not lovable. Coriolanus is lovable in some slightly hard to define way: perhaps it's his honesty.

Doran: *Coriolanus* can be viewed from almost every political point of view. You can take a right-wing angle and side wholeheartedly with the patricians, a left-wing agenda and promote the play from the plebeians' angle—"What is the city but the people"—or indeed from a sort of nihilistic perspective, and view both sides as absurd in their own ways. I think Shakespeare doesn't come down on any one side. I think there is frequently a satirical tone, but the play is too complex, too multifaceted to be reduced to a single political perspective. Shakespeare sees both sides, empathizes with both, and yet is critical of both. *Coriolanus* seems to me to be closely akin to *Troilus and Cressida* in that respect, also in its dark humor and its cynical attitude to male posturing.

So I think it's crucial in production not to take sides. Your political affiliations or prejudices are likely to emerge anyway. But it is too easy to send up the plebs as a stupid, fickle mob. They have genuine grievances and are starving to death. At the same time it is very easy to be taken in by the warm affability of the apparently eminently trustworthy Menenius, whereas actually he is a wily, manipulative, reactionary old bastard. I think part of the success of Will Houston's performance [as Coriolanus] was his ability to marry the ruthless warrior on the battlefield with the volatile child in the drawing room.

So it is vital to see every character from their own point of view and not automatically believe the enemy propaganda about them. We found that job hardest with the tribunes. Was there ever a more self-serving, cowardly, vicious, pusillanimous pair in all literature? They are right to defend the people from the man who would "vent their musty superfluity" in battle; on the other hand, when they have secured Coriolanus' banishment from Rome they realize that they have effectively dismantled their nuclear deterrent only to have that same weapon, doubled in power, pointed right at their walls. The play is a rollercoaster ride in performance, a real thriller, if you engage passionately with the rhetoric, and invest each side with real conviction.

What was your take on Menenius and his fable of the body?

Farr: Menenius is trying to express, in as affable a way as possible, the point that the plebeians who feel hard done by and neglected are actually fundamentally connected to the aristocracy and in need of them. I suppose it is a conservative justification of what I have been describing. Menenius puts a delicate and kindly spin on what is actually a very tough worldview.

Doran: The fable of the body is a total fraud. If the senators are the belly of Rome, then their job is to distribute the nourishment through the arteries of the body to the outer extremities—the plebeians—and they are palpably not doing that. By hoarding corn they are depriving the plebeians of food and therefore threatening their survival. Unfortunately Menenius doesn't seem to be aware that the story actually works against him. Nor does the crowd happen to notice that this elegant fable cannot be comfortably applied.

And on the role of the Tribunes?

Farr: We played them as two highly skilled politicians who genuinely believe in the need for an increasingly transparent and accountable society and who are at a crucial moment in their society's history. They know that the old order and the old world is breaking down, they know that the introduction of technology is increasing accountability and increasing the democratic process. Therefore personally there are lots of opportunities for power which would not have been available to them before because they weren't from the aristocratic caste. So this mixture of genuine political idealism and personal ambition is what drives them. That's modern politics, isn't it? Most politicians have some element of political belief and an awful lot of personal ambition which gets confused so that trust in them starts to dribble away. That's very clearly what happens at the end of the play; they don't develop morally in the play in the way that Coriolanus does. We didn't parody or satirize them. I think some of Junius Brutus' speeches are very powerful and the actor, Simon Coates, was a highly skilled orator, very convincing in what he said. But at some level we knew instinctively from the language that this was a man who was driven primarily by ambition. In Junius Brutus and Sicinius you do recognize modern politicians. We all hear that language and associate it with the language of spin, or the way in which PR manipulates how information is communicated to the public, all the stuff that modern politics is all about. Coriolanus cares not one jot for that; he is only interested in his personal morality, and that belongs to a different era which we associate with despotism and tyranny. He associates it with an old aristocracy, a landed aristocracy that has a God-given right to rule. Of course that is repellent to us now, but at the time that was not considered repellent.

Did you find one of the keys to the character of Coriolanus in his anger at being called a "boy"?

Farr: Greg Hicks and I became interested in his drive to self-definition as man and warrior. His two fears and fascinations were the threatened feminization and infantilization of him, which you see his mother do several times. It's completely possible to treat Coriolanus in a Freudian way. He is a man of fearless self-definition, trying to escape the haunting specters of woman and child. His relationship with his wife is far less sexual than his relationship with his mother. His relationship with Tullus Aufidius is an extraordinarily sexual relationship in some subliminal way. You can choose to overtly push that, it's in the language, particularly in Aufidius' language when they meet again. Interestingly, when things go wrong for Coriolanus is when he listens to his mother, who at two different moments appeals to him. In both cases she is the only person he listens to. It is a remarkable, strange, sexual relationship between them. It's worth mentioning here the Roman notion of virtue, which is so different to the Christian notion of virtue. Roman virtue literally means manliness; what it is to be a man. It is about bravery and honesty but it is not about compassion: that was what Christianity brought to the notion of virtue. Coriolanus in his terms loses his virtue in listening to his mother. In a literal sense he loses his manliness. The sexual confusion of that is absolutely fascinating but it only really works if you place it in a world and in a culture where that maleness and that virtue is something that is really esteemed and upheld as a paragon of what it is to be a man.

Doran: When Aufidius attacks Coriolanus and calls him a "boy of tears" the effect is devastating, not only because it is insulting but because underneath it there is a truth. Coriolanus in the end is a mummy's boy, is childlike, and naive in his belief that he can march over to the other side in a fit of pique and for no genuine principle, out of hurt pride, prosecute war on his own people. Aufidius' charge is wounding too because it comes from the man he loves, and it prompts from Caius Martius a vainglorious boast that "like an eagle in a dovecote" he "Fluttered your Volscians in Corioles."

Coriolanus may be capricious, volatile, and naive, but Aufidius is an even less stable character: witness the violence of his mood swings. Trevor White seized upon these with some relish. Aufidius doesn't realize that in his unequivocal welcome of his archenemy he has, as one of his servants says, cut himself in the middle and "is but one half of what he was yesterday." In the very next scene that we see Aufidius he is already disdainfully calling Coriolanus "the Roman" and regretting his precipitous action, jealous of the man's charismatic effect on his own soldiery. "And you are darkened in this action, sir," warns the lieutenant, "Even by your own."

The two men cannot truly be friends, as their characters demand that they are the sole champion, the leader, the best, the cup holder, and there can only be one of those. Rome ain't big enough for the both of them: "the fall of either / Makes the survivor heir of all." By Act 5 Coriolanus is already pushing his new ally around: "My partner in this action, / You must report to th'Volscian lords, how plainly / I have borne this business." Aufidius complains that though he took his enemy into his house and made him his equal, "joint-servant with me," "till at the last / I seemed his follower, not partner." It is hard not to detect under his bitterness a profound sense of slighted affection. His determination that Coriolanus shall die "And I'll renew me in his fall" is jealously neurotic, but with its overtones of ritual sacrifice is also disturbingly revealing.

Which brings us to the question of his relationship with his mother: what did you discover about that?

Farr: That she was as much a warrior as him—if anything, possibly more so. She has to be fearsome, she has to be a woman who amazes. Rome was full of these women who were as politically powerful as the men and it's interesting what happened to that tradition, because we don't seem to have that in the same way. She's as fearsome a warrior as him, she is at times more male than him, and yet crucially the two moments where she intervenes are moments of traditional female supplication: moments where she pleads for him to be gentle, the opposite of what she has brought him up to be, and those moments destroy him. The first time they cause his banishment, the second time they cause his death. That seems to me to be very clearly and archetypally painted by Shakespeare. We know instinctively as an audience watching that his Achilles heel is her, the one person who can persuade him to act against his nature, because she is the person who has created his nature. I think we all instinctively understand and believe that psychologically: that the mother of this kind of man is the one person who can reach him and press buttons in him and make him operate and behave in ways that he would not do for anyone else. It's a brilliant piece of psychological insight on Shakespeare's part and probably the most powerful mother-son relationship in all his work. It's certainly the strangest. Out of nowhere he produces it and writes it and it's as modern and as powerful as anything. It's remarkable.

7. "Possibly the most potent pause in Shakespeare": Janet Suzman's Volumnia waits on Coriolanus (William Houston) to answer her appeal for mercy in Greg Doran's 2007 production at the Royal Shakespeare Theatre, Stratford-upon-Avon.

Doran: Volumnia has bred a monster. He refers to himself as a "dragon," and indeed so does Menenius. Her tragedy is that by finally getting him to give up his attack on Rome, she kills him. Her triumphal reentry into Rome, as its great patroness—"life of Rome!"— is silent. But Janet Suzman and I chose to make her silence eloquent (like the silence of her son in the previous scene, when he takes her by the hand—possibly the most potent pause in Shakespeare). Her entry is heralded by the senator bidding Rome "Unshout the noise that banished Martius." We decided that a speech is expected from her, that she would silence the crowd in order to address them. After all Volumnia is never short of a word or two. She has just delivered a fifty-line appeal to her son, surely one of the longest speeches in Shakespeare. But when it comes to it, she cannot say anything. Even she cannot spin this personal disaster into a civic triumph. She has just killed her son and she knows it. Janet held the moment, trying to articulate some potent propaganda which will glorify her son. It was electrifying. Finally she turned and walked away.

How did you stage the crucial encounter in which Volumnia succeeds in stopping and silencing her son?

Farr: Normally when you direct a scene you read through it three or four times and then rehearse it two or three times in detail before running the whole play. I had an instinct with that long scene between them, with Virgilia also in attendance, that we needed to do it in a very different way. Greg Hicks, Alison Fiske, and Hannah Young were the three actors in this case. It so happened that we had a long rehearsal process and that all of them were available quite a lot, because they didn't have massive roles in the other play that we were paired with. I think we must have rehearsed that scene twelve to fourteen times and we just played different things with it every time. We got it into our skin. It was an instinctive feeling I had, that this was a scene of such psychological complexity that you couldn't just "do" it, you had to "be" with it, for hours. We could have done it for a lot longer; there was an enormous amount there. The only scene that is comparable in my experience of the Shakespeare I've done is the scene between Lear and Gloucester on the heath, when you feel that you could spend six months just with this scene. The quality of "lived-in-ness" in that scene was vital to find. In our play I think we played him at the age of about forty. You obviously can't in the rehearsal process discuss all their shared forty-year history—it would take you forty years. You can only really discuss elements, so the way in which we created that lived-in, real sense of shared history, shared possession of each other's souls, was through endless rehearsal repetition and just physically finding it within the actors' bodies and minds. There was no other way to reach the level where this scene takes place. It's very obvious when you read the play that no one else, even Virgilia, can understand what is really happening between these two people, but we can feel it and we can intuit it when we watch it.

And how did you view the relationships between Coriolanus and his wife and son?

Farr: The Japanese setting gave us strict social and political rules which were very helpful in the approach to the containment of the women and defining the way in which Virgilia dresses and the whole way in which she should be seen or not be seen in relationship to her husband. The boy is so much like I imagined the "boy" of Caius Martius to be. It's just a lovely detail that is added in, but the issue for me was to be able to play Virgilia as a woman who had to obey social and political structures, and then to play Volumnia as a woman who utterly flouts those structures, has probably obeyed them in the past but has achieved such a level of authority and power that she now has total freedom.

There's also the character of Valeria. It feels to me that Shakespeare was saying that this is the archetypal woman in this society, who is only interested in gossip and who very much holds the female line. It worked beautifully in our setting; she comes in delicately dressed and chats—that is what a woman does in this society. Volumnia has broken that paradigm but controls and oppresses poor Virgilia, who is unable to escape from this incredibly potent woman. She totally overshadows her. So when Martius comes home it is his mother he listens to rather than his wife. There is just no other room. I do think that sort of society is far more understandable when a mother and a daughter-in-law live in the same house. Immediately what that does for an audience is to throw them into another world and invite them to invest in the rules and codes of that world, rather than them imposing their own values and judgments. It's very easy to judge it from our value system where it would seem horrific. It requires a clear and compelling visual language that we can enter into and leave our own moral codes behind. This allows the play to become fresh in a way that I found very exciting.

Doran: If your husband, meeting his fellow general in the field, says he is as happy to see him as he was to see his bride on her wedding night, then I don't think there is a lot going for that relationship! There was a wonderful moment in Terry Hands' production when the little boy was brought in to meet his father dressed exactly as Coriolanus had been in Triumph. He was this new little soldier for Volumnia to play with. We didn't necessarily see that; I think the boy was as likely to despise as to emulate his father.

8. "He is a lion / That I am proud to hunt": Coriolanus (Greg Hicks) and Aufidius (Chuk Iwuji) locked in combat in David Farr's 2002 production for the RSC.

Some commentators, and productions, have detected a homo-erotic element in the bond between Coriolanus and his mighty opponent Aufidius—that dream of wrestling on the battlefield . . . did you explore this dimension?

Farr: We explored it. We didn't choose to render it overt but it's in the language: the dream that Aufidius has of them fighting is a highly sexualized dream. I don't feel that in Shakespeare's time there would have been such embarrassment or shame about that. That's also true for Roman times of course, where homosexuality was treated in a completely different way. I think Shakespeare was exploring and enjoying that eroticization of the warrior. Again I go back to not wanting to modernize the play, not wanting to set it somewhere where these things become different to how they were. I think that is probably why this play is not quite as well known as *Macbeth* or *Lear*; the lead character is just as fascinating but it only really makes sense if you embrace that whole world. It has to have some journey from a world that is antiquarian and archaic to a world that we recognize.

Doran: It would be very hard to ignore the theme of homoeroticism and surely willful to do so. The language is full of it, and not only Coriolanus' and Aufidius' language. The comedy servants at Aufidius' house in Antium describe how extravagantly he treats his new guest: "Our general himself makes a mistress of him." Each sees in the other a perfect male fighting machine. They excite each other. Aufidius calls Coriolanus "Thou noble thing" and admits when he sees him that his "rapt heart" dances. Both declare how much they love their wives, but how much more they worship each other (Martius has embraced Cominius on the battlefield, declaring that he is as happy as when he took his bride to bed on their wedding night [1.6.35–38]). Martius says of Aufidius when he is first introduced into the play in Act 1, "were I anything but what I am, / I would wish me only he." That reflected vanity is deeply narcissistic. When Martius hears that the Volsci have regathered their forces, all he wants to know is if Titus Lartius has seen Aufidius and whether Aufidius spoke of him. In an urgent little shared line he neatly expresses his obsession:

CORIOLANUS	Spoke he of me?
LARTIUS	He did, my lord.
CORIOLANUS	How? What?

They even dream of one another. When Caius Martius arrives at Antium in Act 4, Aufidius, in his tumbling speech of obsessional adoration, admits "I have nightly since / Dreamt of encounters 'twixt thyself and me: / We have been down together in my sleep, / Unbuckling helms, fisting each other's throat, / And waked half dead with nothing." Even in a pre-Freudian world the analysis of that has to be pretty clear.

What you do with that in performance, however, is key. We chose, noting the extravagancy of that language, to make the narcissism evident in their characters, and barely sublimated in the fight between them in Act 1. After all, male worship is a Roman obsession. Coriolanus admits he has always been "godded" by Rome, and by Menenius in particular. And his mother has an unhealthy interest in the precise number of her son's scars.

And the staging of Coriolanus' death, the mood at the end of the play?

Farr: The play started at the Swan Theatre and then ended at the Old Vic in London so the stage got bigger, but the bareness remained and was very important, because the heightened visual moments that we wanted were therefore achieved through very simple things. I used a very, very brilliant martial choreographer, Alasdair Monteith, to work alongside a more traditional fight director, Terry King. The Japanese setting also instigates a very interesting fighting style. Of course, the play is enormously about fighting and I spent much more time working on fighting than I would normally do, because fighting became as important as language in defining the emotional relationship between Coriolanus and Aufidius. Their fight in the first half, their duel, was a powerful piece of theater because it was steeped in tradition, in a very strong code of honor. We set up that very strong choreographic code of Samurai swordplay. But then the play develops technologically, as I mentioned before, such as the typewriters used at the trial. Suddenly everything Coriolanus says is written down, which has never happened before, so in a powerful moment his words are thrown back at him. But the other main powerful moment of technology is the fight at the end. Coriolanus realizes that the Volscians wish to kill him and he takes out his sword to fight as a man of honor. Suddenly he is shot from behind by a gun. One of my favorite moments in our production was the total astonishment on his face when he realizes that someone has just shot him and that the era of his way of fighting is over. It was the crystallization of everything that the production was about in terms of the way in which the society was changing forever. It was the moment when this man realizes that everything he believes in has gone. It reminds me a little of when you see one of those wonderful old traditional Westerns when the cowboy realizes that all the codes and everything he's believed in has gone by: that quality of a vanishing world. There was a beautiful sense of heartbreak in that moment for him. At that point the Volscians just pour upon him like wolves and they literally rip him to shreds.

Doran: The terrifying bloodbath is pitiful, and we couldn't but believe that Coriolanus somehow helps to incite it and immolates himself upon Aufidius' sword. When the frenzy is over the image of Aufidius standing on the body of his quondam partner is horrifying in its animal brutality. It seems to shock the lords of the city, who cry out for him to "Hold, hold, hold, hold!" Sublimated sexuality or not, the hunting imagery which runs throughout the description of their relationship culminates in this brutal triumphing over his enemy's body. And it is replaced as suddenly with horror at what he has done. In our production, Aufidius was left trying to lift the body of Coriolanus by himself, as the lords and even his co-conspirators drift away, leaving Aufidius to howl the final word: "Assist!"

SHAKESPEARE'S CAREER
IN THE THEATER

BEGINNINGS

William Shakespeare was an extraordinarily intelligent man who was born and died in an ordinary market town in the English Midlands. He lived an uneventful life in an eventful age. Born in April 1564, he was the eldest son of John Shakespeare, a glove-maker who was prominent on the town council until he fell into financial difficulties. Young William was educated at the local grammar in Stratford-upon-Avon, Warwickshire, where he gained a thorough grounding in the Latin language, the art of rhetoric, and classical poetry. He married Ann Hathaway and had three children (Susanna, then the twins Hamnet and Judith) before his twenty-first birthday: an exceptionally young age for the period. We do not know how he supported his family in the mid-1580s.

Like many clever country boys, he moved to the city in order to make his way in the world. Like many creative people, he found a career in the entertainment business. Public playhouses and professional full-time acting companies reliant on the market for their income were born in Shakespeare's childhood. When he arrived in London as a man, sometime in the late 1580s, a new phenomenon was in the making: the actor who is so successful that he becomes a "star." The word did not exist in its modern sense, but the pattern is recognizable: audiences went to the theater not so much to see a particular show as to witness the comedian Richard Tarlton or the dramatic actor Edward Alleyn.

Shakespeare was an actor before he was a writer. It appears not to have been long before he realized that he was never going to grow into a great comedian like Tarlton or a great tragedian like Alleyn. Instead, he found a role within his company as the man who patched up old plays, breathing new life, new dramatic twists, into tired repertory pieces. He paid close attention to the work of the university-educated dramatists who were writing history plays and tragedies for the public stage in a style more ambitious, sweeping, and poetically grand than anything that had been seen before. But he may also have noted that what his friend and rival Ben Jonson would call "Marlowe's mighty line" sometimes faltered in the mode of comedy. Going to university, as Christopher Marlowe did, was all well and good for honing the arts of rhetorical elaboration and classical allusion, but it could lead to a loss of the common touch. To stay close to a large segment of the potential audience for public theater, it was necessary to write for clowns as well as kings and to intersperse the flights of poetry with the humor of the tavern, the privy, and the brothel: Shakespeare was the first to establish himself early in his career as an equal master of tragedy, comedy, and history. He realized that theater could be the medium to make the national past available to a wider audience than the elite who could afford to read large history books: his signature early works include not only the classical tragedy *Titus Andronicus* but also the sequence of English historical plays on the Wars of the Roses.

He also invented a new role for himself, that of in-house company dramatist. Where his peers and predecessors had to sell their plays to the theater managers on a poorly paid piecework basis, Shakespeare took a percentage of the box-office income. The Lord Chamberlain's Men constituted themselves in 1594 as a joint stock company, with the profits being distributed among the core actors who had invested as sharers. Shakespeare acted himself—he appears in the cast lists of some of Ben Jonson's plays as well as the list of actors' names at the beginning of his own collected works—but his principal duty was to write two or three plays a year for the company. By holding shares, he was effectively earning himself a royalty on his work, something no author had ever done before in England. When the Lord Chamberlain's Men collected their fee for performance at court in the Christmas season of 1594, three of them went along to the Treasurer of the Chamber: not just Richard Burbage the tragedian and Will Kempe the clown, but also Shakespeare the scriptwriter. That was something new.

The next four years were the golden period in Shakespeare's career, though overshadowed by the death of his only son, Hamnet, aged eleven, in 1596. In his early thirties and in full command of both his poetic and his theatrical medium, he perfected his art of comedy, while also developing his tragic and historical writing in new ways. In 1598, Francis Meres, a Cambridge University graduate with his finger on the pulse of the London literary world, praised Shakespeare for his excellence across the genres:

> As Plautus and Seneca are accounted the best for comedy and tragedy among the Latins, so Shakespeare among the English is the most excellent in both kinds for the stage; for comedy, witness his *Gentlemen of Verona*, his *Errors*, his *Love Labours Lost*, his *Love Labours Won*, his *Midsummer Night Dream* and his *Merchant of Venice*: for tragedy his *Richard the 2*, *Richard the 3*, *Henry the 4*, *King John*, *Titus Andronicus* and his *Romeo and Juliet*.

For Meres, as for the many writers who praised the "honey-flowing vein" of *Venus and Adonis* and *Lucrece*, narrative poems written when the theaters were closed due to plague in 1593–94, Shakespeare was marked above all by his linguistic skill, by the gift of turning elegant poetic phrases.

PLAYHOUSES

Elizabethan playhouses were "thrust" or "one-room" theaters. To understand Shakespeare's original theatrical life, we have to forget about the indoor theater of later times, with its proscenium arch and curtain that would be opened at the beginning and closed at the end of each act. In the proscenium arch theater, stage and auditorium are effectively two separate rooms: the audience looks from one world into another as if through the imaginary "fourth wall" framed by the proscenium. The picture-frame stage, together with the elaborate scenic effects and backdrops beyond it, created the illusion of a self-contained world—especially once nineteenth-century developments in the control of artificial lighting meant that the auditorium could be darkened and the spectators made to focus on the lighted stage. Shakespeare, by contrast, wrote for a bare platform stage with a standing audience gathered around it in a courtyard in full day-light. The audience were always conscious of themselves and their fellow spectators, and they shared the same "room" as the actors. A sense of immediate presence and the creation of rapport with the audience were all-important. The actor could not afford to imagine he was in a closed world, with silent witnesses dutifully observing him from the darkness.

Shakespeare's theatrical career began at the Rose Theatre in Southwark. The stage was wide and shallow, trapezoid in shape, like a lozenge. This design had a great deal of potential for the theatrical equivalent of cinematic split-screen effects, whereby one group of characters would enter at the door at one end of the tiring-house wall at the back of the stage and another group through the door at the other end, thus creating two rival tableaux. Many of the battle-heavy and faction-filled plays that premiered at the Rose have scenes of just this sort.

At the rear of the Rose stage, there were three capacious exits, each over ten feet wide. Unfortunately, the very limited excavation of a fragmentary portion of the original Globe site, in 1989, revealed nothing about the stage. The first Globe was built in 1599 with simi-lar proportions to those of another theater, the Fortune, albeit that the former was polygonal and looked circular, whereas the latter was rectangular. The building contract for the Fortune survives and allows us to infer that the stage of the Globe was probably substan-tially wider than it was deep (perhaps forty-three feet wide and twenty-seven feet deep). It may well have been tapered at the front, like that of the Rose.

The capacity of the Globe was said to have been enormous, per-haps in excess of three thousand. It has been conjectured that about eight hundred people may have stood in the yard, with two thousand or more in the three layers of covered galleries. The other "public" playhouses were also of large capacity, whereas the indoor Blackfri-ars theater that Shakespeare's company began using in 1608—the former refectory of a monastery—had overall internal dimensions of a mere forty-six by sixty feet. It would have made for a much more intimate theatrical experience and had a much smaller capacity, probably of about six hundred people. Since they paid at least sixpence a head, the Blackfriars attracted a more select or "private" audience. The atmosphere would have been closer to that of an indoor performance before the court in the Whitehall Palace or at Richmond. That Shakespeare always wrote for indoor production at court as well as outdoor performance in the public theater should make us cautious about inferring, as some scholars have, that the opportunity provided by the intimacy of the Blackfriars led to a significant change toward a "chamber" style in his last plays—which, besides, were performed at both the Globe and the Blackfriars. After the occupation of the Blackfriars a five-act structure seems to have become more important to Shakespeare. That was because of artificial lighting: there were musical interludes between the acts, while the candles were trimmed and replaced. Again, though, something similar must have been necessary for indoor court performances throughout his career.

Front of house there were the "gatherers" who collected the money from audience members: a penny to stand in the open-air yard, another penny for a place in the covered galleries, sixpence for the prominent "lord's rooms" to the side of the stage. In the indoor "private" theaters, gallants from the audience who fancied making themselves part of the spectacle sat on stools on the edge of the stage itself. Scholars debate as to how widespread this practice was in the public theaters such as the Globe. Once the audience were in place and the money counted, the gatherers were available to be extras on stage. That is one reason why battles and crowd scenes often come later rather than early in Shakespeare's plays. There was no formal prohibition upon performance by women, and there certainly were women among the gatherers, so it is not beyond the bounds of possibility that female crowd members were played by females.

The play began at two o'clock in the afternoon and the theater had to be cleared by five. After the main show, there would be a jig—which consisted not only of dancing, but also of knockabout comedy (it is the origin of the farcical "afterpiece" in the eighteenth-century theater). So the time available for a Shakespeare play was about two and a half hours, somewhere between the "two hours' traffic" mentioned in the prologue to *Romeo and Juliet* and the "three hours' spectacle" referred to in the preface to the 1647 Folio of Beaumont and

Fletcher's plays. The prologue to a play by Thomas Middleton refers to a thousand lines as "one hour's words," so the likelihood is that about two and a half thousand, or a maximum of three thousand lines made up the performed text. This is indeed the length of most of Shakespeare's comedies, whereas many of his tragedies and histories are much longer, raising the possibility that he wrote full scripts, possibly with eventual publication in mind, in the full knowledge that the stage version would be heavily cut. The short Quarto texts published in his lifetime—they used to be called "Bad" Quartos—provide fascinating evidence as to the kind of cutting that probably took place. So, for instance, the First Quarto of *Hamlet* neatly merges two occasions when Hamlet is overheard, the "Fishmonger" and the "nunnery" scenes.

The social composition of the audience was mixed. The poet Sir John Davies wrote of "A thousand townsmen, gentlemen and whores, / Porters and servingmen" who would "together throng" at the public playhouses. Though moralists associated female playgoing with adultery and the sex trade, many perfectly respectable citizens' wives were regular attendees. Some, no doubt, resembled the modern groupie: a story attested in two different sources has one citizen's wife making a postshow assignation with Richard Burbage and ending up in bed with Shakespeare—supposedly eliciting from the latter the quip that William the Conqueror was before Richard III. Defenders of theater liked to say that by witnessing the comeuppance of villains on the stage, audience members would repent of their own wrongdoings, but the reality is that most people went to the theater then, as they do now, for entertainment more than moral edification. Besides, it would be foolish to suppose that audiences behaved in a homogeneous way: a pamphlet of the 1630s tells of how two men went to see *Pericles* and one of them laughed while the other wept. Bishop John Hall complained that people went to church for the same reasons that they went to the theater: "for company, for custom, for recreation . . . to feed his eyes or his ears . . . or perhaps for sleep."

Men-about-town and clever young lawyers went to be seen as much as to see. In the modern popular imagination, shaped not least by *Shakespeare in Love* and the opening sequence of Laurence Olivier's

Henry V film, the penny-paying groundlings stand in the yard hurling abuse or encouragement and hazelnuts or orange peel at the actors, while the sophisticates in the covered galleries appreciate Shakespeare's soaring poetry. The reality was probably the other way around. A "groundling" was a kind of fish, so the nickname suggests the penny audience standing below the level of the stage and gazing in silent open-mouthed wonder at the spectacle unfolding above them. The more difficult audience members, who kept up a running commentary of clever remarks on the performance and who occasionally got into quarrels with players, were the gallants. Like Hollywood movies in modern times, Elizabethan and Jacobean plays exercised a powerful influence on the fashion and behavior of the young. John Marston mocks the lawyers who would open their lips, perhaps to court a girl, and out would "flow / Naught but pure Juliet and Romeo."

THE ENSEMBLE AT WORK

In the absence of typewriters and photocopying machines, reading aloud would have been the means by which the company got to know a new play. The tradition of the playwright reading his complete script to the assembled company endured for generations. A copy would then have been taken to the Master of the Revels for licensing. The theater book-holder or prompter would then have copied the parts for distribution to the actors. A partbook consisted of the character's lines, with each speech preceded by the last three or four words of the speech before, the so-called "cue." These would have been taken away and studied or "conned." During this period of learning the parts, an actor might have had some one-to-one instruction, perhaps from the dramatist, perhaps from a senior actor who had played the same part before, and, in the case of an apprentice, from his master. A high percentage of Desdemona's lines occur in dialogue with Othello, of Lady Macbeth's with Macbeth, Cleopatra's with Antony, and Volumnia's with Coriolanus. The roles would almost certainly have been taken by the apprentice of the lead actor, usually Burbage, who delivers the majority of the cues. Given that apprentices lodged with their masters, there would have been ample

9. Hypothetical reconstruction of the interior of an Elizabethan playhouse during a performance.

opportunity for personal instruction, which may be what made it possible for young men to play such demanding parts.

After the parts were learned, there may have been no more than a single rehearsal before the first performance. With six different plays to be put on every week, there was no time for more. Actors, then, would go into a show with a very limited sense of the whole. The notion of a collective rehearsal process that is itself a process of discovery for the actors is wholly modern and would have been incomprehensible to Shakespeare and his original ensemble. Given the number of parts an actor had to hold in his memory, the forgetting of lines was probably more frequent than in the modern theater. The book-holder was on hand to prompt.

Backstage personnel included the property man, the tire-man who oversaw the costumes, call-boys, attendants, and the musicians, who might play at various times from the main stage, the rooms above, and within the tiring-house. Scriptwriters sometimes made a nuisance of themselves backstage. There was often tension between the acting companies and the freelance playwrights from whom they purchased scripts: it was a smart move on the part of Shakespeare and the Lord Chamberlain's Men to bring the writing process in-house.

Scenery was limited, though sometimes set pieces were brought on (a bank of flowers, a bed, the mouth of hell). The trapdoor from below, the gallery stage above, and the curtained discovery-space at the back allowed for an array of special effects: the rising of ghosts and apparitions, the descent of gods, dialogue between a character at a window and another at ground level, the revelation of a statue or a pair of lovers playing at chess. Ingenious use could be made of props, as with the ass's head in *A Midsummer Night's Dream*. In a theater that does not clutter the stage with the material paraphernalia of everyday life, those objects that are deployed may take on powerful symbolic weight, as when Shylock bears his weighing scales in one hand and knife in the other, thus becoming a parody of the figure of Justice who traditionally bears a sword and a balance. Among the more significant items in the property cupboard of Shakespeare's company, there would have been a throne (the "chair of state"), joint stools, books, bottles, coins, purses, letters (which are brought on stage, read or referred to on about eighty occasions in the complete works), maps, gloves, a set of stocks (in which Kent is put in *King Lear*), rings, rapiers, daggers, broadswords, staves, pistols, masks and vizards, heads and skulls, torches and tapers and lanterns which served to signal night scenes on the daylit stage, a buck's head, an ass's head, animal costumes. Live animals also put in appearances, most notably the dog Crab in *The Two Gentlemen of Verona* and possibly a young polar bear in *The Winter's Tale*.

The costumes were the most important visual dimension of the play. Playwrights were paid between £2 and £6 per script, whereas Alleyn was not averse to paying £20 for "a black velvet cloak with sleeves embroidered all with silver and gold." No matter the period of the play, actors always wore contemporary costume. The excitement for the audience came not from any impression of historical accuracy, but from the richness of the attire and perhaps the transgressive thrill of the knowledge that here were commoners like themselves strutting in the costumes of courtiers in effective defiance of the strict sumptuary laws whereby in real life people had to wear the clothes that befitted their social station.

To an even greater degree than props, costumes could carry symbolic importance. Racial characteristics could be suggested: a breastplate and helmet for a Roman soldier, a turban for a Turk, long robes for exotic characters such as Moors, a gabardine for a Jew. The figure of Time, as in *The Winter's Tale*, would be equipped with hourglass, scythe, and wings; Rumour, who speaks the prologue of *2 Henry IV*, wore a costume adorned with a thousand tongues. The wardrobe in the tiring-house of the Globe would have contained much of the same stock as that of rival manager Philip Henslowe at the Rose: green gowns for outlaws and foresters, black for melancholy men such as Jaques and people in mourning such as the Countess in *All's Well That Ends Well* (at the beginning of *Hamlet*, the prince is still in mourning black when everyone else is in festive garb for the wedding of the new king), a gown and hood for a friar (or a feigned friar like the duke in *Measure for Measure*), blue coats and tawny to distinguish the followers of rival factions, a leather apron and ruler for a carpenter (as in the opening scene of *Julius Caesar*—and in *A Midsummer Night's Dream*, where this is the only sign that Peter Quince is a carpenter), a cockle hat with staff and a pair of sandals for a pilgrim or palmer (the disguise assumed by Helen in *All's Well*), bodices and kirtles with farthingales beneath for the boys who are to be dressed as girls. A gender switch such as that of Rosalind or Jessica seems to have taken between fifty and eighty lines of dialogue—Viola does not resume her "maiden weeds," but remains in her boy's costume to the end of *Twelfth Night* because a change would have slowed down the action at just the moment it was speeding to a climax. Henslowe's inventory also included "a robe for to go invisible": Oberon, Puck, and Ariel must have had something similar.

As the costumes appealed to the eyes, so there was music for the ears. Comedies included many songs. Desdemona's willow song, perhaps a late addition to the text, is a rare and thus exceptionally poignant example from tragedy. Trumpets and tuckets sounded for ceremonial entrances, drums denoted an army on the march. Background music could create atmosphere, as at the beginning of

Twelfth Night, during the lovers' dialogue near the end of *The Merchant of Venice*, when the statue seemingly comes to life in *The Winter's Tale*, and for the revival of Pericles and of Lear (in the Quarto text, but not the Folio). The haunting sound of the hautboy suggested a realm beyond the human, as when the god Hercules is imagined deserting Mark Antony. Dances symbolized the harmony of the end of a comedy—though in Shakespeare's world of mingled joy and sorrow, someone is usually left out of the circle.

The most important resource was, of course, the actors themselves. They needed many skills: in the words of one contemporary commentator, "dancing, activity, music, song, elocution, ability of body, memory, skill of weapon, pregnancy of wit." Their bodies were as significant as their voices. Hamlet tells the player to "suit the action to the word, the word to the action": moments of strong emotion, known as "passions," relied on a repertoire of dramatic gestures as well as a modulation of the voice. When Titus Andronicus has had his hand chopped off, he asks, "How can I grace my talk, / Wanting a hand to give it action?" A pen portrait of "The Character of an Excellent Actor" by the dramatist John Webster is almost certainly based on his impression of Shakespeare's leading man, Richard Burbage: "By a full and significant action of body, he charms our attention: sit in a full theatre, and you will think you see so many lines drawn from the circumference of so many ears, whiles the actor is the centre. . . ."

Though Burbage was admired above all others, praise was also heaped upon the apprentice players whose alto voices fitted them for the parts of women. A spectator at Oxford in 1610 records how the audience were reduced to tears by the pathos of Desdemona's death. The puritans who fumed about the biblical prohibition upon cross-dressing and the encouragement to sodomy constituted by the sight of an adult male kissing a teenage boy on stage were a small minority. Little is known, however, about the characteristics of the leading apprentices in Shakespeare's company. It may perhaps be inferred that one was a lot taller than the other, since Shakespeare often wrote for a pair of female friends, one tall and fair, the other short and dark (Helena and Hermia, Rosalind and Celia, Beatrice and Hero).

We know little about Shakespeare's own acting roles—an early allusion indicates that he often took royal parts, and a venerable tradition gives him old Adam in *As You Like It* and the ghost of old King Hamlet. Save for Burbage's lead roles and the generic part of the clown, all such castings are mere speculation. We do not even know for sure whether the original Falstaff was Will Kempe or another actor who specialized in comic roles, Thomas Pope.

Kempe left the company in early 1599. Tradition has it that he fell out with Shakespeare over the matter of excessive improvisation. He was replaced by Robert Armin, who was less of a clown and more of a cerebral wit: this explains the difference between such parts as Lancelet Gobbo and Dogberry, which were written for Kempe, and the more verbally sophisticated Feste and Lear's Fool, which were written for Armin.

One thing that is clear from surviving "plots" or storyboards of plays from the period is that a degree of doubling was necessary. *2 Henry VI* has over sixty speaking parts, but more than half of the characters only appear in a single scene and most scenes have only six to eight speakers. At a stretch, the play could be performed by thirteen actors. When Thomas Platter saw *Julius Caesar* at the Globe in 1599, he noted that there were about fifteen. Why doesn't Paris go to the Capulet ball in *Romeo and Juliet*? Perhaps because he was doubled with Mercutio, who does. In *The Winter's Tale*, Mamillius might have come back as Perdita and Antigonus been doubled by Camillo, making the partnership with Paulina at the end a very neat touch. Titania and Oberon are often played by the same pair as Hippolyta and Theseus, suggesting a symbolic matching of the rulers of the worlds of night and day, but it is questionable whether there would have been time for the necessary costume changes. As so often, one is left in a realm of tantalizing speculation.

THE KING'S MAN

On Queen Elizabeth's death in 1603, the new king, James I, who had held the Scottish throne as James VI since he had been an infant, immediately took the Lord Chamberlain's Men under his direct patronage. Henceforth they would be the King's Men, and for the rest of Shakespeare's career they were favored with far more court performances than any of their rivals. There even seem to have been rumors early in the reign that Shakespeare and Burbage were being considered for knighthoods, an unprecedented honor for mere actors—and one that in the event was not accorded to a member of the profession for nearly three hundred years, when the title was bestowed upon Henry Irving, the leading Shakespearean actor of Queen Victoria's reign.

Shakespeare's productivity rate slowed in the Jacobean years, not because of age or some personal trauma, but because there were frequent outbreaks of plague, causing the theaters to be closed for long periods. The King's Men were forced to spend many months on the road. Between November 1603 and 1608, they were to be found at various towns in the south and Midlands, though Shakespeare probably did not tour with them by this time. He had bought a large house back home in Stratford and was accumulating other property. He may indeed have stopped acting soon after the new king took the throne. With the London theaters closed so much of the time and a large repertoire on the stocks, Shakespeare seems to have focused his energies on writing a few long and complex tragedies that could have been played on demand at court: *Othello*, *King Lear*, *Antony and Cleopatra*, *Coriolanus*, and *Cymbeline* are among his longest and poetically grandest plays. *Macbeth* only survives in a shorter text, which shows signs of adaptation after Shakespeare's death. The bitterly satirical *Timon of Athens*, apparently a collaboration with Thomas Middleton that may have failed on the stage, also belongs to this period. In comedy, too, he wrote longer and morally darker works than in the Elizabethan period, pushing at the very bounds of the form in *Measure for Measure* and *All's Well That Ends Well*.

From 1608 onward, when the King's Men began occupying the indoor Blackfriars playhouse (as a winter house, meaning that they only used the outdoor Globe in summer?), Shakespeare turned to a more romantic style. His company had a great success with a revived and altered version of an old pastoral play called *Mucedorus*. It even featured a bear. The younger dramatist John Fletcher, meanwhile, sometimes working in collaboration with Francis Beaumont, was pioneering a new style of tragicomedy, a mix of romance and royalism laced with intrigue and pastoral excursions. Shakespeare experimented with this idiom in *Cymbeline* and it was presumably with his blessing that Fletcher eventually took over as the King's Men's company dramatist. The two writers apparently collaborated on three plays in the years 1612–14: a lost romance called *Cardenio* (based on the love-madness of a character in Cervantes' *Don Quixote*), *Henry VIII* (originally staged with the title "All Is True"), and *The Two Noble Kinsmen*, a dramatization of Chaucer's "Knight's Tale." These were written after Shakespeare's two final solo-authored plays, *The Winter's Tale*, a self-consciously old-fashioned work dramatizing the pastoral romance of his old enemy Robert Greene, and *The Tempest*, which at one and the same time drew together multiple theatrical traditions, diverse reading, and contemporary interest in the fate of a ship that had been wrecked on the way to the New World.

The collaborations with Fletcher suggest that Shakespeare's career ended with a slow fade rather than the sudden retirement supposed by the nineteenth-century Romantic critics who read Prospero's epilogue to *The Tempest* as Shakespeare's personal farewell to his art. In the last few years of his life Shakespeare certainly spent more of his time in Stratford-upon-Avon, where he became further involved in property dealing and litigation. But his London life also continued. In 1613 he made his first major London property purchase: a freehold house in the Blackfriars district, close to his company's indoor theater. *The Two Noble Kinsmen* may have been written as late as 1614, and Shakespeare was in London on business a little over a year before he died of an unknown cause at home in Stratford-upon-Avon in 1616, probably on his fifty-second birthday.

About half the sum of his works were published in his lifetime, in texts of variable quality. A few years after his death, his fellow actors began putting together an authorized edition of his complete *Comedies, Histories and Tragedies*. It appeared in 1623, in large "Folio" format. This collection of thirty-six plays gave Shakespeare his immortality. In the words of his fellow dramatist Ben Jonson, who contributed two poems of praise at the start of the Folio, the body of his work made him "a monument without a tomb":

And art alive still while thy book doth live
And we have wits to read and praise to give . . .
He was not of an age, but for all time!

SHAKESPEARE'S WORKS: A CHRONOLOGY

1589–91	*? Arden of Faversham* (possible part authorship)
1589–92	*The Taming of the Shrew*
1589–92	*? Edward the Third* (possible part authorship)
1591	*The Second Part of Henry the Sixth*, originally called *The First Part of the Contention Betwixt the Two Famous Houses of York and Lancaster* (element of coauthorship possible)
1591	*The Third Part of Henry the Sixth*, originally called *The True Tragedy of Richard Duke of York* (element of co-authorship probable)
1591–92	*The Two Gentlemen of Verona*
1591–92; perhaps revised 1594	*The Lamentable Tragedy of Titus Andronicus* (probably cowritten with, or revising an earlier version by, George Peele)
1592	*The First Part of Henry the Sixth*, probably with Thomas Nashe and others
1592/94	*King Richard the Third*
1593	*Venus and Adonis* (poem)
1593–94	*The Rape of Lucrece* (poem)
1593–1608	*Sonnets* (154 poems, published 1609 with *A Lover's Complaint*, a poem of disputed authorship)
1592–94/ 1600–03	*Sir Thomas More* (a single scene for a play originally by Anthony Munday, with other revisions by Henry Chettle, Thomas Dekker, and Thomas Heywood)
1594	*The Comedy of Errors*
1595	*Love's Labour's Lost*

1595–97	*Love's Labour's Won* (a lost play, unless the original title for another comedy)
1595–96	*A Midsummer Night's Dream*
1595–96	*The Tragedy of Romeo and Juliet*
1595–96	*King Richard the Second*
1595–97	*The Life and Death of King John* (possibly earlier)
1596–97	*The Merchant of Venice*
1596–97	*The First Part of Henry the Fourth*
1597–98	*The Second Part of Henry the Fourth*
1598	*Much Ado About Nothing*
1598–99	*The Passionate Pilgrim* (20 poems, some not by Shakespeare)
1599	*The Life of Henry the Fifth*
1599	"To the Queen" (epilogue for a court performance)
1599	*As You Like It*
1599	*The Tragedy of Julius Caesar*
1600–01	*The Tragedy of Hamlet, Prince of Denmark* (perhaps revising an earlier version)
1600–01	*The Merry Wives of Windsor* (perhaps revising version of 1597–99)
1601	"Let the Bird of Loudest Lay" (poem, known since 1807 as "The Phoenix and Turtle" [turtledove])
1601	*Twelfth Night, or What You Will*
1601–02	*The Tragedy of Troilus and Cressida*
1604	*The Tragedy of Othello, the Moor of Venice*
1604	*Measure for Measure*
1605	*All's Well That Ends Well*
1605	*The Life of Timon of Athens*, with Thomas Middleton
1605–06	*The Tragedy of King Lear*
1605–08	? contribution to *The Four Plays in One* (lost, except for *A Yorkshire Tragedy*, mostly by Thomas Middleton)

1606	*The Tragedy of Macbeth* (surviving text has additional scenes by Thomas Middleton)
1606–07	*The Tragedy of Antony and Cleopatra*
1608	*The Tragedy of Coriolanus*
1608	*Pericles, Prince of Tyre*, with George Wilkins
1610	*The Tragedy of Cymbeline*
1611	*The Winter's Tale*
1611	*The Tempest*
1612–13	*Cardenio*, with John Fletcher (survives only in later adaptation called *Double Falsehood* by Lewis Theobald)
1613	*Henry VIII (All Is True)*, with John Fletcher
1613–14	*The Two Noble Kinsmen*, with John Fletcher

THE HISTORY BEHIND THE TRAGEDIES: A CHRONOLOGY

Era/Date	Event	Location	Play
Greek myth	Trojan War	Troy	*Troilus and Cressida*
Greek myth	Theseus king of Athens	Athens	*The Two Noble Kinsmen*
c. tenth–ninth century BC?	Leir king of Britain (legendary)	Britain	*King Lear*
535–510 BC	Tarquin II king of Rome	Rome	*The Rape of Lucrece*
493 BC	Caius Martius captures Corioli	Italy	*Coriolanus*
431–404 BC	Peloponnesian War	Greece	*Timon of Athens*
17 Mar 45 BC	Battle of Munda: Caesar's victory over Pompey's sons	Munda, Spain	*Julius Caesar*
Oct 45 BC	Caesar returns to Rome for triumph	Rome	*Julius Caesar*
15 Mar 44 BC	Assassination of Caesar	Rome	*Julius Caesar*
27 Nov 43 BC	Formation of Second Triumvirate	Rome	*Julius Caesar*
Oct 42 BC	Battle of Philippi	Philippi, Macedonia	*Julius Caesar*
Winter 41–40 BC	Antony visits Cleopatra	Egypt	*Antony and Cleopatra*
Oct 40 BC	Pact of Brundisium; marriage of Antony and Octavia	Italy	*Antony and Cleopatra*
39 BC	Pact of Misenum between Pompey and the triumvirs	Campania, Italy	*Antony and Cleopatra*

39–38 BC	Ventidius defeats the Parthians in a series of engagements	Syria	*Antony and Cleopatra*
34 BC	Cleopatra and her children proclaimed rulers of the eastern Mediterranean	Alexandria	*Antony and Cleopatra*
2 Sep 31 BC	Battle of Actium	On the coast of western Greece	*Antony and Cleopatra*
Aug 30 BC	Death of Antony	Alexandria	*Antony and Cleopatra*
12 Aug 30 BC	Death of Cleopatra	Alexandria	*Antony and Cleopatra*
Early first century AD	Cunobelinus/ Cymbeline rules Britain (and dies before AD 43)	Britain	*Cymbeline*
During the reign of a fictional (late?) Roman emperor		Rome	*Titus Andronicus*
c. ninth–tenth century AD	Existence of legendary Amleth?	Denmark	*Hamlet*
15 Aug 1040	Death of Duncan I of Scotland	Bothnguane, Scotland	*Macbeth*
1053	Malcolm invades Scotland	Scotland	*Macbeth*
15 Aug 1057	Death of Macbeth	Lumphanan, Scotland	*Macbeth*
7 Oct 1571	Naval battle of Lepanto between Christians and Turks	The Mediterranean, off the coast of Greece	A context for *Othello*

FURTHER READING
AND VIEWING

CRITICAL APPROACHES

Adelman, Janet, *Suffocating Mothers: Fantasies of Maternal Origin in Shakespeare's Plays* (1992). Influential psychoanalytical reading: chapter 6 deals with Macbeth and Coriolanus.

Alexander, Catherine M. S., ed., *Shakespeare and Politics* (2004). Contains two useful political, historically informed essays: Anne Barton's "Livy, Machiavelli and Shakespeare's *Coriolanus*" and David George's "Plutarch, Insurrection and Death in *Coriolanus*."

Cantor, Paul A., *Shakespeare's Rome: Republic and Empire* (1976). Lucid overview of the Roman plays.

Charney, Maurice, *Shakespeare's Roman Plays: The Function of Imagery in the Drama* (1963). Detailed, in-depth discussion.

Del Sapio Garbero, Maria, ed., *Identity, Otherness and Empire in Shakespeare's Rome* (2009). Sophisticated collection of essays including Janet Adelman's "Shakespeare's Romulus and Remus: Who Does the Wolf Love?" and Manfred Pfister's "Acting the Roman: *Coriolanus*."

George, David, ed., *Coriolanus.* Shakespeare: The Critical Tradition (2004). Judicious selection of writing from late seventeenth century to 1940. Invaluable resource on play's historical reception.

Jagendorf, Zvi, "*Coriolanus*: Body Politic and Private Parts," *Shakespeare Quarterly*, Vol. XLI (1990), pp. 455–69. Deftly interwoven analysis of the relationship between politics and the personal.

Kahn, Coppélia, *Roman Shakespeare: Warriors, Wounds, and Women* (1997), pp. 144–59. Characteristic work of an influential feminist critic.

Marshall, Cynthia, "Wound-man: *Coriolanus*, Gender, and the Theatrical Construction of Interiority," chapter 4 in *Feminist Readings of Early Modern Culture* (1996), ed. Valerie Traub, M. Lindsay Kaplan, and Dympna Callaghan, pp. 93–118. Strong feminist reading.

Parker, Barbara, *Plato's Republic and Shakespeare's Rome: A Political Study of the Roman Works* (2004). Chapter 3 on *Coriolanus* examines its representation of political theory and Rome's political degeneration.

Poole, Adrian, *Coriolanus*. Harvester New Critical Introductions to Shakespeare (1988). Perceptive close reading.

Smith, Bruce R., *Shakespeare and Masculinity* (2000). Explores the constitution and performance of masculinity in Shakespeare's culture and plays.

Steible, Mary, *Coriolanus: A Guide to the Play*, Greenwood Guides (2004). Useful, straightforward.

Wells, Robin Headlam, *Shakespeare on Masculinity* (2000). Chapter 5, "Flower of Warriors: *Coriolanus*," sees the play as an exploration, and finally a denunciation, of heroic values.

Wheeler, David, ed., *Coriolanus: Critical Essays* (1995). Good selection of important historical criticism with useful reviews at end of volume.

THE PLAY IN PERFORMANCE

Bedford, Kristina, *Coriolanus at the National: "Th'Interpretation of the Time"* (1992). Detailed account of Peter Hall's 1991–92 production; both Ian McKellen and Greg Hicks contribute.

Berkoff, Steven, *Coriolanus in Deutschland* (1992). Personal journal of the charismatic Berkoff's experience of directing his critically acclaimed German version.

Daniell, David, *"Coriolanus" in Europe* (1980). Detailed account of the European tour of Terry Hands's successful 1979 RSC production.

George, David, *A Comparison of Six Adaptations of Shakespeare's Coriolanus, 1681–1962: How Changing Politics Influence the Interpretation of Text* (2008). Detailed historical account spanning Nahum Tate to Bertolt Brecht.

Ripley, John, *Coriolanus on Stage in England and America 1609–1994* (1998). Detailed and perceptive, an invaluable resource.

Smallwood, Robert, ed., *Players of Shakespeare 4* (1998). Includes an interview with Philip Voss on playing Menenius in David Thacker's 1994 production, in which Toby Stephens played Coriolanus.

AVAILABLE ON DVD

Coriolanus, directed by Elijah Moshinsky, BBC Shakespeare (1984, DVD 2006). One of the best of this series with Alan Howard as Coriolanus, Joss Ackland as Menenius, and Irene Worth as Volumnia: uses television's intimacy well, emphasizes the play's homoerotic potential.

Coriolanus, directed by Elijah Moshinsky (2011). Ralph Fiennes's directing debut sets play in war-torn Belgrade, with Fiennes as Coriolanus, Brian Cox as Menenius, and Vanessa Redgrave as Volumnia.

REFERENCES

1. Samuel Taylor Coleridge, *Lectures and Notes on Shakspere and Other English Poets* (1811–1818), ed. T. Ashe (1900), p. 309.
2. William Hazlitt, *Characters of Shakespear's Plays* (1817), p. 50.
3. George Brandes, *William Shakespeare* (1898, English translation 1920), pp. 533–34.
4. Paul A. Cantor, *Shakespeare's Rome: Republic and Empire* (1976), p. 66.
5. Brandes, *William Shakespeare*, p. 551.
6. Jan Kott, *Shakespeare Our Contemporary* (1961), p. 141.
7. Norman Rabkin, *Shakespeare and the Common Understanding* (1967), p. 135.
8. Rabkin, *Shakespeare and the Common Understanding*, p. 138.
9. A. P. Rossiter, *Angel with Horns and Other Shakespeare Lectures* (1961), p. 250.
10. G. K. Hunter, "The Last Tragic Heroes" (1966), in *Shakespeare, Coriolanus: A Casebook*, ed. B. A. Brockman (1977), p. 162.
11. James L. Calderwood, "*Coriolanus*: Wordless Meanings and Meaningless Words," *Studies in English Literature* 6 (1966), pp. 211–24 (pp. 217–18).
12. Coppélia Kahn, *Man's Estate: Masculine Identity in Shakespeare* (1981), p. 167.
13. A. C. Bradley, "Character and the Imaginative Appeal of Tragedy in *Coriolanus*," from "*Coriolanus*," Second Annual Shakespeare Lecture, *Proceedings of the British Academy* (1912), in Brockman, *Shakespeare, Coriolanus: A Casebook*, p. 56.
14. Calderwood, "*Coriolanus*," p. 215.
15. Rabkin, *Shakespeare and the Common Understanding*, p. 143.
16. Anne Barton, "Livy, Machiavelli and Shakespeare's *Coriolanus*" (1985), in her *Essays, Mainly Shakespearean* (1994), pp. 136–60 (p. 144).
17. Rossiter, *Angel with Horns and Other Shakespeare Lectures*, p. 238.
18. Barton, "Livy, Machiavelli and Shakespeare's *Coriolanus*," pp. 156–57.
19. Derek A. Traversi, "The World of *Coriolanus*" (1969), in Brockman, *Shakespeare, Coriolanus: A Casebook*, p. 186.
20. Coppélia Kahn, *Roman Shakespeare: Warriors, Wounds, and Women* (1997), pp. 156–57.

21. Kahn, *Man's Estate*, p. 157.
22. Kahn, *Roman Shakespeare*, p. 149.
23. Janet Adelman, *Suffocating Mothers: Fantasies of Maternal Origin in Shakespeare's Plays, Hamlet to The Tempest* (1992), pp. 146, 150, 152.
24. Adelman, *Suffocating Mothers*, p. 149.
25. Stanley Cavell, *Disowning Knowledge in Six Plays of Shakespeare* (1987), p. 156.
26. Maurice Charney, *Shakespeare's Roman Plays: The Function of Imagery in the Drama* (1963), p. 143.
27. Traversi, "The World of *Coriolanus*," p. 183.
28. Charney, *Shakespeare's Roman Plays*, p. 162.
29. Kott, *Shakespeare Our Contemporary*, p. 166.
30. *Stratford-upon-Avon Herald*, 30 April 1926.
31. Nahum Tate, *The Ingratitude of a Commonwealth* (1682), Epistle Dedicatory.
32. *Coriolanus: Or, The Roman Matron. A Tragedy* (1755), Advertisement.
33. John Ripley, *Coriolanus on Stage in England and America, 1609–1994* (1998), p. 144.
34. Ripley, *Coriolanus on Stage in England and America*, p. 183.
35. *Stratford Herald*, 18 August 1893.
36. *Birmingham Daily Post*, 1 May 1915.
37. *Daily Telegraph*, 23 April 1919.
38. *Birmingham Post*, 24 April 1926.
39. *Daily Telegraph*, 24 April 1926.
40. *Birmingham Mail*, 25 April 1933.
41. Lucy Munro, "*Coriolanus* and William Poel's Platform Stage," in *Shakespeare in Stages*, ed. Christine Dymkowski and Christie Carson (2010), p. 50.
42. Wilhelm Hortmann, *Shakespeare on the German Stage* (1998), p. 149.
43. *Birmingham Mail*, 10 May 1939.
44. *The Times*, London, 10 May 1939.
45. *Daily Telegraph and Morning Post*, 10 May 1939.
46. *Daily Herald*, 14 March 1952.
47. *Daily Herald*, 14 March 1952.
48. *Sunday Times*, 28 February 1954.
49. Ripley, *Coriolanus on Stage in England and America*, p. 284.
50. Lewis Casson, quoted in Ripley, *Coriolanus on Stage in England and America*, p. 274.
51. *Daily Express*, 8 July 1959.

52. Lawrence Guntner, "Shakespeare on the East German Stage," in *Foreign Shakespeare*, ed. Dennis Kennedy (1993), pp. 110–11.

53. Keith Gregor, *Shakespeare in the Spanish Theatre 1772 to the Present* (2010), p. 139.

54. *Theater heute*, 23 September 1970.

55. Kristina Bedford, *Coriolanus at the National: "Th'Interpretation of the Time"* (1992), p. 117.

56. Quoted in Hortmann, *Shakespeare on the German Stage*, p. 457.

57. *Sunday Telegraph*, 14 April 1991.

58. *Guardian*, 28 November 1990.

59. *Sunday Times*, 21 May 1995.

60. *Mail on Sunday*, 18 June 2000.

61. *The Times*, London, 29 March 2001.

62. Gregor, *Shakespeare in the Spanish Theatre*, p. 145.

63. Mary Steible, *Coriolanus: A Guide to the Play* (2004), p. 132.

64. Ripley, *Coriolanus on Stage in England and America*, p. 315.

65. Milton Shulman, *Evening Standard*, 13 April 1967.

66. Ripley, *Coriolanus on Stage in England and America*, p. 316.

67. Peter Lewis, *Daily Mail*, 13 April 1967.

68. Frank Marcus, *Sunday Telegraph*, 16 April 1972.

69. Ripley, *Coriolanus on Stage in England and America*, p. 317.

70. John Mortimer, *Observer*, 16 April 1972.

71. Peter Thomson, "No Rome of Safety: The Royal Shakespeare Season 1972 Reviewed," *Shakespeare Survey* 26 (1973), pp. 139–50 (pp. 143–44).

72. Jean Vaché, *Cahiers Elisabéthains*, No. 14 (1978), p. 111.

73. Terry Hands in an interview with John Higgins, *The Times*, London, 19 October 1977.

74. Irving Wardle, *The Times*, London, 22 October 1977.

75. Carol A. Chillington, Review of *Coriolanus* in *Educational Theatre Journal*, Vol. 30, No. 2 (May 1978), pp. 258–59 (p. 258).

76. Peter Holland, *Shakespeare Survey* 44 (1992), p. 163.

77. Ripley, *Coriolanus on Stage in England and America*, p. 324.

78. Holland, *Shakespeare Survey* 44, p. 164, quoted in Ripley, *Coriolanus on Stage in England and America*, pp. 324–25.

79. Russell Jackson, *Shakespeare Quarterly*, Vol. 46 (1995), p. 345.

80. Holland, *Shakespeare Survey* 44, p. 215.

81. Holland, *Shakespeare Survey* 44, pp. 215–16.

82. Jackson, *Shakespeare Quarterly*, Vol. 46, p. 345.

83. Jackson, *Shakespeare Quarterly*, Vol. 46, p. 345.

84. Russell Jackson, "Shakespeare at Stratford-upon-Avon: Summer and Winter, 2002–2003," *Shakespeare Quarterly*, Vol. 54 (2003), pp. 167–85 (p. 183).

85. Benedict Nightingale, *The Times*, London, 28 November 2002.

86. Jackson, "Shakespeare at Stratford-upon-Avon," p. 184.

87. Philippa Prankard, *Stratford Herald*, 8 March 2007.

88. Ripley, *Coriolanus on Stage in England and America*, p. 316.

89. Ripley, *Coriolanus on Stage in England and America*, p. 314.

90. Ripley, *Coriolanus on Stage in England and America*, p. 314.

91. Ripley, *Coriolanus on Stage in England and America*, p. 314.

92. John Barton, Program Notes, RSC *Coriolanus*, 1967.

93. Alan Brien, *Sunday Telegraph*, 16 April 1967.

94. Peter Lewis, *Daily Mail*, 13 April 1967.

95. Irving Wardle, *The Times*, London, 13 April 1967.

96. John Barber, *Daily Telegraph*, 12 April 1972.

97. John Mortimer, *Observer*, 16 April 1972.

98. Thomson, "No Rome of Safety," p. 143.

99. Irving Wardle, *The Times*, London, 22 October 1977.

100. Chillington, Review of *Coriolanus*, pp. 258–59.

101. Peter Holland, *Shakespeare Survey* 44, pp. 164–65.

102. Jackson, *Shakespeare Quarterly*, Vol. 46, pp. 346–47.

103. John Peter, *Sunday Times*, 1 December 2002.

104. Benedict Nightingale, *The Times*, London, 28 November 2002.

105. Paul Taylor, *Independent Review*, 4 December 2002.

106. Robert Hanks, *Independent*, 8 March 2007.

107. Michael Billington, *Guardian*, 8 March 2007.

ACKNOWLEDGMENTS AND PICTURE CREDITS

Preparation of "*Coriolanus* in Performance" was assisted by a generous grant from the CAPITAL Centre (Creativity and Performance in Teaching and Learning) of the University of Warwick for research in the RSC archive at the Shakespeare Birthplace Trust.

The second half of the introduction ("From Mob to Mother: The Critics Debate") draws extensively on a longer overview of the play's critical history prepared for us by Sarah Carter.

Thanks as always to our indefatigable and eagle-eyed copy editor Tracey Day and to Ray Addicott for overseeing the production process with rigor and calmness.

Picture research by Michelle Morton. Grateful acknowledgment is made to the Shakespeare Birthplace Trust for assistance with picture research (special thanks to Helen Hargest) and reproduction fees.

Images of RSC productions are supplied by the Shakespeare Centre Library and Archive, Stratford-upon-Avon. This library, maintained by the Shakespeare Birthplace Trust, holds the most important collection of Shakespeare material in the UK, including the Royal Shakespeare Company's official archive. It is open to the public free of charge.

For more information see www.shakespeare.org.uk.

1. Frank Benson as Coriolanus (1893). Reproduced by permission of the Shakespeare Birthplace Trust
2. Directed by Peter Hall (1959). Angus McBean © Royal Shakespeare Company
3. Directed by Trevor Nunn (1972). Joe Cocks Studio Collection © Shakespeare Birthplace Trust